Some comments from students and readers:

"I was skeptical when I bought your book. I needed to learn how to use FrameMaker very quickly and didn't think any resource would be able to help me. Your book taught me how to use FrameMaker so quickly even my boss was amazed. You correctly anticipated the order in which I needed to learn this application and the questions I had. It was almost as though you were there, looking over my shoulder the entire time. Thank you!"

"This book is great! It teaches people how to use FrameMaker in a logical way that makes it easy to learn. A definite 'must have' for anyone who wants to learn FrameMaker or refresh their skills!"

"Fantastic course on a topic that is EXTREMELY difficult to teach. The course is very well laid out, with great explanations for someone who is unfamiliar with the field of technical writing. Janet is phenomenal and I most definitely will look for any future courses or books she offers."

"Janet Underwood is organized, knowledgeable, and encouraging. This course pushes through the thicket of its subject matter about as far as possible for an introductory course."

"This is an excellent course!!! I have recommended it to several other people."

"Ms. Underwood has put together a VERY fine course. It teaches you what you need to know in a way that's easy to understand and follow. Ms. Underwood's knowledge and ability to explain FrameMaker concepts is exemplary. She really knows her stuff."

"This course met all of my immediate needs to get me up and running in a knowledgeable state. My employer was impressed and pleased at how quickly the turnaround has been with his current document conversion since my taking this course. Thanks a lot."

"Janet is an amazing teacher. She is one of, if not the best teachers that I've had the pleasure of learning from."

"Very comprehensive, really gets you started with the complex world of FrameMaker!"

"This course gave me a better understanding of the material than I likely would have gained on my own."

"Janet has created an excellent introduction to this not-so WYSIWYG application and accurately anticipated areas that can be challenging for beginners. Well done Janet, and thank you!"

i

Mastering the Basics (and more) of Adobe FrameMaker 10

By Janet S. Underwood

WordWorx Publishing

Belton, MO

This book is dedicated to my "brat pack" for all of their patience with my late nights and preoccupation in finishing this book.

Adobe® FrameMaker® is a product of Adobe Systems Incorporated. Adobe FrameMaker screen shots are reprinted with permission from Adobe Systems Incorporated.

For information, contact

WordWorx Publishing
wordworx.online@ymail.com

ISBN-13: 978-1461013877

ISBN-10: 1461013879

Printed in the U.S.A.

Table of Contents

Table of Figures

Table of Tables

This page is intentionally left blank.

Introduction

Learn why technical writers like FrameMaker so much, how to set up your workspace, and how to open and save FrameMaker templates.

For years, experienced technical writers have thought that FrameMaker is the best application for creating and maintaining very large technical documents. It has a reputation that is almost mythical in the technical writing industry. Even people who have never had to use it in their jobs feel that they can't really consider themselves to be highly skilled technical writers until they have learned how to use FrameMaker.

But, even with the improved user interfaces in Version 10, FrameMaker is an intimidating application. Even people who generally can figure out how to use any software on their own often are stumped when it comes to FrameMaker. Many want some training or at least some books to help them, but both can be difficult to find. And when you do find them, they may be more expensive than you thought they would be.

Despite these things, FrameMaker is one of the most popular applications used by technical writers. There are several reasons for its popularity: First, it handles large documents very well. While word-processing programs can behave erratically when documents become large or contain many graphics, documents created in FrameMaker generally remain stable even if they have hundreds or even thousands of pages. FrameMaker manages the pagination, tables of contents, and indexes in large documents better than most other desktop-publishing applications.

Second, FrameMaker has features that help technical writers create more consistent documents. This is important because technical writers often work in teams with many writers working on the same document at the same time.

Third, while FrameMaker can crash (as any software can), it's a much more stable application than many others you might have used. Additionally, if you open your FrameMaker file on a different computer with a different printer driver, your formatting isn't as likely to change as it would with other word-processing applications.

Fourth, FrameMaker can be used on different platforms. The documents you produce on one platform can be opened on other platforms. For example, if you create a document using FrameMaker on a UNIX computer, you can open it in FrameMaker on a PC without having to convert the file. Since the user interface is almost identical in both Windows and UNIX versions, if you learn how to use FrameMaker for Windows, you can easily learn how to use FrameMaker for UNIX.

What's New in this Book

My goal in writing this book is to give you a good foundation for mastering unstructured FrameMaker 10. To achieve that goal, I'll help you become familiar with many of FrameMaker's windows, dialog boxes, and tools that enable you to create and publish documents and graphics. When you've finished this book, you'll be able to create the types of documents and books in FrameMaker that you'll create most often. In addition, you should have the confidence to explore FrameMaker's many features on your own so you can do even more.

My *Introduction to Adobe FrameMaker 9 for Windows* book was based upon an online class that I taught at numerous colleges and universities around the world.

This book updates the content to reflect the FrameMaker 10 changes, plus it adds more information, such as the following:

- A chapter discussing conditional text.
- A chapter discussing how to create templates.
- A glossary (*See Appendix A: Glossary of Terms*).
- FrameMaker's history (*See Appendix B: A Short History of FrameMaker*).
- An explanation of points and picas (*See Appendix C: Picas and Points*).
- Keyboard shortcuts and explanations of dialog boxes, panels, and pods by their menu options (*See Appendixes D through L*).

Now, let's start mastering the basics and more of FrameMaker 10 by setting up the work area.

Setting Up Your Work Area

When you open FrameMaker for the first time, you'll be asked to choose between two interfaces: **FrameMaker** mode (the unstructured side) and **Structured FrameMaker** mode. You need a good understanding of unstructured FrameMaker before you can feel comfortable using structured FrameMaker, so select **FrameMaker**. FrameMaker will always open in this mode until you change it through the Preferences dialog box that we'll look at soon.

After you've selected which mode you want to use, the application continues to load and the **Welcome** screen opens on the FrameMaker window:

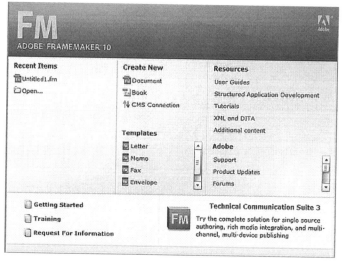

Figure 1: Welcome screen

The Welcome screen will be displayed each time you open FrameMaker. From this screen, you can open a new document, book, or Content Management System (CMS) connection; open a document you've been working on from a list that's displayed at the left; open a document based on a template; access tutorials and other helpful resources; contact Adobe; and more.

You also can do all of these things from the menu options in the menu bar. You often can do things in more than one way in FrameMaker.

Setting Your Preferences

If you ever want to change from the unstructured FrameMaker mode to the structured FrameMaker mode, you must use the Preferences dialog box. To look at the Preferences dialog box, click **File > Preferences > General** from the menu bar. The Preferences dialog box opens. (If you don't see this option on your menu, please check the Frequently Asked Questions at the end of the chapter.)

Product Interface

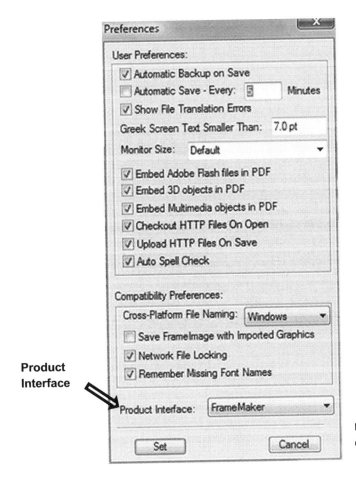

Figure 2: Preferences dialog box

At the bottom of the Preferences dialog box, click the arrow on the button next to the **Product Interface** label. This is where you can switch between unstructured and structured FrameMaker. If you make a change, click the **Set** button. You'll be prompted to restart the application for the change to go into effect. Other options you can set on this dialog box are the following:

- **Automatic Backup on Save**
  The first two options will automatically save your work. The first option, **Automatic Backup on Save**, will create a backup copy of your file automatically when you save it.

- **Automatic Save – Every: [X] Minutes**
  This option will automatically save a backup copy of your file at the intervals you designate. You can select this option or the first one individually, or you can select both of them by placing checkmarks in front of them.

- **Show File Translation Errors**
  When you place a checkmark in front of this option, a list will be generated of errors that have occurred when, for example, you're opening a file that's been created on another platform or saving a file to HTML.

- **Greek Screen Text Smaller Than:**
  With this option, text that's smaller than the point size you designate in the box at the right will be greeked (displayed as nonsense words) on your computer screen, but the text will still print correctly. *(See Appendix C for an explanation of picas and points.)*

- **Monitor Size**
  If you leave the setting at **Default**, FrameMaker will determine what size your monitor is. Choose the size from the list that appears when you click the arrow at the end of the field if your document will be displayed on a monitor of a specific size.

- **Embed Adobe Flash files in PDF**
  If checked, FrameMaker embeds Adobe Flash files as bitmap images in documents that are saved as Portable Document Format (PDF) files. When readers click the images, the Flash files play. If you want readers to be able to play Flash files when PDFs are opened, be sure there's a checkmark in front of *Embed Adobe Flash files in PDF.*

- **Embed 3D objects in PDF**
  If checked, FrameMaker embeds 3D objects in documents saved as PDFs. The 3D objects are embedded as bitmap images in PDFs. When readers click the images, they can view the 3D

objects. If you want readers to be able to do this when PDFs are opened, be sure there's a checkmark in front of *Embed 3D objects in PDF*.

- **Embed Multimedia objects in PDF**
  If checked, FrameMaker embeds multimedia objects in documents saved as PDFs. The multimedia objects are embedded as bitmap images in the PDFs. When readers click the images, they can view the multimedia objects. If you want readers to be able to do this when PDFs are opened, be sure there's a checkmark in front of *Embed Multimedia objects in PDF*.

- **Checkout HTTP Files On Open**
  HTTP stands for *HyperText Transfer Protocol*. FrameMaker files can be saved on WebDAV servers. WebDAV is a protocol that enables users to collaborate on files that are saved on a remote Web server. Place a checkmark in front of this option if you will be checking out files from a WebDAV server.

- **Upload HTTP Files On Save**
  This setting only is applied if you're working with WebDAV, a protocol that enables users to collaborate on files that are saved on a remote Web server. If you place a checkmark in front of this setting, your files will be uploaded to the remote Web server when you save them.

- **Auto Spell Check**
  If you want FrameMaker to underline words it thinks are misspelled as you type, place a checkmark in front of this option. If you type a word that the application thinks is misspelled or use punctuation incorrectly, the possible errors will be underlined with a wavy red or green line. If you right-click on the word or punctuation that is marked, a menu shows you words FrameMaker thinks you might have meant and options to tell FrameMaker to correct it. You can disable automatic spell

checking by removing the checkmark in front of it on the Preferences dialog box.

- **Cross-Platform File Naming**
  If the document you're working on will be opened on a UNIX or Macintosh computer, place a checkmark in front of this option and select the platform that will be using this file. Note that Adobe no longer produces a Mac version of FrameMaker.

- **Save FrameImage with Imported Graphics**
  In the early days of FrameMaker, FrameImage provided a common format for imported raster images for all three platforms you could use FrameMaker on at that time. While you could probably still use it today with mif (a format you can save FrameMaker files to), FrameImage is mostly an unneeded artifact.

- **Network File Locking**
  Select this to warn a user on a network when a document is already opened by another user.

- **Remember Missing Font Names**
  If selected, FrameMaker saves a list of fonts that are used in a document but aren't available on the computer you're using. If the document is opened on a computer that has those fonts installed, the original fonts will reappear even if you've saved the document with substitute fonts.

- **Product Interface**
  Use this to select whether you want to run unstructured or structured FrameMaker.

With the exception of the Product Interface choices, you don't have to restart your computer for these options to take effect immediately.

FrameMaker's Work Area

After you've opened FrameMaker and looked at the preferences you can set, open a blank document by doing one of the following:

- Click **Document** under **Create New** if the Welcome screen is open, or
- Click **File > New > Document** from the menu bar.

The New dialog box opens:

Figure 3: New dialog box

At the top of the window where it says **Use Blank Paper,** there are three buttons labeled **Portrait**, **Landscape**, and **Custom**. Below that, you'll see several folders with FrameMaker templates.

For now, let's say that you want to open a blank document. To do that, you'll select one of the three buttons at the top of the dialog box. Here's what they mean:

- **Portrait**

  If you click the **Portrait** button, a blank document will open that's standard size for your version. *Portrait* means that it'll be longer along the sides than the top and bottom.

- **Landscape**

  If you click the **Landscape** button, a blank document will open that's standard size for your version and is longer along the top and bottom than the sides.

- **Custom**

  Click the **Custom** button and the Custom Blank Paper dialog box opens:

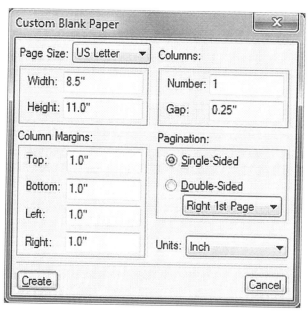

Figure 4: Custom Blank Paper dialog box

If you click the arrow next to the **Page Size** box, you can choose different page sizes. The measurements listed in the other boxes will change if you choose a different size. You also can define a paper size that's different from the ones that are listed by entering the width and height of the page you want on this dialog box. You can define the following:

- The number of columns you want on the page
- The amount of space between the columns (the "Gap")
- Whether your document will be printed on one side of the page or both sides
- Whether you want the first page to be a right-hand or a left-hand page
- The unit of measurement you want to use

Getting Familiar with the Work Area

For now, open a blank portrait document. If you're looking at the Custom Blank Paper dialog box, click **Cancel** to close it. Then click **File > New > Document** to open the New dialog box again and click **Portrait** on the New dialog box. A blank page opens in the work area. You'll see that there's a lot going on in the work area.

At the top right side of the window is a new tool called the **Workspace Switcher**. Click the arrow to the right of a word there. The following is displayed:

Figure 5: Workspace Switcher

When you select the **Authoring, Design, Manage Graphics,** or **Review** options, your workspace changes. The pods and panels that are commonly used when performing those tasks are displayed. (We'll talk more about pods and panels in a bit.) You can add more panels and pods to these options or modify them if you wish.

If you don't want any of the pods or panels to be displayed while you're working, select **Blank**.

If you have developed a workspace with pods and panels that you like displayed, you can save that workspace with a name of your choice by selecting **Save Workspace**.

If you want to rename or delete an option, you can do that by selecting **Manage Workspace**.

Finally, there's a feature here that is very important to most people when they're first learning how to use an application—the option to reset the workspaces back to their original settings by selecting **Reset Workspace**.

Try the different options to see how they change your workspace. Later, you can select the options you want when working in different stages of your document. When you're finished for now, however, select **Blank** so you can look at the following elements around your document window.

Menu bar

The first element to look at is the menu bar. It's located at the top of the window and has the names of menu options such as **File, View, Format**, etc. By clicking any of the menu options, menus drop down with options you can choose. *(See Appendixes D through L for an explanation of the different menus, their options, and shortcut keys you can use to access them.)*

Important! Menu options can be different when you're looking at different types of pages or working with different types of files.

Toolbars

The next elements to look at are the toolbars. Toolbars are generally added below the menu bar and consist of shortcuts to commonly used commands. If you don't see any toolbars below the menu bar, click **View > Toolbars** on the menu bar and click the ones you want to be displayed. Your options are as follows:

- **Show All**
  This displays all of the toolbars listed on this menu.

- **Hide All**
  This hides all of the toolbars listed on this menu.

- **Graphics Toolbar**
  This displays FrameMaker's graphics Tools palette, which is an exception to the statement above that toolbars are displayed below the menu bar. We'll talk more about the Tools palette in Chapter 5.

- **Quick Access Bar**
  This toolbar consists of icons to perform common commands, such as Help, New Document, Open, Save, Import File, Print, Toggle View, Clear, Cut, Copy, Paste, Undo, Redo, History, Character Catalog, Paragraph Catalog, Find/Change, Find Next, Spelling Checker, Anchored Frame, Footnote, Insert Table, Symbols.

- **Text Formatting**
  This toolbar enables you to format your text manually by providing options to boldface, italicize, or underline your text (or remove all manual formatting by clicking **Plain**); increase or decrease the size of the type; change it to lowercase, title case, or uppercase; select a different typeface; or select a different size.

- **Table Formatting**
  This toolbar enables you to format your tables by selecting from the options provided, such as selecting rows, columns, column body cells, and tables; move the insertion point; add and remove rows or columns; align text; straddle (merge) cells; change column widths; and apply custom rulings and shadings. Note that you must have a table inserted for most of the toolbar options to be active, and you must have selected some cells for the alignment options to be active.

- **Paragraph Formatting**

  This displays options for formatting your paragraphs, including setting tab stops; aligning your paragraphs (flush left, centered, flush right, or justified); setting the width between lines; and selecting the paragraph tag to be applied to a paragraph.

- **Object Alignment**

  This displays options for moving graphics and other objects. Use this toolbar to move objects up, down, left, or right; align them on different points; rotate objects; and make lines dashed or solid.

- **Object Properties**

  This displays options for setting the properties of different objects, such as grouping or ungrouping two or more objects; moving an object to the front or sending it to the back; distributing two or more objects; making changes to objects (reshaping them, smoothing or un-smoothing, flipping objects up, down, left, or right); setting object properties; and setting snap and gravity options.

- **Track Text Edits**

  This displays options for tracking changes to text, such as enabling or disabling tracking; showing edits; accepting or rejecting edits; and previewing original or edited text.

Status bar

The next element to look at is the Status bar at the bottom of the overall window. This contains information about the document and has controls for zooming and moving through the document. Be sure to explore this a bit. Once we start adding panels and pods, it could become difficult to see the Status bar.

Borders, Text Symbols, and Rulers

Click **View** on the menu bar again and make sure there are checkmarks in front of **Borders, Text Symbols**, and **Rulers**. After all of these are activated, look at your workspace again. Immediately above your document and along the left side are the document rulers. Notice also that there are symbols and guides within your document. Your text frame has a border around it and if you type some words, you probably will see some symbols in your text. Common text symbols that you'll see are shown in Figure 6.

- To show or hide borders, click **View > Borders**.
- To show or hide text symbols, click **View > Text Symbols**.

Text Symbol	Definition
¶	End of paragraph
§	End of flow and end of table cell
⟩	Tab
⊥	Anchored frame and table anchor
T	Marker
⟨	Forced return
|	Manual equation alignment point
⊔	Nonbreaking space
⊤	Discretionary hyphen
▬	Suppress hyphenation

Figure 6: Common Text Symbols

Panels and Pods

Panels and pods were added in FrameMaker version 9 as a new way to arrange elements on your workspace.

- **Panels**

  Panels contain modified dialog boxes that are used often (for example, the Character, Paragraph, and Table Designers, plus the Marker, Variables, Spelling Checker, Find/Change, and Cross-Reference panels). Panels typically are docked at the right side of the work area. The purpose of the panels is to help you monitor and modify your work. You can minimize, group, or stack panels, as well as move panels out of the docked area by "grabbing" them at the top and then dragging them to another position while holding down the left-mouse button.

- **Pods**

  Pods contain modified dialog boxes that, like the ones in the panels, are used often (for example, the Variables, Cross-Reference, Marker, and Conditional Text pods). The interface has been modified to help users, especially if they have more than one document open. Pods typically are docked along the bottom of the work area.

We'll talk more about the dialog boxes included in the pods and panels as we go through the book.

Interface Preferences

Set your preferences for showing panels and documents by clicking **File > Preferences > Interface** on the menu bar. (If you don't see this option on your menu, please check the Frequently Asked Questions at the end of the chapter.) The Interface Preferences dialog box opens where there are a number of options for displaying your panels and documents as follows:

- **Auto-Collapse Iconic Panels**
  If this is checked, the panels that are displayed as icons will collapse automatically after use.

- **Auto-Show Hidden Panels**
  Select this to show hidden panels automatically.

- **Hide Panels on Close**
  If checked, FrameMaker hides panels when you close them.

- **Open Documents as Tabs**
  If checked, FrameMaker organizes open documents with tabs along the top of the work area. If you remove the checkmark in front of this option, the document windows become floating windows and you'll only see a reference to the document you're looking at currently.

- **Hide Single Tabs in Documents**
  If checked, only the name of floating document windows will be displayed in the title bar. If you remove the checkmark, the name of the document file name appears in both the title bar and the tab bar.

- **Prevent Document Tabbing when Dragging**
  This would be used to prevent users from dragging document windows when the documents are displayed in tabbed windows.

- **Open Composite Documents as Tabs**
  A composite document is a type of FrameMaker file used in an XML-based architecture called Darwin Information Typing Architecture (DITA). If this is checked, FrameMaker opens composite documents as tabbed documents. If you remove the checkmark, the composite document windows become floating windows.

- **Tool Tips**

  Choose how you want to view tool tips from the drop-down menu.

- **UI Brightness**

  "UI" stands for *User Interface*. Slide the bar on the scale to determine how bright your FrameMaker screen and dialog boxes will be.

When you're finished making any changes you want on the Interface Preferences dialog box, click **OK** to save your changes or **Cancel** to close the box without making any changes.

FrameMaker's Templates

Before you leave this chapter, take a quick look at FrameMaker's templates.

FrameMaker comes with standard templates for letters, memos, reports, newsletters, outlines, books, and viewgraphs. You also can use documents as templates.

To understand templates better, look at some of the ones that are included in your FrameMaker package.

Where to Find Templates

Open FrameMaker, and then click **File > New > Document** or press **CTRL + N** to open the New dialog box. Until you change it, the **Templates** folder is selected in the **Look in** box. In the large pane in the middle of the dialog box, you'll see several folders. This is where you'll find FrameMaker's templates. It's also a good place to store your own templates.

You can use a document as a template in FrameMaker. If you want to create a template based on another document, click the arrow at the end of the **Look in** box, and then navigate to the document you want to use.

Also, you can click the folder icon to the right of the **Look in** box to go up one level in the directory, click the folder icon to the right of that one to create a new folder, or click the icon at the far right to view the contents of the current folder in different ways. You can identify the names of each of these icons by moving your cursor slowly over them and pausing until the screen tips are displayed.

FrameMaker comes with several templates that you can use. In addition to the templates that you see by default, you can click the arrow to the right of the **Look in** box to navigate to your Adobe FrameMaker folder on your hard drive. In that folder, look for a folder named "Samples" where you'll find even more templates.

To open a template, click a folder in the large pane or navigate to the folder you want, and then select the template you want to use or the document you want to use as a template.

Standard Templates Dialog Box

Before you do that, however, look at the large buttons at the bottom of the New dialog box. Click the one that says **Explore Standard Templates.** The Standard Templates dialog box opens:

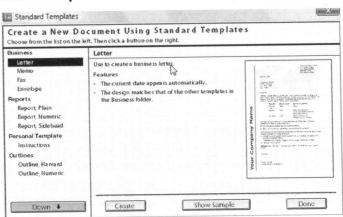

Figure 7: Standard Templates dialog box

This is a handy way to learn about templates that are already loaded on your computer. In addition to the thumbnail image of the document, you'll see a short description of the document and a list of the features of the template.

Notice the three buttons at the bottom of the window. To create a document based on the template you're viewing, click **Create**. All of the margins, typeface settings, etc., will be already defined in your document, but there won't be any text.

To see a sample of a document based on this template, click **Show Sample**. To exit this dialog box without selecting anything, click **Done**.

Note: You may see an error message that tells you that this template uses unavailable fonts. It's not unusual to see this error message often when using FrameMaker. Just click **OK** and proceed.

Before you continue, take a few minutes to explore the different templates by using the Standard Templates dialog box. Highlight each one, and then read the description and features of the individual templates. If you like, look at samples of different ones. When you finish, close the Standard Templates dialog box and return to this chapter.

Open a Document Based on a FrameMaker Template

Open a document that's based on the Memo template in the Business folder by doing the following:

1. Click **File > New > Document** on your menu bar or press **CTRL + N** (the shortcut key combination for this command). The New dialog box opens.

2. Click the **Business** folder in the large pane of the New dialog box to open it, and then double-click **Memo**.

For now, take a look at the Master Pages behind this document, but don't change any of the elements on this page.

Looking at Master Pages

When you're working with a FrameMaker document, you can move back and forth between Master Pages and Body Pages. The page that you're looking at now is called a *Body Page*. Body Pages are where you type new information. *Master Pages* are where you set up elements that you want to appear on the Body Pages of all documents of this type.

To look at the Master Pages of the Memo template, click **View > Master Pages** on the menu bar. The Master Page of the Body Page you were looking at is displayed. Notice that the text frame and column borders are displayed on the Master Page, along with certain text that appears on the Body Page. If the text appears on the Master Page, you have to change it here if you wish to do so. You can't change this text on the Body Pages.

Notice too that the vertical text that says "Your Company Name" along the left side of the Body Page here says *Running H/F 1*. (You may have to scroll down to see this.) Running headers and footers are a special category of elements that you can use when you create your FrameMaker documents. We'll talk more about them in later chapters.

For now, switch back to your Body Page by clicking **View > Body Pages** on the menu bar. At the upper-right side of the page, highlight the words *Your Company Name*, and then type in a new name, such as *ABC Corporation* or the name of the company for which you work. Notice that the vertical text at the left side of the page is changed. If it doesn't change, first try changing the view to Master Pages and then back to Body Pages to refresh the page. If the text still looks skewed with some of the old text remaining, save your document, close it, and then open it again. The text should say the same thing that you typed on the first line in the upper-right corner.

Save Your Template

Now save this template in your own personal template folder by following these steps:

1. Click **File > Save As** on your menu bar.

2. Navigate to the **Program Files** on your hard drive, and then select **Adobe > FrameMaker 10**.

3. Open the **Templates** folder, and then click the **New Folder** icon at the top of the window.

4. Change the name of the new folder to one that you'll identify as being your own templates.

5. After you've named your new folder, double-click it to open it. Notice that while you were doing all of this, the default name of your document is listed in the **File Name** box.

6. Change the name of the file to one that you'll recognize in the future. For example, I saved my memo template to a folder called *Janet* and I called the file *memo*.

   Note: If you're using a trial version of FrameMaker, you may not be able to save your template to a new folder in this location. Save your template to the location suggested by FrameMaker instead. This means that you'll have to navigate to find this folder when you're opening a new document based upon this template.

7. Click **Save**. The next time you click **File > New > Document**, you'll see that your folder has been added to the list and your memo file is inside of that folder.

After you've saved your template, close the document window and then close FrameMaker if you wish. Good job!

FrameMaker has one of the highest learning curves of all high-end desktop publishing applications, so be patient and take your time while learning. We'll go over the material we discussed in this chapter in more detail later, so don't worry if you don't thoroughly understand how FrameMaker works right now. There's much more to come!

Frequently Asked Questions

Q: *I see a message telling me that the "history" will be lost if I do something. What does this mean?*

A: There's actually some interesting history (no pun intended) about this one. Until version 7.2, only a few years ago, FrameMaker didn't have multiple "undo" capability. You could only undo one action that you'd just done. When Adobe added the capability to undo or redo more than one action, they also created a history file that keeps track of the actions you perform in FrameMaker.

If you want to stop seeing these messages, click **File > Preferences > Alert Strings**. The Alert Strings dialog box opens:

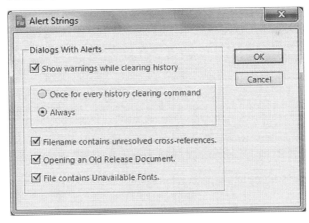

Figure 8: Alert Strings dialog box

Add or remove the checkmarks in front of options as you wish.

Q: *Why do I see a message saying that the document I'm writing uses unavailable fonts so much?*

A: When FrameMaker displays this message, it means that some typefaces used in the document aren't available on your computer. This can be due to a variety of reasons: The document may have been edited on a different system with typefaces and fonts that aren't installed on the system you are using; a typeface or font may have been removed or become damaged; or the default printer for your system may have been changed.

Regardless of the reason, most FrameMaker users simply click **OK** when this message appears and let FrameMaker make the necessary font substitutions. While some of the line breaks may change, the basic formatting will remain the same.

If you want to stop seeing this message, click **File > Preferences > Alert Strings** on the menu bar and remove the checkmark in front of "File contains Unavailable Fonts."

Q: *I installed FrameMaker 10 on my computer, but I'm not seeing all of the menu options I should be seeing. For example, when I click **File** on the menu bar in the Body Pages view, I don't have the options to set preferences. What's wrong?*

A: FrameMaker allows you to open your menus either as Quick menus (shortened versions) or as Complete menus. It sounds as though somehow you have changed the setting to Quick menus. To change this, click **View > Menus** on the menu bar. Select **Complete**. You should see all of the menu options now.

t

Master Pages and Text Flows

Look at Master Pages, create a new Master Page and apply it to a Body Page, create headers and footers, and learn about text flows.

Most word-processing applications only use one type of page for writing documents—the page you see on the screen when you open the application. FrameMaker is different. It uses three types of pages to create a document. These types of pages are as follows:

- **Body Pages**
  This is where you type your text. Body Pages also display the background text and graphics from their corresponding Master Pages.

- **Master Pages**
  You'll use these pages to design the page layout and the background text for Body Pages (for example, page headers and footers). Master Pages are a big part of the templates for your documents and the primary subject of this chapter.

- **Reference Pages**

  These pages hold information that is used to determine how some of the elements in your documents will behave (such as mappings for HTML). They also can hold graphics that you can use throughout a document and templates for some elements of your document. We'll cover them in more detail in later chapters.

  When you open a new document, FrameMaker automatically creates a Body Page, a Master Page (the default is a right-hand page), and Reference Pages. Page layouts are done on your Master Pages. Here's where you'll specify column widths, number of columns, and other aspects of your page layout.

  Some documents require several page layouts. For example, you might create special layouts for the first page of a chapter, a rotated page, or a page with a different number of columns. You can use Master Pages to design custom page layouts for different elements within your document, such as title pages, indexes, and tables of contents.

  In this chapter, you'll create a new document that has right and left Master Pages, and then you'll create a custom Master Page and make some modifications to your Master Pages.

Create a New Document

Create a new document by following these steps:

1. Open FrameMaker and click **File > New > Document** on the menu bar. The New dialog box opens.

2. Click **Portrait** at the top of the box to open a blank portrait page.

3. Before we go on, save your document by clicking **File > Save As** from the menu bar.

4. In the Save Document dialog box, navigate to the folder where you want to save your document.

5. In the **File name** box, type *MyFirstDoc.fm* and click **Save**.

   Note: So this document can be accessible to people using FrameMaker on other platforms (such as UNIX), follow naming conventions that will work on all possible platforms that might open your document. UNIX filenames can't have spaces in the name, so we're running these words together. Also, note that the extension at the end of the file name is *fm* for FrameMaker.

   Because we'll be designing our Master Pages, click the arrow at the right top corner of the window and select **Design** from the Workspace Switcher.

6. Place your cursor on the blank page in the document if it isn't already there, and then press and hold the **ENTER** key to create three blank pages with carriage returns along the left margin.

7. So FrameMaker will generate both a right and left Master Page, click **Format > Page Layout > Pagination** on the menu bar. The Pagination dialog box opens:

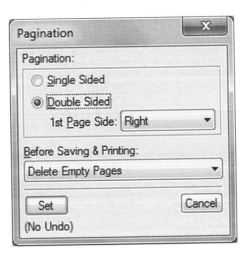

Figure 9: Pagination dialog box

8. Click the radio button in front of **Double Sided** and be sure that the 1st Page Side is "Right."

9. Click **Set**. You can't see them until you go to the Master Pages view, but FrameMaker has now generated a left Master Page to go with the right Master Page that was generated when you opened the new document.

Create a Custom Master Page

Click **View > Master Pages** on the menu bar to open the Master Pages view. Look at the Status bar at the bottom of the window and you'll see that it either says "Right (2 of 2)" or "Left (2 of 2)" (depending upon which type of page your cursor was on when you left the Body Pages).

Scroll up and down so you can see both Master Pages that FrameMaker generated. Notice that these pages contain header, main text, and footer frames, each outlined with dashed lines.

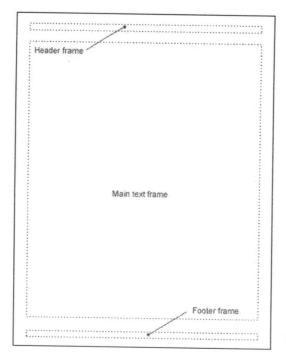

Figure 10: Master Page

Create a custom Master Page that will have a different layout for the first page of chapters by following these steps:

1. While still in the Master Pages view, click **Format > Page Layout > New Master Page** on the menu bar. The Add Master Page dialog box opens.

   Note: One reason that FrameMaker is difficult to learn is because you may get different results when you select some of the menu options, depending on the type of page you're on when you make your selection. If the dialog box that opens doesn't look like the one below, check to be sure that you're in the Master Pages view.

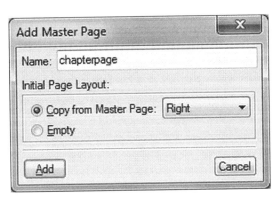

Figure 11: Add Master Page dialog box

2. In the **Name** field of the Add Master Page dialog box, type *chapterpage*.

3. Be sure the **Copy from Master Page** field is selected and that **Right** is the designated Master Page to copy. (A publishing convention is to always start new chapters on a right-hand page to make it easier for readers to find.)

4. Click **Add**.

   Notice that the Status bar at the bottom of your FrameMaker window displays the name of the new Master Page when you add it. That's because your cursor now is on this page.

Create Headers and Footers

You now have three Master Pages—the right Master Page, the left Master Page, and the chapterpage Master Page. Right now, they all look alike. Let's make some changes to them by creating headers and footers. First, you'll create a new header frame on the chapterpage Master Page, and then you'll modify the footer.

Create a Header Frame

To create a new header frame, first check to be sure you're on the *chapterpage* Master Page by positioning your cursor on the Master Page and looking at the name of the page in the Status bar at the bottom of the window. Then follow these steps:

1. Press and hold the **CTRL** key, and then click inside the existing header frame (refer to the graphic above called "Master Page" if you need help remembering which frame is the header frame). Notice that handles appear around the header frame.

2. Press the **DELETE** key to remove the existing header frame.

3. Select **Graphics > Tools** on the menu bar. The Tools palette shown in Figure 12 opens.

Place a Text Frame icon

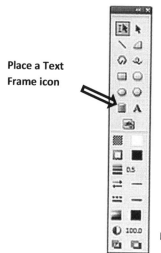

Figure 12: Tools palette

4. Move your cursor slowly over the icons on the Tools palette. The screen tip that appears when you move your cursor over the sixth icon from the top on the left side of the Tools palette should say **Place a Text Frame**. Click this icon.

5. When you clicked the **Place a Text Frame** icon, your cursor changed to two crossed lines. Position the cursor so that there's a little line under the one-inch mark on the horizontal ruler at the top of the window and a little line next to the one-half-inch mark on the vertical ruler along the left side of the window.

6. Press and hold your left-mouse button while drawing a new header frame approximately 6.5 inches long by .25 inches high. Notice that as you draw, the dimensions of the frame are displayed in the lower-left corner of the Status bar.

7. When you finish drawing your header text frame, release the left-mouse button. The Add New Text Frame dialog box opens:

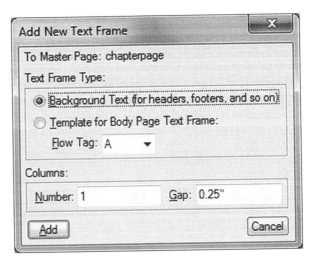

Figure 13: Add New Text Frame dialog box

8. If it isn't already selected, select **Background Text**, which means that the text you type in this frame will appear on your Body Pages, but you can only edit it on your Master Pages.

9. Leave the column settings as they are.

10. Click **Add** to insert the header frame.

11. Click outside the header frame to deselect the frame.

12. Click within the header frame and type *My First FrameMaker Document*.

13. With your cursor still on the line you just typed, locate the Paragraph Formats box on the Paragraph Formatting toolbar at the top of the window. (If it isn't visible, click **View > Toolbars > Paragraph Formatting**.)

14. Click the arrow next to the box and select **Title** from the list to apply the Title paragraph tag to your text. The words you typed should be in a larger type size, bolded, and centered in your header frame.

Adding Page Numbers to Footers

Next, add page numbers to the footer by doing the following:

1. Scroll to the bottom of the chapterpage and click within the footer frame. (If you can't remember which one is the footer frame, please refer to the graphic above called Master Page.) With your cursor in the footer frame, click **Special > Variables** on the menu bar. The Variables pod at the bottom of the screen is displayed, or if it was already displayed, it becomes active.

Insert Selected Variable icon

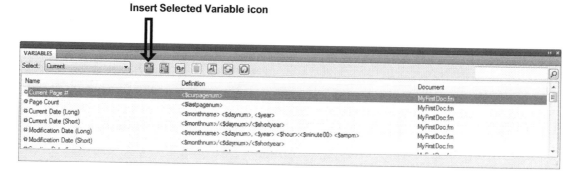

Figure 14: Variables pod

2. Click **Current Page #** in the Variables pod, and then click the **Insert Selected Variable** icon as shown above. The # symbol is inserted in the footer. This symbol is the current page number variable.

3. Place your cursor in front of the # symbol, and then press the **TAB** key on your keyboard one time to position the page number in the center of the footer frame.

4. Go to your right and left Master Pages and repeat these steps to insert the page number variable in the footers of these pages.

5. After you've inserted the page number variable on all of your Master Pages, click **View > Body Pages** to return to your Body Pages.

Applying Master Pages to Body Pages

To apply your custom chapterpage Master Page to the first Body Page in your document, follow these steps:

1. Place your cursor on the first Body Page in your document, and then select **Format > Page Layout > Master Page Usage**. The Master Page Usage dialog box opens:

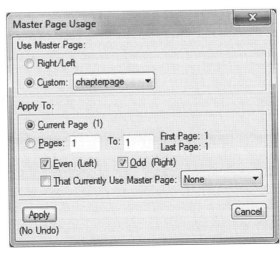

Figure 15: Master Page Usage dialog box

2. Click the radio button in front of **Custom**.

3. Select **chapterpage** from the pull-down list. Notice that in the **Apply To** area of the Master Page Usage dialog box, you can specify the Body Pages that will use the Master Page you select. Since we want this Master Page to be applied to the current page, be certain **Current Page** is selected.

4. Click **Apply**. The current Body Page now uses chapterpage as its Master Page. Note that you can't select or edit the text or graphics that you added to the Master Page on the Body Page. You must modify this information from the Master Page.

Renaming a Master Page

You can't rename the left and right Master Pages that are generated when you open a new document, but you can rename *custom* Master Pages by following these steps:

1. Select **View > Master Pages** on the menu bar, and then place your cursor on the Master Page you want to rename.

2. The name of your Master Page is displayed in the Status bar. Click the name of the Master Page in the Status bar. The Master Page Name dialog box opens:

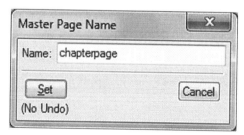

Figure 16: Master Page Name dialog box

3. Type the new Master Page name over the highlighted name, and then click **Set**. You've renamed the Master Page, and all Body Pages that use that Master Page are still formatted by the renamed page.

Text Frames

In FrameMaker, you type content in *text frames*. Master Pages can contain two types of text frames: *background text frames* and *template text frames*.

In the last section, you looked at the Master Pages FrameMaker generated when you opened a new document. You also created a custom Master Page based on one of them. As you may recall, there were three text frames on those pages: a header frame, a main text frame, and a footer frame.

The header and footer text frames are examples of *background text frames*. You may also recall that you can add content to these text frames only when you're on the Master Page. You can't add content to these text frames while you're on the Body Pages associated with that particular Master Page. You'll typically use background text frames for page headers and footers.

The main text frame is an example of a *template text frame*. Template text frames define the layout of the body text of your document. Template text frames work in the opposite manner as the background text frames. If you type in the template text frames while you're on the Master Pages, what you type won't show up on any of the Body Pages that are associated with that Master Page. Many writers like to use these text frames on the Master Pages to type notes about the template.

Text Flows

In FrameMaker, template text frames have *text flows*. Text flows are the way the text flows throughout the document. They're identified by names that are called *flow tags*. When FrameMaker generated your Master Pages, the text flow tag for the text frame was named "A." All text frames named "A" are automatically connected by default. This means that if you fill up a text frame in Flow A on the first Body Page with content, whatever you add automatically flows to the next text frame that has the flow tag "A."

When you have only one text flow in your document, FrameMaker adds Body Pages as necessary and automatically uses the page layout from the left or right Master Pages. FrameMaker handles the text frame connections for you.

If you want to have more than one text flow in your document, or you don't want the content to flow automatically to the next text frame with the same name, you can turn off Autoconnect by doing the following:

1. Select the text frame you want to disconnect by holding down **CTRL** while left-clicking on the border of the frame.

2. Click **Graphics > Object Properties** on the menu bar. The Object Properties dialog box opens.

3. Remove the checkmark in front of **Autoconnect** and click **OK**.

   Note: While you can do this on Body Pages or Master Pages, if you disconnect the flow while on a Body Page, the change becomes an override and is applied only to the specific page you're on when you perform this action.

Add a Template Text Frame

To see how to add a template text frame to your layout, add a second template text frame to the *My First FrameMaker Document* by following these steps:

1. If you closed the document you were working on in the last section, open it again.

2. Click **View > Master Pages**.

3. In the Master Pages view, hold down the **CTRL** key and click in the main text frame. The main text frame has text flow "A."

4. Grab one of the handles on the right side of the selected text frame and move the right side of the frame toward the middle of the page to make room for a second frame.

5. Click the **Place a Text Frame** icon on the Tools palette. (If you have closed the Tools palette, open it again by clicking **File > Graphics > Tools** on the menu bar.)

6. Draw a text frame in the right side of the page.

7. When you finish drawing the new text frame, release the left-mouse button. The Add New Text Frame dialog box opens:

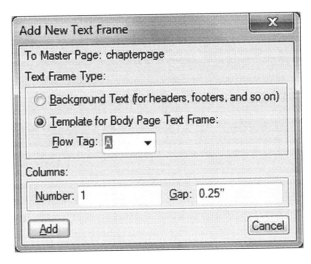

Figure 17: Add New Text Frame dialog box

8. Click the radio button in front of **Template for Body Page Text Frame**. Note that at this time, you only have one choice for the Flow Tag: A.

9. Click **Add**. FrameMaker displays a message telling you that the new frame has been connected to the end of the first one.

When you did this, if you fill up the first text frame with text, your text will automatically flow to the new text frame you just added because both of them have the same flow tag.

Disconnecting Text Frames

At this point, both of the frames are connected. You must start typing in the first text frame because there's a paragraph mark in that text frame where you can insert your cursor, but there isn't a similar mark yet in the frame you just added.

Let's say that you want to make the second text frame a different text flow so you can start typing a different part of your text there (such as a new story, as in a newsletter, or a sidebar to the main text you're typing). To do that, you first need to disconnect the text frames by doing the following:

1. Select the first text frame by holding down the **CTRL** key while clicking on the line around it until handles are displayed around it.

2. Click **Format > Customize Layout > Disconnect Next**. The following message will be displayed:

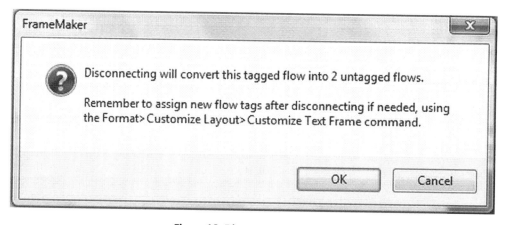

Figure 18: Disconnect message

3. Click **OK**. Notice that both of the text frames now have a paragraph mark that would enable you to insert your cursor in them.

Assigning Text Flows to Frames

At this point, neither of the text frames on this Master Page has a text flow. To assign the text flows to them, follow these steps:

1. Place your cursor in the original text frame, and then click **Format > Customize Layout > Customize Text Frame** on the menu bar. The Customize Text Frame dialog box opens.

2. Type "**A**" in the Tag box.

3. So the text in this frame will flow automatically to the next text frame that has text flow A assigned to it, click the box in front of **Autoconnect**.

4. Click **Set**. Notice that in the left corner of the Status bar, it now says that this is Flow: A.

5. Insert your cursor in the second text frame on this page, and then click **Format > Customize Layout > Customize Text Frame** on the menu bar. The Customize Text Frame dialog box opens:

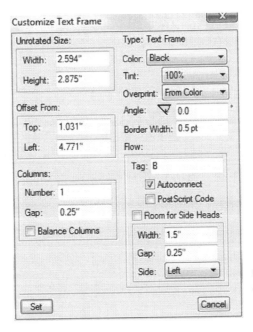

**Figure 19:
Customize Text
Frame dialog box**

6. Type "**B**" in the Tag box.

7. So the text in this frame will flow automatically to the next text frame that has text flow B assigned to it, click the box in front of **Autoconnect**.

8. Click **Set**. Notice that in the left corner of the Status bar, it now says that this is Flow: B.

You can always keep track of which text flow you're working with by clicking your cursor on a page, and then checking the Status bar at the bottom of the FrameMaker window. The current text frame's flow tag appears in the **Tag** area of the Status bar and says "Flow:" followed by the flow tag as follows:

```
Flow: A
```

Check Text Frame Characteristics

To view the characteristics of the text frames in your document, do the following:

1. Select the text frame or position your cursor inside of it.

2. Click **Graphics > Object Properties** or **Format > Customize Layout > Customize Text Frame** on the menu bar. The Customize Text Frame dialog box opens. This dialog box tells you the settings for your text frame.

In addition to changing the flow tag, you also can make changes to the text frame size, side head space (which we'll talk about in a later section), columns, and other text frame properties.

If you've modified any of the text frames while on Body Pages, they're called *layout overrides.* You'll need to confirm whether you want to keep these overrides or remove them when you move from the Master Page view to the Body Page view. If you modify a Master Page that is applied to several Body Pages and you've made changes to the text frames on one of the Body Pages, selecting **Keep overrides** will retain the overrides you made to that page while changing the layout for the other pages that have this modified Master Page applied to them.

Modify All Text Frames in a Text Flow

While you can use the Customize Text Frame dialog box to modify a single text frame, you can modify all of the text frames in the text flow by using the Column Layout dialog box. Practice changing the margins and number of columns on your Master Pages by doing the following:

1. Click **View > Master Pages** on the menu bar to open your Master Pages.

2. Go to the left Master Page so you can change the number of columns only on your left Master Page.

3. Position your cursor inside of the main text frame of the left Master Page.

4. Click **Graphics > Object Properties** on the menu bar. The Customize Text Frame dialog box opens.

5. In the Columns section, change the number of columns to **2**, and then click **Set**.

6. Scroll down and look at your right Master Page. Notice that it has only one column, while the left Master Page has two. Your Body Pages will look the same as your Master Pages.

If we had not used the chapterpage Master Page to learn how to add a text frame with a different text flow, you could modify all of your Master Pages to have two columns as follows:

1. Change your left Master Page back to a one-column layout by placing your cursor in the text frame of the left Master Page, and then click **Graphics > Object Properties** on the menu bar.

2. Change the number of columns in the **Columns** section to **1**, and then click **Set**.

3. Change all of the text frames in the text flow "A" to a two-column layout by clicking **Format > Page Layout > Column Layout**. The Column Layout dialog box is displayed.

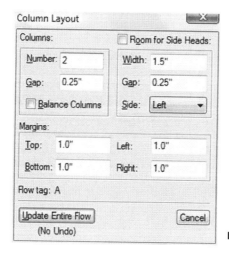

Figure 20: Column Layout dialog box

4. Change the number of columns to **2**. Before you go on, notice that it says **Flow tag: A** at the bottom. This tells you that it will change all text frames associated with the flow tag A.

5. Click **Update Entire Flow**. All of your Master Pages that have Text Flow A will now have a two-column layout. These columns will be the same width and will be separated by a uniform gap.

    Note: If your custom Master Page (*chapterpage*) doesn't have two columns, you will have to do this manually by placing your cursor on the custom Master Page, and then clicking **Graphics > Object Properties** on the menu bar, and changing the number of columns to **2** before clicking **Set**.

As you can see, text frames are an important part of FrameMaker. Practice changing the text frames on your Master Pages and your Body Pages to see what kind of layouts you can achieve!

Frequently Asked Questions

Q: *How can I select several text frames at once?*

A: To select several frames, do one of the following:

- While holding down the left-mouse button, drag your cursor across the frames you want to select as though you were drawing a box. An outline is displayed around the frame as you press the mouse button. When you release the mouse button, the outline disappears and all of the frames within that outline are selected.
  Or
- While pressing **CTRL,** click on the first frame, and then click the second frame, and so on.
  Or
- Click outside the main text frame and press **CTRL + A**. This selects all objects on the page.

This page is intentionally left blank.

Character and Paragraph Tags

Format your documents more consistently and easily by using character and paragraph tags; explore the Character and Paragraph Designers; and create tags you can use in your documents.

Formatting your text can take a great deal of time when you're writing documentation. If you're working with a team of writers, disagreements about formatting can cause conflict or inconsistency in the documentation. In this chapter, we'll discuss a FrameMaker feature that eliminates many arguments about formatting. This feature is called a *tag*.

There are two kinds of tags in FrameMaker: *paragraph tags* and *character tags*. These tags are sets of formatting characteristics that you use to change the look of your text. Paragraph tags enable you to format a paragraph, while character tags enable you to format a character or few words within a paragraph without changing the formatting of the rest of the paragraph.

All text in FrameMaker has some type of tag applied to it. The default paragraph tag is the *Body* paragraph tag. Heading, footer, bulleted list, and figure title tags are more examples of types of paragraph tags. *Emphasis* is a good example of a character tag. You can apply this tag to one or more words within a paragraph and only those words you selected would be changed.

Designers

To create or modify paragraph and character tags, you'll use what FrameMaker calls **Designers**. In FrameMaker 10, these Designer dialog boxes have become part of the panels arranged at the right side of the screen. When you've selected the Design mode in the Workspace Switcher at the right top of the window, these Designers are displayed, or you can open them at any time by using the Format menu on the menu bar. Designers enable you to create the formatting you want for different types of tags.

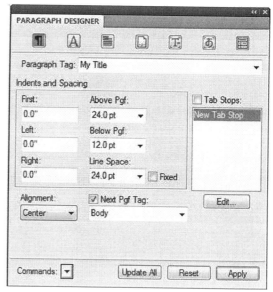

Figure 21: Character and Paragraph Designers

Catalogs

After you've created your tags, their names are displayed in the **Character Catalog** or the **Paragraph Catalog**.

- To open the Character Catalog, click **Format > Characters > Catalog** on the menu bar. The Character Catalog opens as a panel:

Figure 22: Character Catalog

- To open the Paragraph Catalog, click **Format > Paragraphs > Catalog** on the menu bar. The Paragraph Catalog opens as a panel:

Figure 23: Paragraph Catalog

You can move these catalogs by clicking on the dark area at the top of them, and then holding down the left-mouse button while moving them.

Collapse or expand them by clicking on the double arrows in their top banners.

Close them by clicking the **X** in their top banners or by right-clicking while your cursor is in the dark strip at the top of the catalog and selecting **Close** from the menu that's displayed.

Notice that at the bottom of each catalog, you have the following three buttons: **Delete, Options,** and **Refresh Catalog**. Let's look at each of these individually.

- **Delete**
  This opens the Delete Formats from Catalog dialog box where you can select a character or paragraph tag that you want to delete from the catalog. After you click **Delete** to remove it, if it isn't removed immediately, click the **Refresh Catalog** button. Note that while some references say this deletes the format from the catalog in all of your documents, in my experience, it just deletes the format from the document I was working with when I deleted the format.

- **Options**
  If you click this, the Set Available Formats dialog box is opened.

Figure 24: Set Available Options dialog box

This is where you can select how you will view the tag names. Your options are the following:

- **Show all**

  If you select this, all of the tags in your catalog will be displayed. If you click the box beneath this, the tags that are in use will be displayed in the catalog above the ones that are not being used in this document. Notice that tags that are being used have checkmarks in front of their names.

- **Show only used formats**

  If you select this, only the tags that are being used in the document will be displayed in the catalog.

- **Show only unused formats**

  If you select this, only the tags that aren't being used in the document will be displayed in the catalog.

- **Delete unused formats**

  If you select this, the tags that are not being used in the document will be deleted from the current catalog. This doesn't delete the tags from catalogs associated with other templates.

- **Customized List**

  If you select this and then select **Edit**, the Customize List of Available Formats dialog box opens:

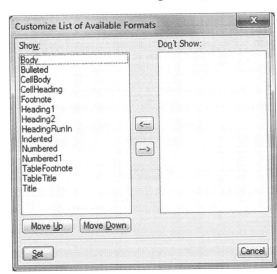

Figure 25: Customize List of Available Formats dialog box

This allows you to list the tags you want in the order that you want. In previous versions of FrameMaker, tags always were displayed alphabetically. Now you can list them in the order that makes the most sense for you.

- **Refresh Catalog**
  The last button on the catalogs is the **Refresh Catalog** button. If you click this, your catalog will be refreshed.

Why You Should Use Tags

Before you look at designers and tags in more depth, I want to take a moment to explain why you should always use tags instead of manually formatting your text.

First, tags help you save time. Instead of manually applying several formatting characteristics to a certain paragraph, you simply select the tag name and apply it to the text you want. All of the formatting characteristics associated with that tag are applied to your text at the same time.

Second, tags help you produce documents that are more consistent. If you work on large documents or work with other people on the same document, tags make it easy to maintain consistency.

Third, if you make changes to your formatting as you work on your document, you can modify the tag just once instead of searching for and modifying the text that you applied certain formatting characteristics to throughout your document. If you use a tag for the formatting, you change the tag and all text that has that tag applied to it will be changed.

Character Tags

As mentioned earlier, character tags define the format of selected characters within a paragraph without changing the format of the rest of the paragraph. For example, if you want to emphasize certain words in your document, you could create a character tag that would format these words the same way each time they're used. Character tags are also important when you're dealing with variable text, cross-references, and autonumbers (these will be discussed later).

To apply a character tag to text, do one of the following:

- Select the text to which you want to apply a character tag and click **Format > Characters > Catalog**. Select the character tag you want to apply to the text you've highlighted.

- Select the text, and then click **Format > Characters > Designer** on the menu bar or press **CTRL + D** to display the Character Designer or make it active. Select a tag name from the **Character Tag** name drop-down list and click **Apply To**.

- Highlight the word you want to change, press **CTRL + 8**, and then select the character tag you want from the pop-up menu that appears on the Status bar.

- To apply a character format using the Copy and Paste commands, first select text that's tagged with a character tag. Select **Edit > Copy Special > Character Format**. Select text that you want to apply the character format to, and then choose **Edit > Paste**.

To remove a character tag, do one of the following:

- Select text that's formatted with a character tag, open the Character Catalog, and then click **Default Font**.

51

- To remove a character tag from the Character Catalog, open the Character Designer. Make sure the name of the character tag you want to delete is displayed in the Character Tag box at the top of the designer, and then click the Commands button. Click **Delete Format** from the list of options.

Paragraph Tags

Apply paragraph tags to your text by placing your cursor in a paragraph or highlighting several paragraphs, and then doing one of the following:

- Click **Format > Paragraph > Catalog** on the menu bar. The Paragraph Catalog opens and you can select the tag you want.

- Select the name of the paragraph tag you want from the Paragraph Tag box on the Paragraph Formatting task bar.

- Click **Format > Paragraph > Designer** on the menu bar. The Paragraph Designer opens. Select the tag you want from the drop-down list at the end of the Paragraph Tag box.

Paragraph tags are always applied to the entire paragraph. To apply a tag to a word or a few words within a paragraph, you must use character tags.

Notice that the Tag area on the left side of the Status bar (at the bottom of the window) displays the name of the tag applied to the paragraph where your cursor is located.

The Paragraph Designer

When you're designing your document or a template, you'll spend a lot of time using FrameMaker's Paragraph Designer. Pay special attention to the names that you give the paragraph tags you create. Since paragraph tag names are displayed in the Paragraph Catalog and are also used with other FrameMaker features such as variables, cross-references, and generated files, give short, consistent, easy-to-understand names to any paragraph tags you create.

To explore the Paragraph Designer, open FrameMaker, and then open either the document you were working on in the last chapter or a new one. Click **Format > Paragraphs > Designer** on the menu bar or select it from the panels. The Paragraph Designer opens:

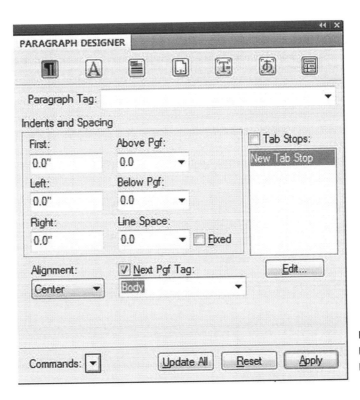

Figure 26: Paragraph Designer

There are seven icons at the top of the Paragraph Designer, representing the seven tabs of the Paragraph Designer. These icons mean the following:

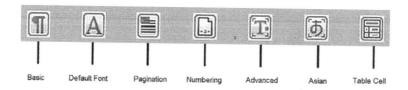

Figure 27: Paragraph Designer icons

Each tab has several settings that you can apply to your paragraph tags. You can work with all or some of the settings when defining paragraph formats, but the following fields and buttons are the same on all tabs:

- The **Paragraph Tag box** at the top of the tabs displays the name of the paragraph tag that's applied to the text where your cursor is located or that you've chosen from the drop-down list at the end of the box.

- The **Update All, Reset,** and **Apply** buttons are important ones to understand. After modifying the settings on one of the tabs for a specific Paragraph Designer property, you must take one of the following actions:

  - Apply those changes to the paragraph where your cursor is located by clicking the **Apply** button,
  - Apply those changes to all paragraphs that this paragraph tag is applied to by clicking the **Update All** button, or
  - Reset all of the settings that you haven't saved yet to what they were by clicking the **Reset** button.

If you click the **Apply** button, the changes you made aren't applied to any other paragraphs with the same paragraph tag and aren't included in the settings for this paragraph tag for future use. Using **Apply** also creates a format override for the paragraph or paragraphs that are currently selected. Format overrides result from a change that you made to a particular selection that no longer matches the predefined format. An asterisk (*) in the Status bar Tag area indicates there's a format override in the text. Try to avoid overrides as much as possible because they can cause inconsistencies in documents.

Note: If you press **ENTER** after making changes in the Paragraph Designer without pressing Apply, Update All, or Reset, **Apply** is selected by default

In addition, FrameMaker doesn't allow you to switch to another tab unless you click **Apply, Reset,** or **Update All.** If you forget to click one of these after making changes on a tab, the Apply Changes dialog box opens and prompts you to apply the changes to the selection, update all, not to apply the changes (in which case they're lost), or to cancel to dismiss the window and return to the property tab you were working with.

The **Commands** button is another important part of this dialog box. Click the arrow next to it to see the following commands:

- **New Format**
  When this is selected, the New Format dialog box opens. This is where you type the name of the new paragraph tag you're creating and indicate whether you want to add this new tag to the catalog and apply it to the text where your cursor is located.

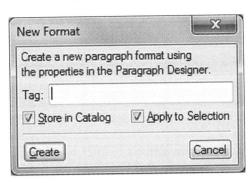

Figure 28: New Format dialog box

- **Global Update Options**

    If you select **Global Update Options,** the Global Update Options dialog box is displayed. To update the paragraph tag you're changing with the changes you've made on all of the property tabs, select **All Properties** option.

    Under this option is an option that is named according to the tab you're on (i.e., if you're currently on the Basic properties tab, this option will say "Basic Properties Only"). If you select this, this tag is updated only with changes that you make on the named property tag.

    In the Update Paragraph Formats section, you choose which paragraph formats will be updated.

Figure 29: Global Update Options dialog box

- **Delete Format**

    If you select **Delete Format**, the Delete Formats from Catalog dialog box opens. Use this to delete the paragraph tag or tags that you select from the list of formats.

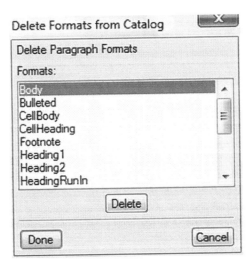

Figure 30: Delete Formats from Catalog dialog box

- **Set Window to As Is**

  Use this option to update specific properties of a tag. When set to **As Is**, the text boxes are blank, the check boxes are dim and the pop-up menus display **As Is**. This is a tricky setting. You think you've made a change, but actually all you've set it to is "As Is," meaning that it only changes to whatever is currently displayed, which can mean that nothing will be changed. Be sure to watch this one carefully.

- **Reset Window From Selection**

  This resets the paragraph tag according to the formatting of the text where your cursor is located.

  Now, let's take a closer look at each of the property tabs.

Basic Properties Tab

This is where you'll define indents, alignment, line spacing, tabs, and next-paragraph characteristics of your text.

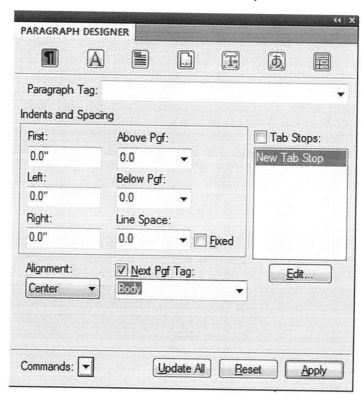

Figure 31: Basic properties tab

The settings are as follows:

- **Indents—First, Left and Right**
  - **First** sets the left indent for the first line of the paragraph.
  - **Left** sets a left indent for the second and subsequent lines of the paragraph.
  - **Right** sets a right indent for each line of the paragraph, including the first line.

- **Alignment**
  This option sets the alignment of the paragraph. You have four choices:

  - **Left** (all lines are even on the left margin and can be uneven on the right margin).
  - **Center** (all lines are centered).
  - **Right** (all lines are even on the right margin and can be uneven on the left margin).
  - **Justified** (all lines are even on both the left and right margins).

- **Above and Below Pgf**
  Pgf stands for *paragraph.* If you usually press the **ENTER** key to add a space between paragraphs, you're actually adding a blank line that has a paragraph tag attached to it. If that paragraph tag is used for other things, such as creating cross-references and generating lists, you may have errors in your document. Use the **Above Pgf** field instead to add a fixed amount of space above the current paragraph and the **Below Pgf** field to add a fixed amount of space below a paragraph.

  Note: If a fixed amount of space is added below a paragraph and a fixed amount of space is added above paragraphs using the same tag, and you have two or more of these paragraphs in a row, FrameMaker doesn't add these spaces together. Instead, it uses only the larger of the two settings as the space before or after a paragraph.

- **Line Space**
  This sets the amount of space between lines in a paragraph (called *leading*).

- **Fixed**
  If this is checked, the amount of space between lines remains the same even if you use superscripts or subscripts (letters that rise above or dip below the baseline of the text). If unchecked,

the amount of space between lines changes if you use superscripts or subscripts.

- **Next Pgf Tag**

  This sets the default paragraph tag for the next paragraph after you press **ENTER**. Place a checkmark in the **Next Pgf Tag** check box, and then select the paragraph tag you want from the drop-down menu.

- **Tab Stops**

  This is where you set tab stops for the paragraph. Unlike most other word-processing programs, FrameMaker doesn't have default tab stops. You must set them. Until you set your tab stops, pressing the **TAB** key has no effect. We'll explore this more later.

Default Font Properties Tab

This is where you set the default font and other typographical characteristics for the paragraph tag. This tab and the Character Designer are identical except for their names.

Figure 32: Default Font properties tab

The settings are as follows:

- **Family**
  Select the typeface you want from the drop-down list.

- **Size**
  Select the type size from the drop-down list.

- **Angle**
  Select the angle of the letters from the drop-down list.

- **Weight**
  Select the weight of the letters from the drop-down list.

- **Variation**
  This setting lists variations that may be available in a typeface, such as compressed type or small caps. The choices available vary by typeface selected in the *Family* setting.

- **Color**
  Select the color you want your text to be from the drop-down list.

- **Spread**
  This is where you can adjust the space between letters. The default is 0.0%.

- **Stretch**
  This is where you can change the shape of the letters. The default is 100% (normal).

- **Language**
  This sets the language of the paragraph. FrameMaker uses this to determine which dictionary to use for spell checking and hyphenation. If you don't want FrameMaker to spell-check certain paragraphs, choose **None** (useful for paragraphs of code samples, for example). This setting doesn't affect your ability to spell-check paragraphs with other tags applied to them—just the paragraphs to which you apply the tag you set this setting for in its definition.

- **Underline**
  If you place a checkmark in front of this box, and then select **Underline**, the text will be underlined. Or you can click the down arrow and select **Double Underline** to insert two lines under your text, or you can select **Numeric Underline**, which is one underline that is similar to the Underline setting, but the underline is placed a little farther from the text.

- **Overline**
  If you place a checkmark in front of this, a line will be placed over the text.

- **Strikethrough**
  If you place a checkmark in front of this, a line will be placed through the text.

- **Change Bar**
  If you select this, a vertical line will be placed in the margin of the page next to the text where changes are made.

- **Superscript, Subscript**
  If you place a checkmark in front of this box and select **Superscript**, the text will be placed above the baseline. If you select **Subscript**, the text will be placed below the baseline.

- **Small Caps, Lowercase, Uppercase**
  If you place a checkmark in front of this box and select **Small Caps**, the text will be displayed with all small caps. If you select **Lowercase**, all of the text will be lowercase, and if you select **Uppercase**, all of the text will be uppercase.

- **Pair Kern**
  Kerning means to adjust the spacing between letters to improve readability. As a general practice, Pair Kern should be turned on for all paragraph tags except those that use monospace typefaces such as Courier.

- **Tsume**
  If you're using Japanese characters and want the characters to be closer to each other, place a checkmark in front of this.

- **Background Color**
  If you place a checkmark in front of this and select a color from the drop-down list, that color will be added behind all text written with this paragraph tag applied to it.

Pagination Properties Tab

This tab allows you to define where the paragraph will be placed on the page and other paragraph characteristics.

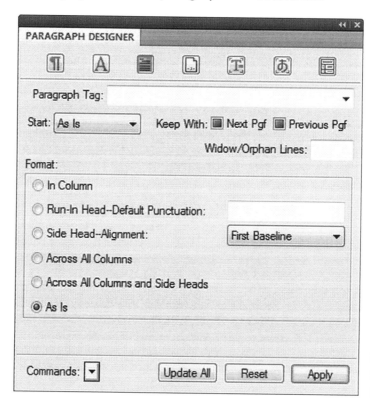

**Figure 33:
Pagination
properties tab**

The settings are as follows:

- **Start**
  Defines where the paragraph starts on a page. Your choices are **Anywhere**, **Top of Column**, **Top of Page**, **Top of Left Page**, and **Top of Right Page** (this one is commonly used for chapter titles).

- **Keep With**
  Your choices are **Next Pgf** (keeps the current paragraph attached to the next paragraph—commonly checked for heading tags that you want to keep on the same page as the first paragraph after

them) or **Previous Pgf** (keeps the current paragraph with the previous paragraph).

- **Widow/Orphan Lines**
  Widow is a printing term for a single word or a few words at the end of a paragraph that are printed at the top of the next page. *Orphan* is a printing term for the first line of a paragraph isolated at the bottom of a page. Neither is acceptable. This setting enables you to set a minimum number of lines that can appear on their own at the top or bottom of a page.

- **Format**
  You have many options in the Format section as follows:

  - **In Column**
    If you select **In Column**, the paragraph will be positioned in the main text column.

  - **Run-In Head—Default Punctuation**
    If you select **Run-In Head—Default Punctuation**, the heading will be placed at the beginning of the body-text paragraph that comes after it. The heading runs into the paragraph text. In the Default Punctuation field of this setting, specify the punctuation you want after the run-in head, such as a period or a colon. For example, you could create a heading paragraph tag that is 16 pt. boldface Times Roman. In addition to setting those specifications, you could set the Next Pgf Tag on the Basic tab to be Body. When you press **ENTER** after typing your run-in heading text, the paragraph tag would change to Body and you could continue typing your body text on the same line as the heading.

  - **Side Head—Alignment**
    If you select **Side Head—Alignment**, the paragraph will be positioned so that it's on the same line as the following paragraph, but the heading is in a separate column.

- o If you choose **First Baseline**, the first line of text in the column next to the side head will be aligned with the baseline of the first line of your side head.

- o If you choose **Top Edge**, the top of the letters of the first line of text in the column next to the side head will be aligned with the top of the letters in the first line of your side head.

- o If you choose **Last Baseline**, the first line of text in the column next to the side head will be aligned with the baseline of the last line of your side head.

- **Across All Columns**
  If you select **Across All Columns**, the paragraph will span all text columns except the side head area.

- **Across All Columns and Side Heads**
  If you select **Across All Columns and Side Heads**, the paragraph will span all text columns and all side head areas.

- **As Is**
  If you select **As Is**, the paragraph will inherit the setting that was previously applied.

Numbering Properties Tab

This tab enables you to set up automatic properties such as step numbers, chapter numbers, bullets, and repeated words (such as *Note:*). You can use *Building Blocks* (codes) that are displayed in the Building Blocks pane to refine the autonumbered text you define.

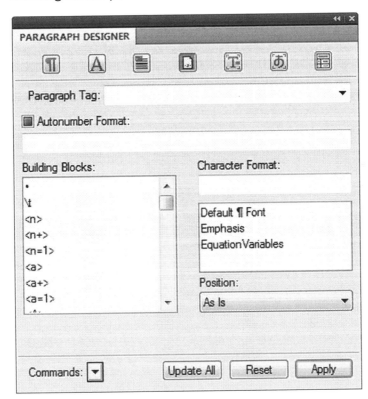

Figure 34: Numbering properties tab

The settings are as follows:

- **Autonumber Format**
  Place a checkmark in the box in front of this to set the definition of the numbering for the paragraph. You can use text, building blocks, or a combination of the two.

- **Building Blocks**

  These are codes that you insert into the Autonumber Format field, or you can type them. Here's what they mean:

Table 1: Autonumber Building Blocks

Building Block	Function	Description
* or \b	Bullet	Inserts a bullet.
\t	Tab	Inserts a tab space. You must define the tab space on the Basic properties tab.
<n>	Numeric value	Displays the current numeric value (e.g., 1, 2, 3, etc.).
<n+>	Numeric value plus one	Increments the numeric value by 1 and displays the new value.
<n=1>	Set numeric value	Set the value to 1 or other number you enter after the equal sign.
<a>	Lowercase alphabetic value	Displays the current alphabetic value in lowercase letters (e.g., a, b, c).
<a+>	Alphabetic value plus one	Increments the alphabetic value by one letter and displays the new value in lowercase.
<a=1>	Set alphabetic value	Set the value to the first letter of the alphabet if you indicate "1" or to another letter of the alphabet according to the number you enter after the equal sign. For example, if you want the value set to "c," you would type "3" after the equal sign. Letters are displayed in lowercase.
<A>	Uppercase alphabetic value	Displays the current alphabetic value in uppercase letters (e.g., A, B, C).
<A+>	Alphabetic value plus one	Increments the alphabetic value by one letter and displays the new value in uppercase.
<A=1>	Set alphabetic value	Sets the value to the first letter of the alphabet if you indicate "1" or to another letter of the alphabet according to the number you enter after the equal sign. For example, if you want the value set to "C," you would type "3" after the equal sign. Letters are displayed in uppercase.

Table 1: Autonumber Building Blocks (continued)

Building Block	Function	Description
<r>	Value in lowercase Roman numerals	Displays the current value in lowercase Roman numerals (e.g., i, ii, iii, iv, v, etc.).
<r+>	Plus one value in lowercase Roman numerals	Increments the value by one Roman numeral and displays the new value in lowercase Roman numerals.
<r=1>	Set value using lowercase Roman numeral	Set the value in lowercase Roman numeral to the numeral you enter after the equal sign.
<R>	Value in uppercase Roman numerals	Displays the current value in uppercase Roman numerals (e.g., I, II, III, IV, V, etc.).
<R+>	Plus one value in uppercase Roman numerals	Increments the value by one Roman numeral and displays the new value in uppercase Roman numerals.
<R=1>	Set value using uppercase Roman numeral	Sets the value in uppercase Roman numeral to the numeral you enter after the equal sign.
<$volnum>	Volume number	Displays the current value of the volume number.
<$chapnum>	Chapter number	Displays the current value of the chapter number.
<$sectionnum>	Section number	Displays the current value of the section number.
<$subsectionnum>	Subsection number	Displays the current value of the subsection number.
<>	Placeholder counters	Suppresses the display of a counter but does not change its value. Notice the space between the angle brackets. This was commonly used in numbering series in early versions of FrameMaker.

There are additional building blocks after these that are used in Asian documentation.

- **Character Format**

  Displays a list of character tags you can use to format the autonumbered text for the paragraph.

- **Position**

  Sets whether the autonumber element is added at the beginning or end of the paragraph.

Advanced Properties Tab

This is where you set characteristics such as hyphenation, justification, and lines above or below paragraphs.

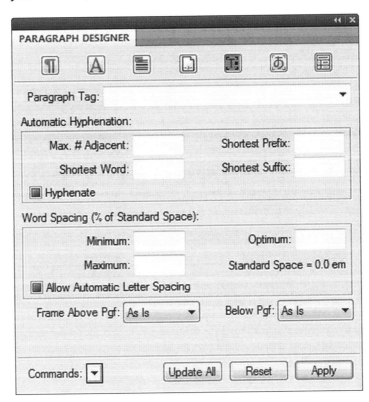

Figure 35: Advanced properties tab

The settings are as follows:

- **Max. # Adjacent**
  This option sets the number of consecutive lines in a paragraph that can end in a hyphen.

- **Shortest Prefix**
  This option sets the minimum number of letters before a hyphen. If you set *3* as the minimum, a word with two letters in the prefix couldn't be hyphenated.

- **Shortest Word**

  This option sets the minimum number of letters in a hyphenated word.

- **Shortest Suffix**

  This option sets the minimum number of letters after a hyphen.

- **Hyphenate**

  If you check this, FrameMaker can hyphenate words. If you don't check this, FrameMaker can't hyphenate words in paragraphs that have a tag with this setting applied to them. FrameMaker will hyphenate words according to the dictionary for the language you chose on the Default Font tab. If you don't choose a language there, the words in paragraphs with this tag can't be hyphenated.

- **Word Spacing—Minimum, Maximum, Optimum**

  This option controls how much FrameMaker can alter the space between words when *Justified* has been selected on the Basic tab.

- **Allow Automatic Letter Spacing**

  If checked, FrameMaker may add space between characters as well as words when justifying text.

- **Frame Above Pgf**

  This option enables you to add a graphic frame with a line or other graphic above this paragraph.

- **Frame Below Pgf**

  This option enables you to add a graphic frame with a line or other graphic below this paragraph.

Asian Properties Tab

This tab enables you to set properties when writing documentation using Asian text.

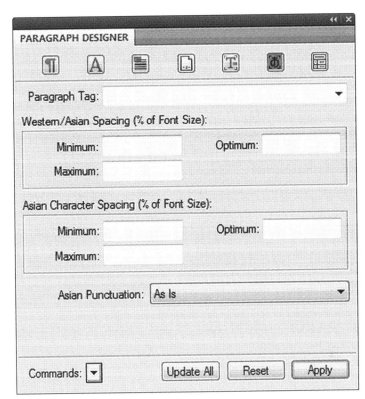

The settings are as follows:

- **Western/Asian Spacing (% of Font Size)**
  If you're using both Western and Asian characters in your document, use these settings to adjust the amount of space between them.

- **Asian Character Spacing (% of Font Size)**
  Use these settings to adjust the amount of space between Asian characters only.

- **Asian Punctuation**

  These options designate the amount of space between Asian punctuation marks and Asian characters.

  - **Squeeze as Necessary** means that the amount of space between them will be reduced only when special punctuation handling occurs.
  - **Never Squeeze** means that the space between them will never be reduced.
  - **Always Squeeze** means that space between them will always be reduced.

Table Cell Properties Tab

This tab enables you to set properties for the text within tables. Some of the settings here interact with settings you make on the Table Designer (discussed in the next chapter).

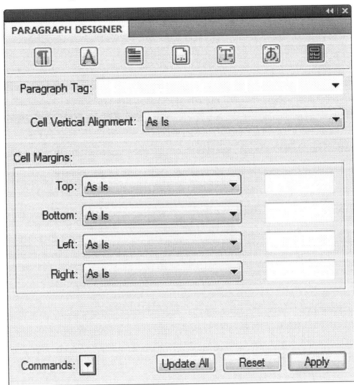

Figure 37: Table Cell properties tab

The two settings on this tab are as follows:

- **Cell Vertical Alignment**
  This option sets the vertical alignment of the text within the table cell.

- **Cell Margins**
  This option sets the margins of the text within the table cell. These properties interact with the default cell margins set in the Table Designer that we'll discuss in the next chapter.

Creating Paragraph Tags

Now that you know about the settings on the Paragraph Designer, let's create some paragraph tags. First, let's create a new heading tag by modifying one of FrameMaker's existing tags. To modify an existing tag, follow these steps:

1. Open FrameMaker, and then open a new document.

2. Type *New Heading* anywhere in your document. Don't press **ENTER**.

3. With your cursor still on the line you just typed, apply the **Heading1** paragraph tag to that line (select the paragraph tag from the Paragraph Catalog or the Paragraph Formats box on the Paragraph Formatting toolbar).

4. Open the Paragraph Designer by clicking **Format > Paragraph > Designer** on the menu bar or selecting it from the panels at the right of the work area.

5. Click the Commands button and select **New Format**.

6. In the New Format dialog box, type *NewHeading1* in the Tag text box. Make sure the **Store in Catalog** and **Apply to Selection** check boxes are selected.

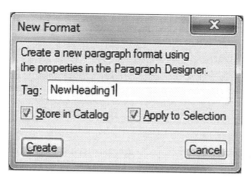

Figure 38: New Format dialog box

7. Click **Create**. The new tag is now available from the Paragraph Catalog.

8. Click the **Default Font** properties tab on the Paragraph Designer.

9. From the **Family** pull-down list, select **Arial**.

10. From the **Angle** pull-down list, select **Italic**. Your settings tab should look similar to this:

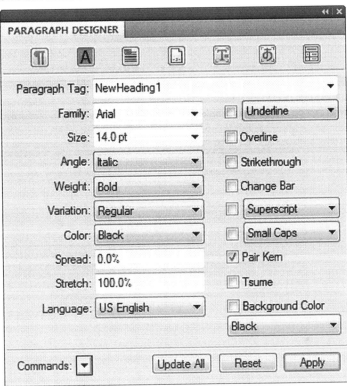

Figure 39: Default Font properties tab

11. Click **Update All**.

12. Because you want a body paragraph to follow the heading, go to the Basic properties tab, place a checkmark in the Next Pgf Tag setting, and then select **Body** from the list. Click **Update All**. You've just created a new heading paragraph tag.

Creating tags for ordinary body text is pretty much the same as it is for headings. For example, you might want to change the font of your body text or perhaps you want to change the tabs or indents. Notice that you don't have to change all of the settings on every properties tab when you're creating tags—just the ones that need to be changed.

Deleting Paragraph Tags

You can delete a paragraph tag in a FrameMaker document by selecting **Delete Format** from the **Commands** list on the Paragraph Designer, and then selecting the tag you want to delete from the list that's displayed. Deleting a tag removes it only from the catalog. Text that the tag was applied to retains the tag's format even after it's deleted.

Creating Bulleted List Tags

Vertical lists are important in technical documents. You may want to create bulleted lists for many levels of your lists or to create new types of lists.

To illustrate how to create a paragraph tag for a bulleted list, create one now by doing the following:

1. On a blank page, type *Apples, Peaches, Pears, Oranges*. Press **ENTER** after each word to create a vertical list.

2. Highlight all lines in your vertical list by placing your cursor in front of the first word, and then holding down the left-mouse button while dragging your cursor to a position after the last word.

3. Open the Paragraph Designer.

4. Select **Bulleted** from the list of paragraph tags at the top of the dialog box.

5. Click **Apply**.

6. If it isn't already displayed, click the first icon at the top to open the **Basic** properties tab.

7. Change the **First Indent** to **1.0 inches** and the **Left Indent** to **1.25 inches**.

8. Since FrameMaker doesn't have any preset tab stops, you can add tabs to your paragraph tags, but until you set them, they won't work. Set a new tab for this paragraph style by selecting the existing tab stop (.25) in the pane, and then click **Edit** under the **Tab Stops** area at the right of the Basic properties tab. The Edit Tab Stop dialog box opens.

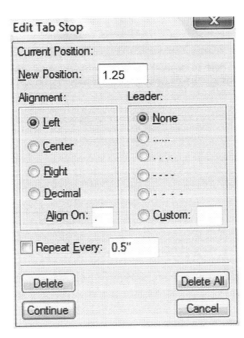

Figure 40: Edit Tab Stop dialog box

9. In the Edit Tab Stop dialog box, type *1.25* in the **New Position** box and then click **Continue**.

10. Select **New Format** from the **Commands** pull-down menu, and then type *MyBullet1* in the **Tag** text box. Make sure the **Store in Catalog** and **Apply to Selection** check boxes are selected.

11. Click **Create.** Your new bulleted list should be correctly formatted.

12. Click behind the last word to deselect the list, and then press **ENTER.**

13. Apply the *Body* paragraph tag to the blank line after the last bulleted item.

14. Close the Paragraph Designer if you wish.

Creating a Note Paragraph Tag

Notes, warnings, and cautions often are used in technical documents to make important information stand out. To make it easier to be consistent when adding these, create paragraph tags. To create a paragraph tag for a note, press **ENTER** a few times to move to a new area of your document. Open the Paragraph Designer if you closed it earlier, and then follow these steps:

1. Select **New Format** from the Commands pull-down menu, and then type *Note* in the **Tag** text box. Make sure the **Store in Catalog** and **Apply to Selection** check boxes are selected.

2. On the **Basic** properties tab, click **Edit** under the **Tab Stops** area.

3. In the Edit Tab Stop dialog box, type *.50* in the **New Position** field.

4. From the **Alignment** section, select **Left**, and then click **Continue**.

5. Click **Update All**, and then click the **Numbering** tab icon.

6. Select the **Autonumber Format** check box as shown in Figure 41.

7. In the **Autonumber Format** text box, type *Note:\t*. To italicize the word *Note*, select **Emphasis** from the **Character Format** section.

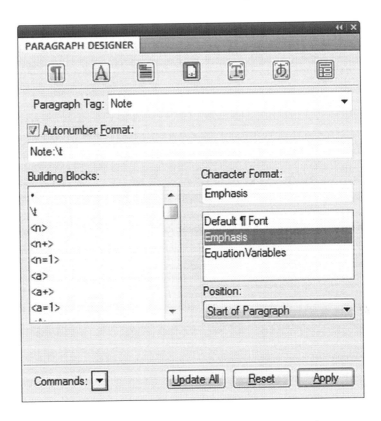

Figure 41: Numbering properties tab with Note settings

8. Click **Update All** to apply the Note tag to your paragraph. Then close the Paragraph Designer window. Try typing a couple of lines of text behind the word *Note:* to see how it aligns.

9. Press **ENTER** at the end of your note.

10. Apply the Body paragraph tag to the blank line. Note that you also could have designated that the Body paragraph tag would be applied to the next line on the Basic properties tab of the Paragraph Designer.

Creating a Paragraph Tag for Side Heads

Side heads are headings that are placed in a narrow column at the left of the page. They're often used in technical documents.

First, you need to change the layout of your pages to accommodate side heads. You'll create a narrow column on the left side of your pages where your headings will be located, and then you'll create a wider column on the right side of the pages where the body text and graphics will be located. After the columns are set on your pages, you'll create the side head paragraph tag that will enable you to move between the columns. Start with creating the columns on your pages by doing the following:

1. Open a new blank document by clicking **File > New > Document** on the menu bar and selecting **Portrait**.

2. Type the word *Overview* on the first line.

3. Click **Format > Page Layout > Column Layout** on the menu bar. The Column Layout dialog box opens:

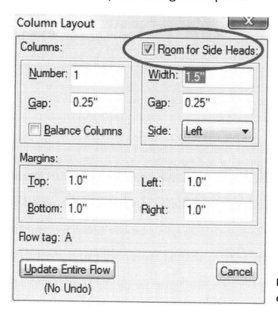

Figure 42: Column Layout dialog box

4. On the Column Layout dialog box, place a checkmark in front of **Room for Side Heads.** Note that you can designate the width, gap (space between the side head and the body text), and location of the side head from the appropriate fields. For now, however, accept the default settings.

5. Click the **Update Entire Flow** button. This will change the position of your headers and footers as well as the text you've previously typed on this page. Also, side head settings are always applied to the entire flow.

Now, create the side head paragraph tag by doing the following:

1. Open the Paragraph Designer if you closed it earlier.

2. Click the Commands button and select **New Format** from the menu. The New Format dialog box opens.

3. Type *Sidehead* in the Tag text box as the name of the new paragraph tag.

4. You want the text where your cursor is currently located to be a side head, so check the check box in front of **Apply to Selection**. Also, place a checkmark in front of **Store in Catalog** so you can use this tag again.

5. Click the **Basic** icon to open the Basic properties tab.

6. Place a checkmark in front of **Next Pgf Tag** and designate a tag for the next paragraph, such as *Body*. This ensures that when you finish typing your side head and press **ENTER**, your cursor will move to the other side of the text frame and the text you type will have the Body paragraph tag applied to it.

7. Click **Update All**.

8. Click the **Pagination** icon to open the **Pagination** properties tab.

9. Click the radio button in front of **Side Head—Alignment** and change the alignment as you wish from the dropdown list. Typically, you'd select **First Baseline** as the alignment.

10. Click **Update All**. The word *Overview* moves to the sidehead area of your page.

11. Be sure your cursor is at the end of the word, and then press **ENTER.** Your cursor will move to the wider column and the Body paragraph tag will be applied to it.

12. Type some text in this column to see how it looks.

13. To add your next side head, press **ENTER** at the end of your text.

14. Click the arrow at the end of the Paragraph Tag box on the Paragraph Designer, select **Sidehead** from the list, and then click **Apply**. Or select **Sidehead** from the list of paragraph styles in the Paragraph Formats box on the Paragraph Formatting toolbar.

These are some common paragraph tags that you'll work with. Creating paragraph tags may seem complicated now, but as you work with FrameMaker, you'll soon master them!

Tips for Working with Tags

Here are some tips for working with your paragraph and character tags:

- If possible, base new tags on existing ones. It's easier to modify an existing tag than to create a new one.
- When you create a new tag, give it a simple, short name that will identify its use. Since these tags are used with other features and will be added to the catalogs, you'll want names that are easy to find and remember.
- When you're designing tags, it's better to use restraint. Don't use too many different typefaces in your documents or too many extra-large type sizes. Strive for overall balance in your formatting.
- Try to avoid formatting overrides as much as possible. Overrides occur when you make changes to a tag and apply it to the

current selection instead of updating the tag style. Formatting overrides lead to inconsistencies in your formatting.

Frequently Asked Questions

Q: *How can I get the numbers in my numbered lists to restart after I apply the Numbered Paragraph tag?*

A: This is one of those simple, but quirky characteristics of FrameMaker that can cause a lot of confusion when you're first learning to use the application. To correctly number your lists and start new ones, you have to use two paragraph tags. First, to prevent the numbering from continuing from a previous list, you must start each new list with a paragraph tag that tells FrameMaker that this is the start of a new list. You then must apply another paragraph tag to the list items under that item that will number those items incrementally from that point forward. To see how this works, look at the default paragraph tags. Notice that there are two numbered paragraph tags: **Numbered** and **Numbered1**. The Numbered1 paragraph tag starts the numbering of each new list with a number "1." The Numbered paragraph tag is applied to the rest of the items in the list and numbers them incrementally.

Examining the settings of these two paragraph tags, especially on the Numbering properties tab of the Paragraph Designer, may help you understand how these tags work more clearly. When you're looking at the settings for these styles, notice that the paragraph tag that starts your list with "1," for example, will require using the <n=1> building block in its definition. The paragraph tag that automatically adds the numbers that follow in our example list will use the <n+> building block. If you look at the list of building blocks shown in the description of the Numbering properties tab earlier, you'll see that there are similar building blocks that you can use if you wish to use letters or Roman numerals instead of Arabic numbers in your numbered lists.

Q: *How can I create second-level lists in my numbered lists?*

A: To create second-level lists (also called *nested lists*), follow these steps. For this example, we'll create a second-level list that's indented and uses lowercase letters instead of numbers. The first-level list uses numbers.

1. Open a new blank document in FrameMaker.

2. Type several lines, pressing **ENTER** at the end of each line.

3. Click the first line and apply the Numbered1 paragraph tag.

4. Highlight the remaining lines and apply the Numbered tag.

5. Place your cursor at the end of the second line and press **ENTER**. Notice that the number *3* is placed at the beginning of the line. This is where we'll insert a second-level list.

6. Open the Paragraph Designer and click the **Numbering** icon to go to the Numbering properties tab.

7. Click the Commands button, and then select **New Format** from the menu. The New Format dialog box opens.

8. Type *secondlist1* in the Tag text box. The "1" at the end of the tag name tells us that this is the paragraph tag to apply to the first list item with this formatting.

9. Click **Create**.

10. In the Autonumber Format text box, change <n+> to <a=1>, leaving the tab building block behind it.

11. Click **Update All**. The number *3* changes to the letter *a*.

12. To indent the list, click the **Basic** icon to open the Basic properties tab.

13. Change the **First Indent** to 0.25 inches and the **Left Indent** to 0.50.

14. Double-click 0.25-inch left tab setting in the pane at the right of the tab. The Edit Tab Stop dialog box opens.

15. In the New Position box, type *0.50* inches, and then click **Continue**.

16. Click **Update All**.

In addition to the secondlist1 paragraph tag, you also have to create a paragraph tag for items that will be listed under the first one. To do this, follow these steps:

1. Press **ENTER** to move to the next line in your new list. Notice that it's numbered *a*.

2. Click the **Numbering** icon on the Paragraph Designer to open the Numbering properties tab.

3. Click the Commands button and select **New Format** from the menu. The New Format dialog box opens.

4. Type *secondlist* in the Tag text box, and then click **Create**.

5. In the Autonumber Format text box on the Numbering properties tab, change the building block that says <a=1> to <a+>. Leave the tab building block intact.

6. Click **Update All**. Your second-level paragraph tags are ready to use.

Q: *How can I achieve a monospace look with my Japanese characters?*

A: To do this, choose **Never Squeeze** from the Asian Punctuation spacing pop-up box on the Asian properties tab of the Paragraph Designer and turn off **Tsume** on the Default Fonts properties tab of the Paragraph Designer.

Q: *Can I copy the formatting of a paragraph instead of applying a paragraph tag?*

A: Yes, you can. Click anywhere in a paragraph that has the format you want to copy and select **Edit > Copy Special > Paragraph Format** from the menu bar. Place your cursor in the paragraph that you want to apply the format to, and then select **Edit > Paste**.

Tables

Learn how to design and insert tables, format them as you like, and use FrameMaker's Table Designer.

Tables provide readers with rapid access to information and allow them to compare data. The best use of tables is for organizing numerical data, although you can use them to present other information, too. They're often used for illustrating comparisons of similar data. A table typically has heading rows, body rows, and a title. It also may have a footing row.

In this chapter, you'll learn how to insert a table into a FrameMaker document and modify it. You'll notice that your new table will come equipped with rows and columns where you can add your text. It will also have a format that defines its look. You can use FrameMaker's table styles or you can create your own, using FrameMaker's Table Designer .

Just like the control you get from the Paragraph Designer and the Character Designer, the Table Designer lets you define the properties of your table. You decide where to position the table, where the cell margins will be, what kind of borders will be around the table, and whether your table will have a title. After you insert a table, you can perform custom formatting tasks, such as straddling rows or applying shading to selected cells.

The Table Catalog

Like paragraph and character tags, FrameMaker stores table formats in a catalog—the Table Catalog. In previous versions of FrameMaker, the Table Catalog appeared only in the Table Format list in the Insert Table dialog box. In version 10, FrameMaker still displays the available table formats in the Insert Table dialog box, but it also has a Table Catalog that opens as a panel when you click **Table > Format > Catalog** on the menu bar.

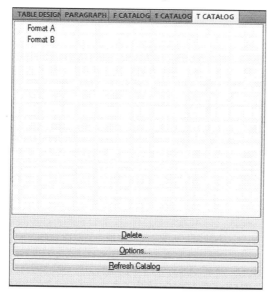

Figure 43: Table Catalog

You can move this catalog like you move the Paragraph and Character catalogs. Click the dark area at the top of the catalog, and then hold down the left-mouse button while moving the panel.

Collapse or expand the panel by clicking on the double arrows in its top banner. Close the panel by clicking the **X** in its top banner or by right-clicking while your cursor is in the dark strip at the top of the catalog and selecting **Close** from the menu that's displayed.

Notice that at the bottom of the table catalog, you have the following three buttons: Delete, Options, and Refresh Catalog. Let's look at each of these individually.

- **Delete**

    This opens the Delete Formats from Catalog dialog box where you can select a table format that you want to delete from the catalog, and then click **Delete** to remove it.

Figure 44: Delete Formats from Catalog dialog box

- **Options**

    If you click this, the Set Available Formats dialog box opens:

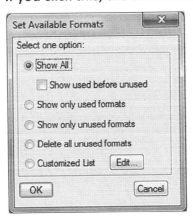

Figure 45: Set Available Formats dialog box

This is where you can select how you will view options. This is a new feature in FrameMaker 10 that will make it easier for you to manage your table formats when you're writing or developing templates. Your options here are the following:

- **Show all**

  If you click this, all of your existing table formats will be displayed in the catalog. If you click the checkbox in front of **Show used before unused**, the formats that are being used will be listed above the ones that aren't in use.

- **Show only used formats**

  If you select **Show only used formats**, only the table formats that are being used in the document will be displayed.

- **Show only unused formats**

  If you select **Show only unused formats**, only the table formats that aren't being used in the document will be displayed.

- **Delete unused formats**

  If you select **Delete unused formats**, the table formats that aren't being used in the document will be deleted from the current catalog. Note that this doesn't delete the tags from catalogs associated with other templates.

- **Customized List**

  If you select **Customized List**, and then select **Edit**, the Customize List of Available Formats dialog box opens:

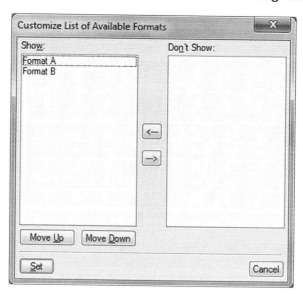

Figure 46: Customize List of Available Formats dialog box

This allows you to list the table formats you want to be displayed in the order that you want.

- The last button on the Table Catalog is the **Refresh Catalog** button. If you click this, the list of table formats in your catalog will be refreshed.

Insert a Table

As mentioned earlier, in addition to listing table formats in the new Table Catalog, table formats also are listed in the Insert Table dialog box. To see how this works, click **Table > Insert Table** on the menu bar. The Insert Table dialog box opens:

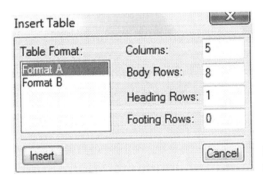

Figure 47: Insert Table
dialog box

Notice that you can choose between two table formats: **Format A** and **Format B**. If these don't meet your needs, you can modify one of them or you can create a new one with the Table Designer. When you create a new table format and save it to the Table Catalog, its name will appear in the Insert Table dialog box.

Anchors

You'll learn a new term in this chapter: *Anchor*. Whenever you insert a table in your document, it will anchor to the point where you inserted it. If you've turned on your text symbols, you'll see an anchor symbol that looks like an upside-down capital *T*.

Figure 48: Anchor symbol

FrameMaker uses anchors for other things besides tables, so they'll be mentioned again as you learn about other features. Let's learn how to insert a table into a document and then modify it.

Insert a Table in Your Document

To insert a table in your document, follow these steps:

1. Open a new blank document by clicking **File > New > Document** on the menu bar. The New dialog box opens.

2. From the Use Blank Paper section of the dialog box, select **Portrait**, and then click **OK**.

3. Click **Table > Insert Table** on the menu bar. The Insert Table dialog box opens:

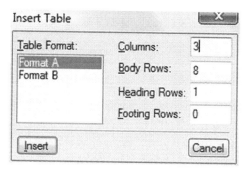

Figure 49: Insert Table dialog box

4. On the left side of the dialog box, select **Format A** from the Table Format list.

5. Change the number of columns by highlighting *5* in the **Columns** box, and then typing *3*.

6. If needed, change the number of rows by typing *8* in the **Body Rows** box.

7. Leave the **Heading Rows** number at *1* and the **Footing Rows** number at *0*.

   Note: Heading rows contain the names of each column in your table. FrameMaker will repeat them if your table breaks to the next page. Footing rows contain text that repeats at the bottom of tables that break across several pages.

8. Click **Insert**. The table is inserted in your document and if your text symbols are turned on, you'll see an anchor symbol at the table's insertion point. If you don't see an anchor symbol, your text symbols may be hidden. Select **View > Text Symbols** to display the symbols. Your table should look similar to the following at this stage:

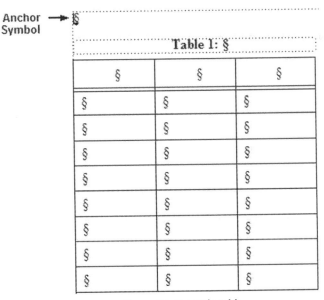

Figure 50: Example table

This table format includes a table title with the words *Table 1:* at the top. If you click the table title, you'll see that it uses the TableTitle paragraph tag (look on the Paragraph Formatting toolbar above the document window or at the left side of the Status bar at the bottom of the document window). This tag automatically numbers, which means that when you add the next table, the numbering in the new table will correctly follow this one.

Adding Text to Your Table

You add information to your table by doing the following:

1. Place your cursor after the colon in the table title, press the spacebar, and then type the title you want to give this table.

2. Press **TAB** to move your cursor to the first heading cell and type the name you want to give this column.

3. Press **TAB** to move to the next heading cell and type the name you want to give that column.

4. Press **TAB** to move to the last heading cell and type the name you want to give that column.

5. Press **TAB** to move to the first cell in the first body row and type some text.

6. Continue to press **TAB** to move to the next cell, adding text to each so you can practice doing the exercises below. It doesn't matter what you type. Single words in each cell will suffice. Add words that start with different letters so you can see more clearly how some of the features we'll talk about in the following sections work.

Rearranging Table Rows

Now that you have a table with some text in it, let's say that you want to move a row to another position in the table (above or below its current position). Move a row by following these steps:

1. Select the row you want to move by holding down your left-mouse button while dragging across the entire row. (You can also place your cursor in a row, and then press the **ESC, t, h,** and **r** keys one at a time to select an entire row.)

2. Click **Edit > Cut** on the menu bar or press **CTRL + x** to cut the selected cells from the table. The Cut Table Cells dialog box opens:

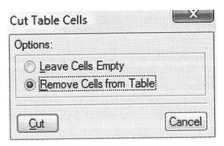

Figure 51: Cut Table Cells dialog box

3. Select **Remove Cells from Table** and click **Cut**. The row is removed from your table.

Place your cursor in the row that's above or below the place where you want to move the row you just cut from the table, and then press **CTRL + v**. The Paste Rows dialog box opens.

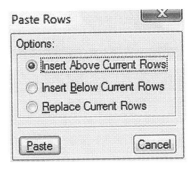

Figure 52: Paste Rows dialog box

4. Select whether you want the row you cut to be inserted above or below the row where you cursor is located, or if you want the row you cut to take the place of the row where your cursor is located.

5. Click **Paste**. Your row is pasted where you indicated.

Sorting Table Rows

Now let's say that you want to sort your rows so the information is arranged alphabetically. To sort the rows of your table, follow these steps:

1. Place your cursor anywhere in the body rows of your table.

2. Click **Table > Sort** on the menu bar. The Sort Table dialog box opens and the body rows are selected.

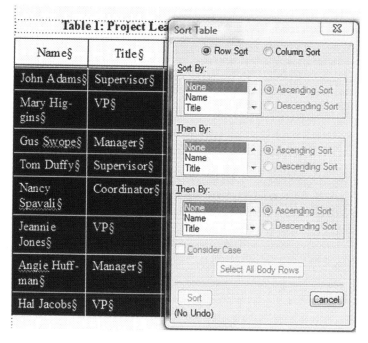

Figure 53: Sort Table dialog box

3. Notice that the table rows are highlighted when you do this, and that you can sort by rows or by columns. If you choose to sort by rows, your options in the Sort by boxes will be related to the words in the rows. If you choose to sort by columns, the columns are listed by number.

4. Select the options that you want, and then click **Sort** to sort your table as you indicated. For example, if you wanted to sort the table illustrated above alphabetically by the names of the project leaders, select "Name" in the first Sort By list, and then click **Sort**.

   Note: You must have text in your table cells to sort them.

Resizing Table Columns

When you insert a table, all of the cells are the same size. If you have written text in a cell that wraps to a second line, however, you may want to resize your columns so all words will fit on one line. You can resize your columns by following these steps. To see how this works, type text that wraps to a second line in a table cell.

1. With your cursor in the table cell with the text that wraps to a second line, select **Table > Format** > **Resize Columns** on the menu bar. The Resize Selected Columns dialog box opens.

   Note: If you have more than one cell where the words wrap to a second line, place your cursor in the cell that has the longest words.

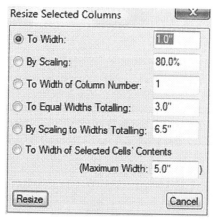

Figure 54: Resize Selected Columns dialog box

2. Select **To Width of Selected Cells' Contents**, and then click **Resize**. Your column should be resized so that the words fit on one line in their cell.

Add Rows or Columns

In some applications, you press the **TAB** key in the last cell of the last row to add another row. If you do this in FrameMaker, the cursor will jump to the table title or the first cell of the table. Here are the steps to add rows or columns to your tables:

1. Place your cursor in the cell that is next to the place where you want to add the row or column.

2. Select **Table > Add Rows or Columns** on the menu bar. The Add Rows or Columns dialog box opens:

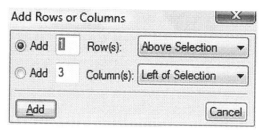

Figure 55: Add Rows or Columns dialog box

3. If you want to add rows, select the radio button in front of **Add X Row(s)** and type the number of rows you want to add.

4. Click the arrow at the right and select where you want the row(s) to be added.

5. Click **Add**. Your new row(s) will be added where you indicated you wanted them to be added.

    Note: You also can add a new row under the row where your cursor is located by pressing **CTRL + ENTER**.

6. If you want to add columns, select the radio button in front of **Add X Column(s)** and type the number of columns you want to add.

7. Click the arrow at the right and select where you want the column(s) to be added.

8. Click **Add**. Your new column(s) will be added where you indicated you wanted them to be added.

Straddling Table Cells

Merging two or more table cells into one cell is called *straddling* in FrameMaker. To merge cells in a table, highlight the cells you want to straddle (merge), and then click **Table > Straddle** on the menu bar. You'll see the two cells merge.

If you need to alphabetize your rows, do that before straddling rows. If you want a single cell in a row with two rows to its right, type the text in the first column (if that's what you're sorting by) in two different rows, do your sort, and then delete the extra text when you straddle the cells.

Aligning Text in a Table Cell

To align the text within a single table cell, do the following:

1. Place your cursor in the cell that contains the text you want to align, and then click the Paragraph Designer panel at the right of the window or click **Format > Paragraphs > Designer** on the menu bar. The Paragraph Designer opens.

2. Select the **Table Cell** tab and select how you want the text in this cell to be aligned. For example, if you merged two cells in a column, you might want your text in that cell to be centered vertically. To do that, you'd locate the Cell Vertical Alignment field and select **Middle** from the pull-down menu.

3. Click **Apply,** but don't click **Update** unless you want all text using the *CellBody* paragraph tag to be altered.

4. Close the Paragraph Designer dialog box.

Change the Ruling and Shading

Change the ruling and shading in your table by doing the following:

1. Select the row or column you want to change.

2. Select **Table > Format > Custom Ruling & Shading** from the menu bar. The Custom Ruling and Shading panel opens:

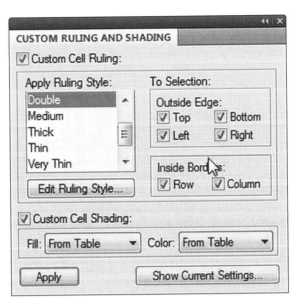

Figure 56: Custom Ruling and Shading panel

3. Select the ruling style you want from the Apply Ruling Style field.

4. In the Outside Edge group of the To Selection field, place checkmarks in front of all selections that you want to use the ruling style.

5. In the Inside Borders group, remove the checkmarks in front of *Row* and *Column* if you don't want the ruling style you selected applied to rules within the borders of the cells you selected.

6. To add shading to a row or column, place a checkmark in front of the words *Custom Cell Shading*.

7. Select a percentage from the Fill drop-down list. These percentages refer to the level of saturation of the color you'll select in the next step.

8. Select the color you want from the Color drop-down list, and then click **Apply**. Your settings should take effect.

The Table Designer

When you're creating large documents, you can use the Table Designer to create a table format for all of the tables in your document.

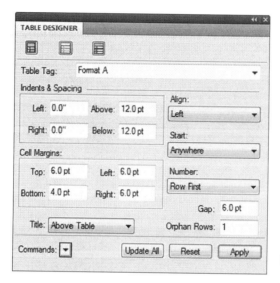

Figure 57: Table Designer

Open the Table Designer by clicking **Table > Format > Table Designer** on the menu bar, by selecting the Table Designer panel at the right side of the window, or by pressing **CTRL + T**.

As with the Paragraph Designer, the Table Designer has more than one tab (represented by the three icons at the top of the dialog box) and there are fields on the dialog box that remain the same on all of the tabs.

The three tabs of the Table Designer are the *Basic* tab, the *Ruling* tab, and the *Shading* tab. Their icons are as follows:

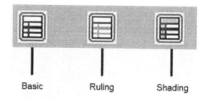

Figure 58: Table Designer icons

At the top of the Table Designer is the *Table Tag* field that displays the name of the current table tag. This field is the same on all of the Table Designer's tabs.

At the bottom of the Table Designer are the other fields that remain the same on all of the tabs. Just like in the Paragraph Designer, you'll see *Commands* with a down arrow next to it. When you click the down arrow, you'll see the same menu of commands:

- **New Format**
  Click this, and then type the name of a new table tag.

- **Global Update Options**
  Click this, and then select **All Properties** (which will update this tag with the changes you make on all of the property tabs) or the option under this (which will update this tag with the changes that you make only on the current tab).

- **Delete Format**
  Click this if you want to delete a selected table tag.

- **Set Window to As Is**
  Use this to update specific properties of a tag. When set to **As Is**, the text boxes are blank, the check boxes are dim, and the pop-up menus display **As Is**.

- **Reset Window From Selection**
  This resets the table tag according to the formatting of the text where your cursor is located.

Use the **Apply** button to apply changes to the table where your cursor is located. To apply the changes to all tables using this table tag, click **Update All.** If you decide that you don't want to make changes before you click Apply or Update All, click the **Reset** button. The settings on this tab will be restored to what they were before you made changes. After you click **Apply** or **Update All**, the **Reset** button will not change the settings back to the original. You'll configure most table tag properties on the individual tabs in the Table Designer. Let's go through the settings on each tab.

Basic Tab

On this tab, you set spacing, alignment, margins, orphan rows, and other properties.

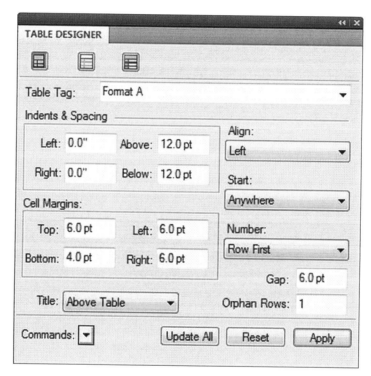

Figure 59: Basic tab

The settings are as follows:

- **Indents & Spacing**
  This lets you set how much space you want between the left or right edge of the text frame and the table, and set the amount of space above and below the table and the paragraphs on both sides of it. Since those paragraphs will have spacing properties too, FrameMaker uses the larger setting of the two.

- **Cell Margins**
  Use this to set the margins inside the table cells. This setting interacts with the Paragraph Designer Table Cell properties tab.

- **Align**
  Use this to set the horizontal position of your table under the previous paragraph. This interacts with the paragraph's pagination settings.

- **Start**
  This designates where the table will be positioned vertically on the page. Most of the choices are self-explanatory, except for *Float*, which means that the table will move (float) to the first text column that has room for the table.

- **Number**
  Use this setting to organize auto-numbered rows or columns. If you select *Row First*, paragraphs in the cells will be numbered by row. If you select *Column First*, paragraphs in the cells are numbered by column.

- **Title**
  This lets you define your table title's placement, whether it's above or below your table or if you don't want a table title at all.

- **Gap**
  Gap is the amount of space between your table and your table title.

- **Orphan Rows**
  Orphan rows are rows that are isolated if a table breaks to another page. Use this setting to indicate the number of table rows that must stay together. If you want to force FrameMaker to fit the entire table on the same page, as in a floating table, specify up to 255 rows.

Ruling Tab

Click the middle icon to open the Ruling tab of the Table Designer. This is where you set the border styles for your table.

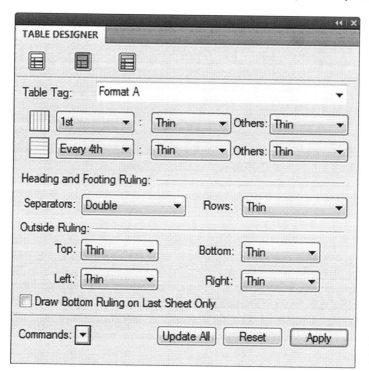

Figure 60:
Ruling tab

The settings are as follows:

- **Column Ruling**
  The Column Ruling settings (in the first row under the Table Tag name) let you set different rules for specified columns. Select the column to have a different type of rule from the first drop-down menu in this row, the type of ruling you want from the second drop-down menu, and then the type of ruling you want applied to the other columns from the third drop-down menu.

- **Body Row Ruling**
  This is the row immediately under the Column Ruling settings. This is where you specify the ruling between rows for designated rows. Select which rows will have a different type of rule between them from the first drop-down menu, the type of ruling you want from the second drop-down menu, and then the type of ruling you want all of the other rows to have from the third drop-down menu.

- **Heading and Footing Ruling**
  This is where you designate what the ruling will be between heading and footing rows. This also is where you'll designate the border for multiple heading and footing rows.

- **Outside Ruling**
  This setting specifies the ruling for the outside border of your table.

- **Draw Bottom Ruling on Last Sheet Only**
  If checked, the bottom border will appear on only the last sheet of a table if it breaks across pages.

Shading Tab

Click the third icon to open the Shading tab. This is where you choose the color and shading for your table.

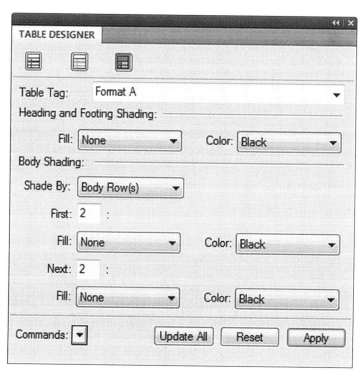

Figure 61: Shading tab

The settings are as follows:

- **Heading and Footing Shading**
  This setting lets you designate the color and saturation for the heading and footing rows. Designate the amount of saturation in the Fill field and select the color from the Color field. If your table has both heading and footing rows, both will be the same color.

- **Body Shading**
  This setting lets you designate the color and saturation for either rows or columns. It also lets you select different colors and

shading for rows or columns. You'll select whether you want to shade rows or columns in the *Shade by* field. You'll designate how many rows or columns you want to be filled with the first color by typing a number in the *First* field. You'll select the amount of color saturation you want for the first rows or columns in the first *Fill* field, and the color you want for the same areas in the *Color* field. And you can follow these same steps for the alternate rows or columns in the *Next* area.

Create a New Table Tag

Now that you know what the settings on the Table Designer mean, create a new table format (also called a *table tag*) by following these steps:

1. Insert a table with the tag that most closely resembles the table you want to create.

2. Press **CTRL + t** to open the Table Designer, and then type a new name in the Table Tag box.

3. Click **Apply**. The New Format dialog box will open with the name you typed in the Table Tag box.

4. Click **Create**, making sure the **Store in Catalog** and **Apply to Selection** check boxes are selected.

5. If the Table Designer closes after you name your new format, open it again.

6. Make the changes you want to the settings on the Table Designer tabs, clicking **Update All** on each tab to save the changes.

7. When you're finished, try inserting a new table. Your new table format should be listed in the Insert Table dialog box.

Format Tables that Break Across Pages

In addition to using the Table Designer to create new table formats, you need to know how to format tables that break across pages. When a table breaks across a page, you'll want to include some information that indicates that the table is continued from the previous page, such as adding the word *continued*.

In FrameMaker, the table title and heading rows automatically repeat when the table breaks to another page. To add the text to show that the table continues, however, you'll need to use a *table continuation variable*. Here's how:

1. Using a table you've already created, place your cursor at the end of your table title.

2. Select the Variables pod at the bottom of the screen.

3. From the list of variables, select **Table Continuation**.

4. Click the **Insert** icon on the Variables pod. A non-breaking space is added to the end of your table title. When the table wraps to the next page, you'll see the word *Continued* in parentheses after the title.

Tabbing within a Table Cell

If you press the **TAB** key while you're in a table cell, your cursor will move to the next table cell. To use your Tab key to indent text within a table cell, press **ESC + TAB**. Remember, however, that if the paragraph style doesn't have tab stops defined for it, you won't be able to tab. If pressing **ESC + TAB** doesn't work, check the tab settings on the Paragraph Designer for the paragraph tag that's applied to the table text.

Tips for Working with Tables

When you're working with tables, here are some tips that might make it easier:

- To select the entire table, double-click the anchor symbol.
- To delete a table, press the **DELETE** key after selecting the table.
- To remove the title of a table, open the Table Designer and select the **Basic** tab. From the Table Position pull-down menu, select **No Title**.

Frequently Asked Questions

Q: *I sometimes have to create tables within other table cells. Can I do that in FrameMaker?*

A: This is something that writers often have to do when they're creating If/Then tables within a table. To create a table within a table, follow these steps:

1. Click inside the cell where you want to insert the table within the table, and then select **Special > Anchored Frame** on the menu bar. The Anchored Frame panel opens:

Figure 62: Anchored Frame panel

2. Select the anchoring position that works best in your situation. You may have to experiment with this a bit to see what works best for your document. I find that "At insertion point" often works well.

3. Set the width and height of the frame you want.

4. Click the **New Frame** button. An anchored frame will be inserted in your table cell.

5. If your anchored frame is larger than the table cell, adjust the size of the table cell by clicking **Table > Resize Columns** on the menu bar. You want the table cell to be slightly larger than the anchored frame.

6. Open the Tools palette by clicking **Graphics > Tools** on the menu bar.

7. Click the **Place a Text Frame** tool on the Tools palette.

   Note: If you move your cursor slowly over the icons on the Tools palette, screen tips will pop up to tell you what each represents.

8. Click inside the anchored frame that you inserted, and then draw a frame inside the anchored frame while holding down the left-mouse button. When you release the mouse button after drawing the frame, the Create New Text Frame dialog box opens:

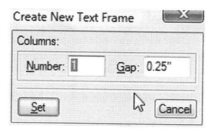

Figure 63: Create New Text Frame dialog box

9. Click **Set**. The text frame is inserted inside the anchored frame.

10. Click one time inside the text frame so that the text frame is deselected and your cursor is inside of the text frame.

11. Select **Table > Insert Table** on the menu bar.

12. Choose the desired table format, and click **Insert**. FrameMaker will insert the table inside the text frame.

Q: *There are times that I need to insert a page break in my tables to make sure they break to the next page where I want them to break. How can I do that?*

A: Here are the steps to do this:

1. Click in the row where you want to insert a break.

2. Select **Table > Format > Row Format** from the menu bar. The Row Format dialog box opens:

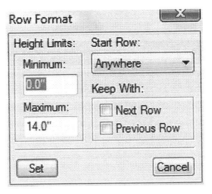

Figure 64: Row Format dialog box

3. From the Row Format dialog box, do one of the following:

   o From the Start Row: pull-down menu, select **Top of Page**

      Or

   o From the Keep With: section, select **Next Row**.

4. Click **Set**.

Q: *What's the best way to move a table to another location?*

A: Select the entire table, and then press **CTRL + x** on your keyboard to cut it from its current location. Now, move your cursor to where you want the table to be displayed and press **CTRL + v** to paste the table in that location.

Q: *Can I resize a table column by dragging the ruling lines?*

A: Yes. Select the column you want to resize (it turns black when selected), and then position your cursor over one of the spots that you see on the outside of the selected area. Your cursor will change to an arrowhead. Press the left-mouse button, and then drag the line to the position you want, perhaps using FrameMaker's rulers as a guide. Note that if you've turned on FrameMaker's Snap to Grid (**Graphics > Snap** on the menu bar), your line will move to the next grid position.

Q: *I want to rotate the text in some of my table cells. How can I do that?*

A: To do this, select the table cell(s) where you want to rotate your text, and then select **Graphics > Rotate** on the menu bar. The Rotate Table Cells dialog box opens. FrameMaker rotates text in 90-degree increments. The directions you can rotate your text are displayed on the Rotate Table Cells dialog box. Click the radio button in front of the option you want, and then click **Rotate**.

Drawing Tools

Use FrameMaker's drawing tools to create graphics that will make your documents look more professional and inviting.

Graphics make documents seem easier to read and more interesting. Graphics help readers understand complex concepts in a way that words alone can't. A picture of a computer screen (called a *screen shot*) helps readers understand what they need to do in a fraction of the time it would take them to read step-by-step instructions. A schematic can quickly illustrate how components interact. Flowcharts help readers understand the correct sequence of steps.

Whenever possible, you should use graphics in your documentation to add information, illustrate complex concepts, add interest, and give your work a more professional look.

In this chapter, you'll learn about FrameMaker's drawing tools and how you can create many drawings without having to use another graphics program. FrameMaker's drawing tools enable you to use lines, arcs, and freehand tools to create many different types of graphics.

FrameMaker's Drawing Tools

To use FrameMaker's drawing tools, you need to open the graphics Tools palette. To look at this palette, open FrameMaker, and then open a blank document. After the new document is displayed, open the graphics Tools palette by clicking **Graphics > Tools** on the menu bar or by clicking **View > Toolbars > Graphics Toolbar** on the menu bar. The graphics Tools palette opens. If you move your mouse slowly over the icons, you'll see that most of them have screen tips that pop up to tell you what they are.

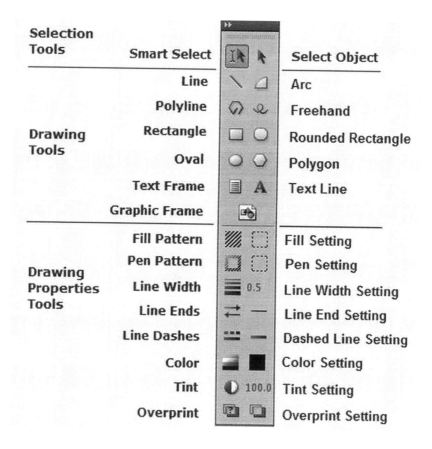

Figure 65: Graphics Tools palette

Selection Tools

Notice that there are three different types of tools on the palette: Selection tools, Drawing tools, and Drawing Properties tools. The top two icons are selection tools.

Use the **Smart Select** tool to select text or objects. If you click this and then press **CTRL**, you can force the selection of an object.

Use the **Select Object** tool to select objects, but not text.

Drawing Tools

The drawing tools are under these two selection tools. To use most of them, click the icon on the Tools palette, and then click where you want to start the shape. Hold down the left-mouse button while drawing the shape. As you draw the shape, you'll see an outline of it on the page. This outline is called the *path* of the object. When you finish drawing the shape, release the left-mouse button and the border of the shape appears. Here are descriptions of the drawing tools and some tips for using some of them.

The **Line tool** draws a line. If you want to draw a straight line that doesn't have any "wobbles," hold down the **SHIFT** key while drawing the line. Even if you move your mouse a bit, the line will remain straight.

The **Arc tool** draws a curved line. To draw a section of a circle, press **SHIFT** while drawing.

The **Polyline tool** draws a line that has several angles. To draw a polyline, select this tool, and then start drawing as normal. When you want to change direction, click the left-mouse button. When you've finished the polyline, double-click the left-mouse button to end the line.

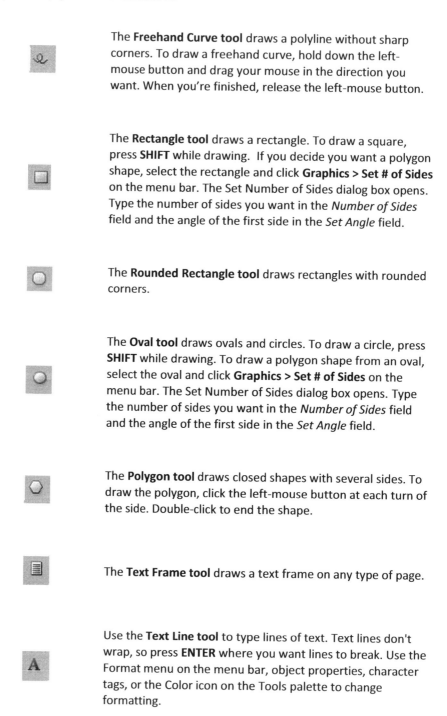

The **Freehand Curve tool** draws a polyline without sharp corners. To draw a freehand curve, hold down the left-mouse button and drag your mouse in the direction you want. When you're finished, release the left-mouse button.

The **Rectangle tool** draws a rectangle. To draw a square, press **SHIFT** while drawing. If you decide you want a polygon shape, select the rectangle and click **Graphics > Set # of Sides** on the menu bar. The Set Number of Sides dialog box opens. Type the number of sides you want in the *Number of Sides* field and the angle of the first side in the *Set Angle* field.

The **Rounded Rectangle tool** draws rectangles with rounded corners.

The **Oval tool** draws ovals and circles. To draw a circle, press **SHIFT** while drawing. To draw a polygon shape from an oval, select the oval and click **Graphics > Set # of Sides** on the menu bar. The Set Number of Sides dialog box opens. Type the number of sides you want in the *Number of Sides* field and the angle of the first side in the *Set Angle* field.

The **Polygon tool** draws closed shapes with several sides. To draw the polygon, click the left-mouse button at each turn of the side. Double-click to end the shape.

The **Text Frame tool** draws a text frame on any type of page.

Use the **Text Line tool** to type lines of text. Text lines don't wrap, so press **ENTER** where you want lines to break. Use the Format menu on the menu bar, object properties, character tags, or the Color icon on the Tools palette to change formatting.

The **Graphic Frame tool** draws a frame to crop or mask objects. It's also used on reference pages to hold objects that you use often.

Drawing Properties Tools

You'll use the next group of icons to define such properties as color, tint, and line width of the drawing-tool objects. Click the icon on the left side of the palette, make your choices, and then the settings you chose are displayed (in one manner or another) in the icons on the right side of the palette. This helps you see the settings for an object at a glance. The icons in this group are as follows:

 When you click the **Set Fill Pattern** icon, the Fill palette opens. From this palette, you choose the pattern you want to fill your object. After you select a pattern, it will be displayed in the icon to the right of the Set Fill Pattern icon.

 When you click the **Set Pen Pattern** icon, the Pen palette opens. From this palette, choose the pattern you want for the border of your object. After you select a pattern, it will be displayed in the icon to the right of the Set Pen Pattern icon.

Note: Some of the striped Fill and Pen Patterns don't display properly when a document is converted to Portable Document Format (PDF). If you plan to convert your document to PDF, create a test document to try out the patterns.

 When you click the **Set Line Widths** icon, the Line Widths palette opens. From this palette, choose the width of the lines in your object. After you select one of these, the numeric size of your choice will be displayed in the icon to the right of the Set Line Widths icon. You can use the slider to set yet more line widths. As you move the slider up and down, the width of the line that would be inserted is displayed in the icon to the right of the Line Widths icon. You don't have to click **Set** for these settings to take effect. If you click **Set**, the Line Width Options dialog box opens. We'll discuss this later.

When you click the **Set Line End Style** icon, the Line End palette opens. From this palette, choose whether you want the lines in your object to have arrows on the ends or not. After you select one of these, your choice will be displayed in the icon to the right of the Set Line End Style icon.

When you click the **Set Dashed Line Pattern** icon, the Line Styles palette opens. From this palette, choose whether you want dashed or solid lines. Your choice will be displayed in the icon to the right of the Set Dashed Line Pattern icon. When you select **Set** on the Set Line Widths, Set Line End Style, or Set Dashed Line Pattern palettes, additional dialog boxes open that can help you to define your lines more precisely.

When you click the **Set Color** icon, the Color palette opens. From this palette, choose the color you want your object to be. After you select one of these, your choice will be displayed in the icon to the right of the Set Color icon.

When you click the **Set Tint** icon, a panel with a slider opens. Move the slider by selecting it and then holding down the left-mouse button to set the percentage of color saturation you want in your object. The top of the slider is 0% and the bottom of the slider is 100%. The percentage is displayed in the icon to the right of the Set Tint icon as you move the slider up and down. When you release the left-mouse button, the percentage you were on is displayed in the icon to the right. You also can click **Set** on the slider to open the Tint Value dialog box, type the percentage you want, and then click **Set**.

When you click the **Set Overprint** icon, the Overprint palette opens. From this palette, choose whether you want FrameMaker to print only the color of the top object (knockout), to print both colors from the overlapped portions of the objects (overprint), or to print the color defined for each object (from color). After you select one of these, your choice will be displayed in the icon to the right of the Set Overprint icon.

Grids

FrameMaker has two grids that will help you draw and align your drawings. One of these is an invisible snap grid that attracts objects to it. To turn the snap grid on or off, click **Graphics > Snap** on the menu bar.

FrameMaker also has a visible grid that appears when you select **View > Grid Lines** on the menu bar. The lines that you see on the grid appear only on your computer screen—they don't appear when you print your document.

To change the spacing of the grid, do the following:

1. Click **View > Options** on the menu bar. The View Options dialog box opens:

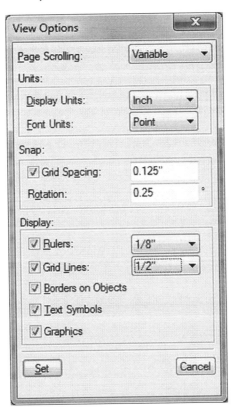

Figure 66: View Options dialog box

2. Under the Display heading in the lower half of the dialog box, look for *Grid Lines*. To the right, click the arrow at the end of the box to display the options you have for changing the spacing of your grid lines.

Before you leave this dialog box, notice that you can set the grid intervals for the snap grid here too. To set this, enter the interval in the Grid Spacing box. You should keep in mind, however, that if you intend to use the visible and invisible grids at the same time, you should make the visible grid spacing a multiple of the snap grid setting. For example, if the snap grid setting is 0.125 inch (the default), the visible grid spacing should be 0.125 inch, 0.25 inch, or 0.5 inch.

After you finish setting the spacing of the grids on the View Options dialog box, click **Set**.

Drawing Shapes

Drawing simple shapes with FrameMaker is fairly straightforward. If you're drawing a closed shape (such as a rectangle or an oval), click the shape you want to create from the Tools palette, position your cursor where you want the shape to appear, and then drag the mouse to the approximate size that you want the shape to be while holding down the left-mouse button. Release the left-mouse button when you have the shape you want.

If you're drawing a shape such as a polygon and you don't want to use the Set Number of Sides dialog box with a rectangle or an oval, follow these steps:

1. Click the **Polygon** or the **Polyline** icon on the Tools palette.

2. Click where you want to start your shape, and then release the left-mouse button.

3. Draw the first side of the shape by dragging your mouse to the point where you want to go a different direction.

4. Click your left-mouse button, release it, and drag your mouse to the next point where you want to change direction.

5. Continue doing this until you have completed the shape.

6. When you're finished, double-click the left mouse button to end.

Note: You can also do this by holding down the left-mouse button and releasing it when you want to change direction, then pressing it down again to continue.

Using the Tools

Click the Smart Select or Select Object icons (the top two icons on the Tools palette) to select your graphics. Most of the time, there are handles around a shape if it is selected. To select several objects at once, press **CTRL** while clicking each object. To delete a graphic, select it and press **DELETE**. If you want to deselect a graphic, click a place that's away from the graphic. If you want to add a fill pattern, color, tint, or other property to a shape, select it, and then click the icons in the lower portion of the Tools palette.

You also can use the **Object Properties** dialog box to change the properties of a graphic. To do this, select the graphic, and then click **Graphics > Object Properties** to open the Object Properties dialog box. Here, I've selected a rectangle shape that I drew:

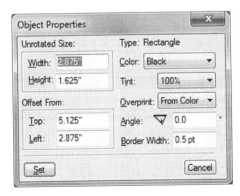

Figure 67: Object Properties dialog box

Notice that you can change the size of the object, where it is located on the page (offset properties), the color and tint of its fill overprint settings, the angle the graphic will be displayed on the page, and the width of the border around it.

You can also change these properties of a graphic by selecting it, and then clicking the Tools palette icons to make changes as follows:

- **To change fill and pen patterns:**
  Click the Set Fill Pattern or Set Pen Pattern icon, and then select the pattern you want.

- **To change line-width options:**
  FrameMaker provides four options for the width of lines: Choose from .5 point, 1 point, 3 points, and 4 points. If you want to change these options, do the following:

  1. Click the **Set Line Width** icon. The Line Widths palette opens.

  2. Click **Set**. The Line Width Options dialog box opens:

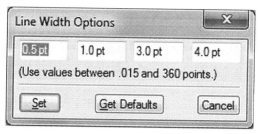

Figure 68: Line Width Options dialog box

  3. Type the values you want in the fields, and then click **Set**. These values are then mapped to the Line Widths pop-up menu.

  4. If you want to change the values back to the original, go back to the Line Width Options dialog box and click **Get Defaults**.

- **To change line-end style options:**
  FrameMaker provides eight default arrowhead line ends. You can change these by specifying the base angle, tip angle, and length if you follow these steps:

1. Click the **Set Line End Style** icon on the Tools palette. The Line Ends palette is displayed. This shows you the four line-end styles you can apply to a line you've drawn with the Line tool (no arrows at ends; an arrow pointing left; an arrow pointing right; arrows on both ends).

2. Click **Set**. The Line End Options dialog box opens:

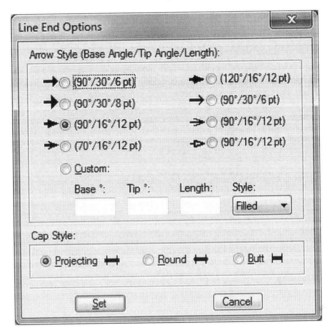

Figure 69: Line End Options dialog box

3. On the Line End Options dialog box, you can do one of the following:

   - Click a radio button for the type of arrow you like, or
   - Click the Custom radio button, and then type the base and tip angle in degrees and the length in points. Choose the arrow style from the Style drop-down list.

4. To change the end of the arrow, click one of the radio buttons in the Cap Style section.

5. Click **Set**. When you apply one of the arrow styles from the Line Ends palette, the arrow will be displayed as you have defined it.

- **To change dashed-line pattern options:**
  FrameMaker also provides eight default dashed line styles. To modify the default dashed line, follow these steps:

  1. Click the **Set Dashed Line Pattern** icon on the Tools palette. The Line Styles palette opens.

  2. Click **Set**. The Dashed Line Options dialog box opens:

Figure 70: Dashed Line Options dialog box

  3. Click the radio button for the line you want to use, and then click **Set**.

Resizing Graphics

You can resize graphics by selecting them and then dragging the handles to the size that you want, using FrameMaker's rulers as your guide (the rulers are located at the top and left sides of your document window). If you want to be more precise about the dimensions of your graphic, right-click it, select Object Properties from the menu that's displayed, and then type the dimensions in the Object Properties dialog box.

If you want to resize a graphic proportionally, say, by increasing its size 50 percent, select the graphic, and then select **Graphics > Scale** on the menu bar. The Scale dialog box opens:

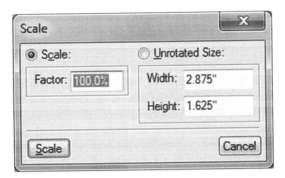

Figure 71: Scale dialog box

Type a percentage in the Factor field, and then click **Scale**. The graphic will be resized proportionally.

Smoothing Corners of Graphics

FrameMaker allows you to smooth the corners of your graphics so you have an even greater variety of shapes to use in your document. Let's say that you've drawn a polygon and you want it to have smooth corners. To do this, select the graphic you want to change, and then select **Graphics > Smooth** on the menu bar. The corners of your graphic will be smoothed. If you want to change it back to the original, select it again and click **Graphics > Unsmooth** on the menu bar.

Cropping Graphics

If you want to crop a graphic, follow these steps:

1. Click the **Graphic Frame** icon on the Tools palette, and then hold down the left-mouse button while drawing your graphic frame.

2. Do one of the following:

   - Draw the graphic you want to crop inside the graphic frame, and then move the frame to crop the graphic, or
   - Drag an existing object into the graphic frame, and then adjust the frame to crop the object.

Masking Graphics

"Masking" a graphic means covering up a portion of it. You do this if you want to create a graphic with a piece missing, as in the following illustrations. (I've left the outline of the masks in these illustrations so you can see them.)

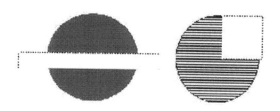

Figure 72: Examples of masking

To mask a graphic, follow these steps:

1. Draw a graphic with a colored fill pattern (so you can see the effects of the masking easier).

2. Click the **Graphic Frame** icon on the Tools palette.

3. Draw a graphic frame over the portion of the graphic that you want to mask.

4. The graphic frame can't be selected along with the graphic, so if you think you might want to move the masked image, instead of

inserting a graphic frame over the existing graphic to mask it, select one of the shape tools (square, circle, etc.). Change the fill and border lines to white, then place it over the other graphic, select both of them, and group them.

Aligning Graphics

If you want to align your graphics, select all of the graphics that you want to align by holding down the **SHIFT** key while you select them. Select the graphic that you want all of the other graphics to be aligned with *last*.

After they're all selected, click **Graphics > Align** on the menu bar. The Align panel opens:

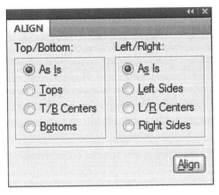

Figure 73: Align panel

If you want to align your graphics horizontally, click the appropriate radio button in the Top/Bottom section. If you want to align your graphics vertically, click the appropriate radio button in the Left/Right section. Click the **Align** button after you've made your selection.

Distributing Graphics

Distributing your graphics means that you're putting an equal amount of space between them. To do this, select all of the graphics that you want to distribute, and then click **Graphics > Distribute** on the menu bar. The Distribute panel opens:

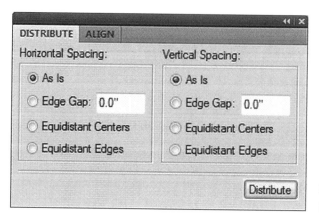

Figure 74: Distribute panel

To align the graphics horizontally, click the appropriate radio button in the Horizontal Spacing section.

To align the graphics vertically, click the appropriate radio button in the Vertical Spacing section. When you're finished, click **Distribute**.

Grouping Graphics

To group two or more graphics, select them, and then click **Graphics > Group** on the menu bar. When you group graphics, they're treated as one object and no longer have handles around the individual graphics. If you change your mind and want to ungroup the graphics, select the grouped graphic, and then click **Graphics > Ungroup** on the menu bar.

Layering Graphics

You can layer your graphics to create new designs. If you layer your graphics, they'll be layered in the order that you created them.

The last object you draw will be the top layer. To layer graphics, simply move them over each other. Once you've layered your graphics, rearrange the layers by doing any of the following:

- To move a graphic to the back layer, click the graphic, and then click **Graphics > Send to Back** on the menu bar.

- To move a graphic to the top layer, click the graphic, and then click **Graphics > Bring to Front** on the menu bar.

- To move a graphic to the middle layer when you have three layers, move one of the other graphics on top of it.

Wrapping Text around Graphics

You can run text around your graphics in several different ways. You can do this by configuring FrameMaker's *runaround properties* as follows:

1. Select the graphic or graphics that you want to run text around, and then select **Graphics > Runaround Properties**. The Runaround Properties panel opens:

Figure 75: Runaround Properties panel

2. If you want the text to flow around the edge of the object, click the **Run around Contour** radio button.

3. If you want the text to flow around an imaginary box surrounding the graphic, click the **Run around Bounding Box** radio button.

4. If you want the text to flow through the graphic, click the **Don't Run Around** radio button.

5. When you finish making your selection, click **Set**.

Rotating Graphics

To rotate a graphic, do the following:

1. Select the graphic you want to rotate.

2. If you want to rotate the graphic clockwise or counterclockwise, select **Graphics > Rotate** on the menu bar, and then type the degree you want to rotate the graphic in the Rotate By field of the Rotate Selected Objects dialog box. Click the **Clockwise** or **Counterclockwise** radio button, and then click **Rotate**.

3. If you want to rotate your object only in a clockwise direction, select **Graphics > Object Properties** on the menu bar, type the degree of angle in the Angle field of the Object Properties dialog box, and click **Set**.

These are just a few of the ways you can manipulate the graphics you create with FrameMaker's tools. As you practice, you'll learn more ways to make your documents more exciting and attractive.

Frequently Asked Questions

Q: *When I move two graphics toward each other, they seem to pull toward each other. Is this normal?*

A: FrameMaker has a feature called *gravity* that causes objects to be attracted to each other and snap together. If you're resizing, moving, or drawing an object, and the corner of the object meets the corner or path of an adjacent object, you'll see this happen. If you don't want them to be as close as they are, select one of the objects and move it away from the other one a bit.

This page is intentionally left blank.

Imported Graphics

Import graphics in different file formats, resize them by changing their dots per inch, and use anchored frames to position your graphics more precisely.

You can import many different graphic file formats into your FrameMaker documents. *Format* refers to the way a graphic is saved to your computer. Different file formats have different extensions to the file names. For example, a graphic that's saved as a bitmap will have a .bmp at the end of the filename. You can import line art, clip art, or photographs in many different formats.

- *Line art* is a graphic that uses lines to draw a diagram, such as an organizational chart or a diagram of a computer network.
- *Clip art* is royalty-free art that you find on the Internet or in clip art libraries of applications that you have on your computer. When working in FrameMaker, you'll probably save the clip art you want to your hard drive and import it into your document.
- *Photographs* and other graphics often are saved as JPEGs, GIFs, or BMPs. You might create these graphics in other applications. *Screen shots* often are saved in one of these formats.

If you're importing a graphic into a Body Page, you'll probably import it into an anchored frame. As we discussed earlier, anchored frames are attached to paragraphs. If you add or delete text above the paragraph to which a frame is anchored, the paragraph and the anchored frame will move.

Anchored Frames

Among their other uses, anchored frames are used for placing graphics in your documents. You can also use anchored frames to crop and mask graphics. Anchored frames can be used on Body Pages, Master Pages and Reference Pages. Whenever you import a graphic, FrameMaker creates an anchored frame around it. The default position for this anchored frame is centered beneath the current line. You may remember that when you have text symbols turned on (click **View > Text Symbols** on the menu bar), the anchored frame symbol looks like an upside-down T. This symbol will appear on the line where your cursor is positioned when you import the graphic.

You also can insert an anchored frame before you import your graphic. Inserting an anchored frame before you import a graphic allows you to align and position it as you wish. To do this, you'll use the Anchored Frame panel. Let's take a look at it now.

1. Open a new blank document.

2. Click in the new document to establish an insertion point, and then click **Special > Anchored Frame** on the menu bar. The Anchored Frame panel opens:

Figure 76: Anchored Frame panel

3. Click the arrow at the end of the Anchoring Position field. Note that there are seven different positions that you can choose:

    *   **Below Current Line**
        This is the default. This position places the anchored frame below the line where your cursor is located.

    *   **At Top of Column**
        This places the anchored frame at the top of the column where your cursor is located.

    *   **At Bottom of Column**
        This places the anchored frame at the bottom of the column where your cursor is located.

    *   **At Insertion Point**
        This places the anchored frame on the line where your cursor is located. The bottom of the anchored frame is aligned with the line and the Anchored Frame panel changes as shown in Figure 77. Instead of having alignment options, you enter a value for the Distance above Baseline. The amount you enter adds space between the anchored frame and the bottom of the text line (called the *baseline*).

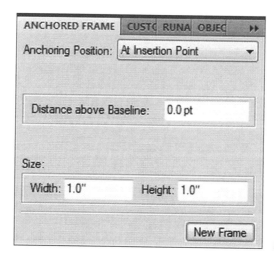

Figure 77: Anchored Frame panel at insertion point

- **Outside Column**

  This places the anchored frame in the *side head* area outside of the text column. Note that if you choose this option, the Anchored Frame panel changes as shown in Figure 78 and you have more alignment options. We'll go over these added options with the other alignment options in our next step.

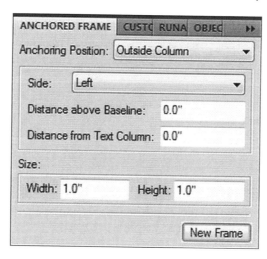

Figure 78: Anchored Frame panel with Outside Column selected

- **Outside Text Frame**

  This places the anchored frame in the margin of the document, outside of the main text column. In a single-column document, this position is the same as the Outside Column position. The alignment and spacing options for this setting are the same as the *Outside Column* setting.

- **Run into Paragraph**
  This places the anchored frame in the text column with the paragraph. Text is displayed around one side of the frame. When you select this option, the Anchored Frame panel changes to allow you to set the gap between the text and the frame. Alignment options are the same as for the *Below Current Line* setting, except that the center alignment isn't available.

4. If it's available in the view you're looking at, click the arrow at the end of the Alignment field. Depending upon which Anchoring Position you chose, you can have up to six different alignments as follows:

- **Left**
  This aligns the anchored frame at the left side of the text column. If the paragraph to which the frame is anchored extends across the side head and columns, the frame is aligned under that paragraph.

- **Right**
  This aligns the anchored frame at the right side of the text column.

- **Side Closer to Binding**
  The bound edge of the document is where the pages are held together. If you're printing on only one side of your pages, this setting will align the anchored frame along the left side of all pages. If you're printing on both sides of your pages, this setting will align the anchored frame on the left side of right-hand pages and the right side of left-hand pages.

- **Side Farther from Binding**
  This setting works in the same way as the *Side Closer to Binding* setting, except that the anchored frame is positioned at the edge that's farthest from the bound edge.

The alignment options for the *Outside Column* and *Outside Text Frame* settings are the same as above, except that they have the following two additional options:

- **Side Closer to Page Edge**
  This aligns the anchored frame closer to the edge of the page in a single-sided document and is the same as the *Side Farther From Binding* in a double-sided document.

- **Side Farther from Page Edge**
  This aligns the frame farther from the edge of the page in a single-sided document and is the same as the *Side Closer to Binding* setting in a double-sided document.

There's just one more section of this panel that you need to understand. When you choose the *Below Current Line*, *At Top of Column*, or *At Bottom of Column* settings, you can apply two additional properties to your frame: **Cropped** and **Floating**.

If you select **Cropped**, the graphic may be cut off by the borders of your text frame or the side head area. No matter what size you specify for the frame in the *Size* section, the image will be contained within the text frame. Any part that falls outside of that text frame will be cropped.

If you select **Floating**, your anchored frame will move to the top of the next column if there isn't enough space at the insertion point for it.

To insert an anchored frame, select the position and alignment (if available), and then complete the additional fields that are displayed. After you type the size of the frame in the Width and Height fields, click the **New Frame** button. An empty frame will be inserted on the page. When you're ready to import a graphic into the frame, click the anchored frame to select it before you import your graphic.

Copying or Importing by Reference

There are two ways you can import graphics into a FrameMaker document: You can **copy** them into the document or you can **create references** to them. Your graphics will look the same when you use either method, but there are advantages and disadvantages to each method of importing graphics.

When you copy a graphic into your document, that graphic becomes a part of your document file. If you move the original document file to another location, you don't have to worry about losing the graphic in your document. Another advantage to copying the graphic to your document is that you don't have to rely only on the original graphic file. If the original is deleted or becomes corrupted, the graphic in your document won't be affected. The primary disadvantage to copying graphics into documents is that it increases the size of the document file.

Importing a graphic by reference means that you don't insert the graphic into your document. Instead, you insert a link in your document to the original graphics file. The graphic still appears in your document, but it's not a part of the document file.

One advantage to this is that your document file size will be smaller. Plus, if you make changes to the original graphics file, the graphic in your document will update automatically. The biggest disadvantage to importing a graphic by reference is that if the link is broken (as would happen if you or someone else moved or deleted the graphics file), your graphic is gone.

It's important to decide before you import graphics whether you want to import them directly into your document or import them by reference. If you decide to import them by reference, you need to decide where you want to store them so they can be updated and moved easily if you need to move your document. Here are some things to consider:

1. What's the best way to organize your graphics files if you're importing them by reference? Because of the structure of FrameMaker documents, it generally isn't a good idea to store graphics in chapter folders. Consider storing all of your graphics in one folder. That way, if you need to link to your graphics again at a later time, you can point FrameMaker to that directory for the first graphic you need to re-link, and then FrameMaker will re-link the rest of the graphics in that folder.

2. What naming conventions should you use? If your graphics have long file names and you want to modify them by using the Object Properties dialog box, you may find it difficult to find the file that you want because long file names are truncated in the Object Properties dialog box.

3. Is it possible that this document and its graphics files will ever be moved onto a different platform? Remember that FrameMaker files can be opened on Windows and UNIX platforms. Follow these conventions when naming your files:

   - For Windows users, include the file name extensions (such as .jpg or .bmp).
   - For UNIX users, use lowercase for your file names.
   - For the most compatibility, don't use spaces, asterisks, quotation marks, slashes, question marks, colons, or other special characters in file names.

Importing a Graphic

To import a graphic into your document, follow these steps:

1. Position your cursor where you want to insert your graphic, or if you've already inserted an anchored frame, select it.

2. Click **File > Import > File** on the menu bar. The Import dialog box opens:

Import by Reference, or Copy into Document buttons

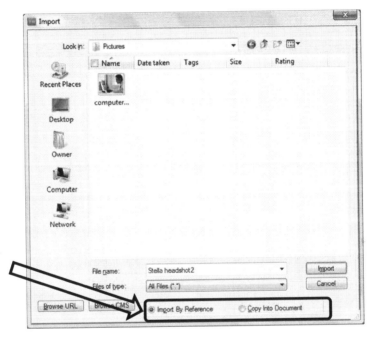

Figure 79: Import dialog box

3. Notice the two radio buttons at the bottom of the dialog box. These allow you to choose whether you want to import by reference or copy the graphic into the document. Whichever one you choose will be the default the next time you import a graphic in this session. If you want to copy graphics into your document in a different session, you'll have to select this again.

4. Navigate to the folder where your graphic is stored.

5. Select the graphic you want by clicking it, and then click the **Import** button.

6. If you're importing a graphic (such as a JPEG or a GIF) and FrameMaker can discern the correct graphics filter to use, the Imported Graphic Scaling dialog box opens:

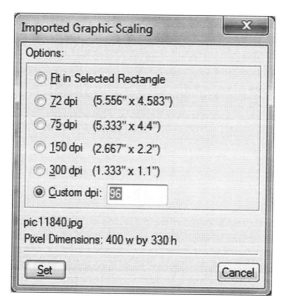

Figure 80: Imported Graphic Scaling dialog box

7. Notice the radio buttons in the Options section of this dialog box. These allow you to change the dots per inch (DPI) of your graphic and the resulting size of it. The size that your graphic would be at each of the DPI is shown to the right of the DPI settings. If *Custom dpi* and a value are selected, this is the current DPI of the graphic.

8. Notice too that the name of the file and its dimensions (in pixels) are displayed near the bottom of the dialog box.

    Note: Avoid selecting the *Fit in Selected Rectangle* option. This setting resizes the graphic to fit in the selected anchored frame and usually distorts the graphic.

9. Click **Set** when you're ready to import the graphic. The graphic will be inserted in your document.

10. If FrameMaker doesn't recognize the format of your graphic, the Unknown File Type dialog box will open:

Figure 81: Unknown File Type dialog box

11. Select your graphic's format from the list provided, and then click **Convert**. The Imported Graphic Scaling dialog box will be displayed. Follow the instructions in step No. 7, and then click **Set** when you're ready to import your graphic. The graphic will be inserted in your document.

Importing SVG Files

FrameMaker supports Scalable Vector Graphics (SVG). SVG is a language for describing two-dimensional graphics and graphical applications in XML. To import an SVG file, follow these steps:

1. Position your cursor where you want to insert your graphic, or if you've already inserted an anchored frame, select it.

2. Click **File > Import > File** on the menu bar. The Import dialog box opens.

3. Choose whether you want to import by reference or copy the graphic into the document.

4. Navigate to the folder where your graphic is stored.

5. Select the SVG graphic you want by clicking it, and then click the **Import** button.

6. After you click **Import**, the Unknown File Type dialog box opens.

7. Select **SVG** from the filters list, and then click **Convert**. The Import SVG dialog box will open:

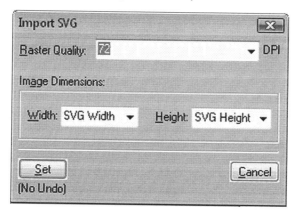

Figure 82: Insert SVG dialog box

8. To resize the graphic by setting the DPI, select a DPI in the Raster Quality drop-down list. This will resize the graphic proportionally. Note that the current DPI of the graphic is the default in this field.

9. If you want to change the dimensions more specifically, click a width in the Width drop-down list and a height in the Height drop-down list. You may distort the image if you resize the image using this method, however.

10. Click **Set**. The graphic will be converted to a bitmap and displayed in your document.

As you can see, importing graphics into your documents requires planning ahead. It's generally best to devise a method of handling your graphics that you like to use and then use that method for all of your documents.

After you import graphics into your document, you may want to change their size, name, or other attributes. In the next section, you'll learn how to do these things in FrameMaker.

Resizing Graphics

If you want to resize an imported graphic, you might think that the best way to do this would be to grab one of the handles around the graphic with your cursor and drag it to the size you want.

While you can resize graphical objects (such as squares and circles you created in the last chapter) and vector graphics proportionally by holding down the **SHIFT** key while dragging a corner, if you do this with a graphic such as a photograph, FrameMaker will reset the DPI of this graphic to *Unknown*. As a consequence, that graphic may not print or export properly. In addition, you may distort the graphic.

The best way to resize an imported graphic is to change the DPI of the graphic. You can do this by selecting the graphic, not the frame. (If you've selected the anchored frame, the handles will be on the outside of the frame; if you've selected the graphic, the handles will be harder to see because they are inside the frame.) After you've selected the graphic, select **Graphics > Object Properties** on the menu bar. Alternately (and usually easier), you can right-click the graphic, and then select **Object Properties** from the drop-down menu. The Object Properties panel opens (Figure 83):

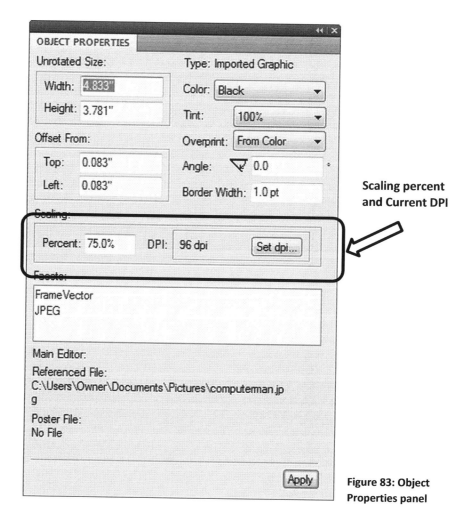

Scaling percent and Current DPI

Figure 83: Object Properties panel

The current DPI of the graphic is displayed to the right of the word *DPI*. To the left of this field is the *Scaling Percent* of this graphic. To resize your graphic, do one of the following:

- Click **Set DPI**. The Imported Graphic Scaling dialog box opens. Select a new DPI, and then click **Set**. Your graphic should be resized , or

- Change the percentage in the Scaling section of the Object Properties dialog box.

Shrink-wrapping Anchor Frames to Fit Graphics

If you're changing the size of your imported graphic, you may have to select the anchored frame that's around it and drag a corner of it to allow you to see the entire graphic.

An alternate way to make the anchored frame fit the graphic is to *shrink-wrap* it by doing the following:

1. Select the anchored frame (not the graphic).

2. Press **ESC, m,** and **p** individually on your keyboard. The anchored frame will shrink or expand to fit its contents.

Shrink-wrapping also changes the anchoring position to *At Insertion Point* and displays the frame zero (0) points above the baseline of the text. If the anchored frame is on the same line as some text, this can cause the graphic to cover the text on the preceding lines. If this is a problem, delete the graphic and press **ENTER** in your document to create a new blank line. Re-import your graphic and shrink-wrap it if needed.

Grouping Graphics

There may be times when you want to group several graphics together in a single frame. This is especially useful when you're creating logos or special design elements that you'll use throughout your document. To do this, follow these steps:

1. Insert an anchored frame in your document, adjusting the settings so that it'll be large enough to hold all of the graphics you intend to insert into it.

2. Import your graphics one by one, always selecting the anchored frame before you import the graphic.

3. Position your graphics as you wish them to appear within the frame by selecting them and moving them with your cursor.

4. When you're satisfied with the layout, select each of the graphics you want to group by pressing **SHIFT** on your keyboard while selecting each graphic.

5. Click **Graphics > Group** on the menu bar. All of the graphics you selected will now appear to be one unit. (If you want to ungroup the graphics, select the grouped graphic and click **Graphics > Ungroup** on the menu bar.)

6. Shrink-wrap the anchored frame by clicking it and then pressing **ESC, m,** and **p** on your keyboard.

Putting Graphics on Reference Pages

You may recall that we mentioned Reference Pages briefly in Chapter 2, when we discussed the different types of pages in a FrameMaker document.

Among other things, Reference Pages can hold boilerplate graphics that you can use throughout a document. FrameMaker automatically generates Reference Pages when you open a new document. Take a look at your Reference Pages now by following these steps:

1. Open a new FrameMaker document.

2. Click **View > Reference Pages** on the menu bar. The first page of your Reference Pages will appear.

The first page of your Reference Pages contains four line styles called *Footnote, TableFootnote, Single Line*, and *Double Line*. Do you remember when we were looking at the Advanced properties tab of the Paragraph Designer and at the bottom of that tab there were the Frame Above Pgf and Frame Below Pgf fields? The choices for those fields were *None, As Is, Footnote, Double Line, Single Line,* and *TableFootnote*. The lines that you see on the Reference Page are the ones that are inserted when you choose them from these fields on the Advanced properties tab.

In addition to these lines, you can store graphics here that you can add to your documents using the Frame Above Pgf and Frame Below Pgf fields on the Advanced properties tab of the Paragraph Designer. This can be a useful way to add warning, caution, or note icons to your documents. You accomplish this by saving the graphics you want to use on your Reference Page in a special way. Once you do that, your graphics are added to the list of items you can designate to be in the **Frame Above Pgf** or the **Frame Below Pgf** fields in the Paragraph Designer. Here's how you do it:

1. Open the Paragraph Designer panel, and then click the **Advanced** properties tab of the Paragraph Designer.

2. At the bottom of the Advanced properties tab, locate the *Frame Above Pgf* field and click the arrow next to it. A list of items you can place in the frame above the paragraph is displayed.

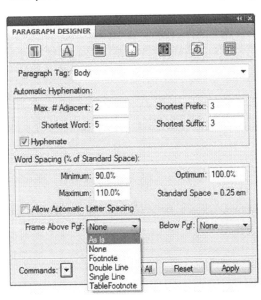

Figure 84: Advanced properties tab with Frame Above Pgf options

In addition to *As Is* and *None*, notice the four options listed. These four options are the same as the line styles that FrameMaker generated on your Reference Page when you opened your document.

Now, let's save a graphic on your Reference Page so it will be added to this list and you can apply it to a paragraph tag to be inserted in the frame above or below the paragraph. But you have to save your graphic in a special way. Let's go through the steps now. You can use any graphic or clip art that you want. Before you work with your Reference Page, save the graphic you want with a name and location you can remember, and then follow these steps:

1. If you aren't looking at your Reference Pages now, click **View > Reference Pages**.

2. While you're on the Reference Page that has the default graphics shown (generally the first page of your Reference Pages), open the Tools palette by clicking **Graphics > Tools** on the menu bar.

3. On the Tools palette, click the **Graphic Frame** icon.

Figure 85: Graphic Frame icon

4. Hold down the left-mouse button and draw a frame on the Reference Page that's approximately the size of your graphic.

5. When you release the left-mouse button, the **Frame Name** dialog box opens.

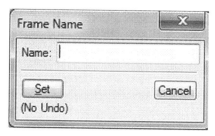

Figure 86: Frame Name dialog box

6. Type the name of this graphic in this dialog box. After you've typed the name in this box, click **Set**. This name will appear in the Paragraph Designer now.

7. With the frame still selected, click **File > Import File**.

8. Navigate to the folder where you stored your graphic on your hard drive, select it, and then click **Import**. The graphic will be inserted into the frame.

Go back to your Body Pages, open the Paragraph Designer, and then click the **Advanced** properties tab. Click the arrow next to the Frame Above Pgf or Frame Below Pgf fields. Notice that the name of your graphic is now in your list.

Try creating a paragraph style that will insert your graphic for the frame above or below the paragraph. I find that a good use for this is adding graphics to warnings and other information I want to stand out.

Placing Graphics on Master Pages

Graphics are often used on Master Pages in the headers and footers. For example, some companies like to place a small version of their logo in the headers of their documents. To insert a graphic on a Master Page, do the following:

1. Select **View > Master Pages** on the menu bar to display the Master Pages.

2. Scroll to the Master Page where you want to add a graphic.

3. It's generally best to insert an anchored frame, and then import the graphic into that anchored frame so you have more precision in positioning your graphic. Place your cursor in the frame where you want to place the graphic, and then click

Special > Anchored Frame on the menu bar. The Anchored Frame panel opens.

4. After you've inserted your anchored frame, click **File > Import > File** on the menu bar.

5. Navigate to the folder that holds your graphic, select how you want to insert it into your document, and then click **Import**.

You learned a lot about working with graphics in this chapter. You can create some interesting things with your graphics. It's important to experiment with graphics. Try creating new designs for your pages that will make it easier for your readers to find the information they need. It's a fun and rewarding way to add interest to your documents.

Frequently Asked Questions

Q: *How can I get my graphics to print better?*

A: Graphics that are imported into FrameMaker documents typically print well if you set their DPI at a number that can evenly divide the DPI of your printer. For example, if your printer has DPI of 600, your graphics would print best if they had a DPI of 100, 120, 150, or 300 DPI.

Q: *Help! When I tried to open my document, an error message called "Missing Files" displayed. How can I open my document now?*

A: Don't panic! This means that the graphic listed at the top of the Missing File dialog box under the words *Looking for* has been renamed, moved, or deleted. To re-link a missing graphic, browse through your folders to find the missing graphic. If it's been moved or renamed, be sure the radio button in front of **Update Document to Use New Path** is selected. If you know the graphic has been deleted, click the radio button in front of **Skip This File**. If you want to skip all missing graphics, click the radio button in front of **Ignore All Missing Files**. After you've made your choices, click **Continue**. Your document will open.

This page is intentionally left blank.

System and User Variables

Learn the difference between system and user variables; how to design, modify, and delete variables; and create variables to automatically update important information in your documents.

Whenever you write technical documents, especially long ones, wouldn't it be great if some of the things in your document, such as dates, would update automatically?

Wouldn't it be nice if you could insert some code and have the header or footer automatically pick up some of the text in the body of your document to display?

And if your company's marketing department decides to change the name of the product after you've finished writing about it, wouldn't it be great if you only had to change the name in one place and it would automatically be updated throughout your entire document?

FrameMaker's variables can do all of these things for you and more. As you'll see in this chapter, variables can help you write your documentation more easily by taking care of tasks that are necessary but difficult to maintain.

FrameMaker variables come in two varieties: *system variables* and *user variables*. *System variables* are installed by default when you install FrameMaker. They take their information from FrameMaker or your computer system (such as your computer's clock). *User variables* are ones that you create.

FrameMaker gives variables abbreviated names that you can choose from when you want to insert one into your document. System variables are comprised of things called *building blocks*. You may remember that we discussed building blocks when we were looking at the Paragraph Designer. The building blocks you use to create your variables aren't the same as those building blocks, so we'll talk in detail about the system variable building blocks in this chapter.

When associated with a system variable, these building blocks define what information will be updated and displayed in your document. As you'll see, all of your system variables have default definitions that you can use or change.

User variables use *character tags* if you want to format the text that you're defining in the variable. As you'll recall from an earlier chapter, character tags primarily add formatting such as boldface and italics to the selected text.

As we look at variables, think of ways you can use them in your documentation. I'm sure you'll quickly see the advantages of using the system variables for automating such things as creating text for headers and footers.

Also, think of ways that user variables could help you. You might want to use them to save the time it takes to type long text strings, such as complicated product names, or you might want to use them in place of typing out names of products that might change before your document is finished.

However you choose to use them, variables can save you a great deal of time, both when you're writing your document and when you're editing it. Let's take a closer look at them.

Understanding Variables

In FrameMaker, a *variable* is information in your document that may need to be changed in the future. The date is a good example of information that's suitable for a FrameMaker variable.

Variables help you save time when you're writing your documents and they can help you be more consistent. Even more important, variables make it easy to update key information throughout your entire document. If, for example, you're writing responses for proposals (RFPs) and you essentially use the same document each time, you could make the name of the company to whom you're sending the RFP a variable. The next time you write an RFP for a different company, you would change the name of the company in your variable and all references to the company name would be changed throughout your document.

As we discussed earlier, there are two types of variables: *system variables* and *user variables*.

System variables display information that's generated by your computer or by FrameMaker. They include such things as page numbers and the date. Each system variable has a name and a definition. You can't add, delete, or rename the system variables that are installed with FrameMaker, but you can modify them.

User variables display information that you've defined. Standard templates don't include any user variables. You need to create them yourself. You can add, delete, and edit your user variables. User variables are used primarily for words that you use often in your documents or words that you might need to change in the future, such as a company or product name.

The Variables Pod

When you're working with variables, you'll probably spend a lot of time with the Variables pod. Let's take a look at it now.

1. Open a new blank page in FrameMaker.

2. After the new page opens, click **Special > Variables** on the menu bar. The Variables pod opens if it wasn't already displayed:

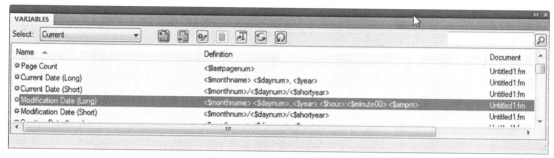

Figure 87: Variables pod

The large pane in the middle of the pod lists the names of the variables on the left side of the pane in the Name column and lists their building blocks in the middle of the pane in the Definition column. System variables are listed first.

There are seven icons at the top of the Variables pod. Here's what they mean:

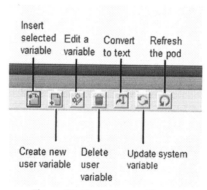

Figure 88: Variables pod icons

These icons represent the following, from left to right:

- **Insert Selected Variable**
  If you want to insert a variable in your document, select the variable you want from the list, and then click the **Insert**

Selected Variable icon. Some system variables can only be placed on certain types of pages, but you don't have to memorize which variables are available on which type of page. If your cursor is on a Body Page when you open the Variables pod, only the variables that you can insert on Body Pages are listed. If it's on a Master Page, only the variables that you can insert on Master Pages are listed.

- **Create New User Variable**
  You'll use the **Create New User Variable** icon when you're creating your user variables. When you click this button, the Add/Edit User Variable panel is displayed. We'll explore this later when we create a user variable.

- **Edit a Variable**
  If you want to modify a system variable, click the **Edit a Variable** icon to open the Edit System Variable panel.

- **Delete User Variable**
  To delete a user variable that you've created, select it in the list of variables, and then click the **Delete User Variable** icon.

- **Convert to Text**
  The **Convert to Text** icon opens the Convert Variables to Text dialog box. Although variables look like standard text in your document, they don't behave like text. When you click a word in a phrase that's a variable in your text, the entire phrase is highlighted, FrameMaker doesn't spell-check variables, and you can't change the spelling of the words in a variable after it's inserted on a page. You have to edit it through the Variables pod. The Convert to Text button converts the selected variable to text. Once converted, it can be treated like the rest of your text.

  However, system variables (such as dates) won't update automatically and you can't convert them back to variables. If you change your mind and want to convert a piece of text back to a variable, you have to insert it as a variable again.

- **Update System Variables**
  The **Update System Variables** icon updates all system variables in the designated document.

- **Refresh**
  Clicking the **Refresh** icon refreshes the list of variables in the Variables pod.

Inserting Variables

A common way to use system variables is in background text frames, such as headers and footers. System variables behave differently on different types of pages.

- When you insert a system variable on a Master Page, its values are updated automatically.

- When you insert a system variable on a Body or Reference Page, its value is updated only when you open or print the document or when you manually update the value of the variable by clicking **Update System Variables** on the Variables pod while the file is open.

You can insert a variable on any page (body, master, or reference) or in a text frame. You can't, however, insert a variable in a line of text that you create using the Text Line tool on the Tools palette. To insert variables into your document, follow these steps:

1. Click where you want the variable to appear on the page.

2. Click **Special > Variable** on the menu bar if the Variables pod isn't displayed, or if it is open already, go to the next step.

3. Select a variable in the Variables list, and then click **Insert**.

Note: You also can insert a variable by clicking where you want the variable to appear on the page, and then clicking the right button of your mouse. Select **Variables** from the pop-up menu. The Variables pod opens. Select a variable in the Variables list, and then click **Insert**.

System Variables and Their Building Blocks

The table below lists the types of system variables that are available on specific types of pages:

Table 2: Available System Variables by Type of Page

Page or Location	Available System Variables
Body, Master, or Reference	Page Count
	Current Date (long or short)
	Modification Date (long or short)
	Creation Date (long or short)
	Filename (long or short)
	Volume Number
	Chapter Number
Master	Current Page #
	Running H/F 1-12
Table title, heading, and footing rows	Table Continuation
	Table Sheet

When you modify these system variables, you'll use building blocks. Let's look at them more closely.

Date and Time Variables

Date variables, such as *Current Date*, can display the month, day, and year in long or short forms. Date variables consist of building blocks that allow you to display the date in different formats by changing their building blocks. You can add time building blocks to some of these variables to show the second, minute, hour, and year. Note that while you can change variables, you can't change the function of a system variable. For example, if you're modifying the Modification Date variable, you can't change it to display the creation date. You must use the Creation Date variable to show the creation date.

The following table shows you the building blocks you can use with Date and Time variables and their descriptions:

Table 3: Building Blocks for Date and Time Variables

Building Block	Description
<$ampm>	Lowercase morning or evening abbreviation (am or pm)
<$AMPM>	Uppercase morning or evening abbreviation (AM or PM)
<$dayname>	Name of day (i.e., Monday)
<$shortdayname>	Abbreviated name of day (i.e., Mon.)
<$daynum>	Number of day (i.e., 15)
<$daynum01>	Number of day with leading zero (i.e., 05)
<$hour>	Hour (i.e., 12)
<$hour01>	Hour with leading zero (i.e., 02)
<$hour24>	Hour in military format (i.e., 17)
<$minute>	Minute (i.e., 10)
<$minute00>	Minute with leading zero (i.e., 05)
<$monthname>	Name of month (i.e., August)

(Continued on next page)

Building Block	Description
<$monthnum01>	Number of month with leading zero (i.e., 08)
<$shortmonthname>	Abbreviated name of month (i.e., Aug.)
<$monthnum>	Number of month (i.e., 8)
<$second>	Seconds (i.e., 8)
<$second00>	Seconds with leading zero (i.e., 03)
<$year>	Year (i.e., 2010)
<$shortyear>	Abbreviated year (i.e., 10)

Numeric Variables

Numeric variables display page, volume, and chapter numbers. The following are the numeric variables:

- **Current Page Number**
  This variable displays the number of the current page. It can only be inserted on Master Pages.

- **Page Count**
  This variable displays the total number of pages in the file.

- **Volume Number**
  This variable displays the volume number of the file.

- **Chapter Number**
  This variable displays the chapter number of the file.

The following table shows you the building blocks you can use with Numeric variables and their descriptions:

Table 4: Building Blocks for Numeric Variables

Building Block	Description
<$curpagenum>	Page number of current page (i.e., 236)
<$lastpagenum>	Page number of the last page in the document (i.e., 566)
<$paranum>	Value of the autonumber field in the paragraph tag (i.e., Step 5)
<$paranumonly>	Numeric value of the autonumber field without punctuation or text (i.e., 5)
<$chapnum>	Chapter number (i.e., 2)
<$volnum>	Volume number (i.e., III)
<$sectionnum>	Section number
<$subsectionnum>	Subsection number
<$chaptertitlename>	Chapter title name

Filename Variables

There are just two Filename variables: Filename (long) and Filename (short). The long file name variable displays the filename and its entire path. The short file name displays only the file name. Below is a table that shows the building blocks:

Table 5: Building Blocks for Filename Variables

Building Block	Description
<$fullfilename>	The document's full file name, including the path to where it is located (i.e., c:\My Documents\Business Docs\Manual)
<$filename>	The document's file name without the path (i.e., Manual.fm)

Table Variables

You already used one of the Table variables when we looked at *continued* lines in the chapter about tables. There are two system variables that you can use only in tables:

- **Table Continuation**
  This is the variable that adds the *continued* line. By default, this displays *(Continued)*. But you can change the text by editing the definition on the Edit System Variable panel.

- **Table Sheet**
  This variable displays the number of the sheet this table is on and the total number of sheets. By default, this variable displays *(Sheet # of #)*. You can change this, too, by editing the definition on the Edit System Variable panel.

The Table Continuation variable doesn't have any building blocks that you can change. The following table shows you the two building blocks that you can use in the Table Sheet variable:

Table 6: Building Blocks for Table Variables

Building Block	Description
<$tblsheetnum>	Displays the sheet number (i.e., 2)
<$tblsheetcount>	Displays the total number of sheets in a table (i.e., 5)

Running Header/Footer Variables

Finally, let's look at the Running Header/Footer Variables. There are 12 of these and they're only available when you're on the Master Pages of your document. As their names suggest, these variables are used to insert information in the headers and footers of your document.

Authors often use different headers for left and right pages, and sometimes for the first pages of chapters or sections, too. For example, you might a header on your left-hand pages that has the name of your document. On the right-hand pages, you might want a header that has the name of the current chapter.

In FrameMaker, you can use the Running H/F variables to create these headers. There are 12 Running Header/Footer variables. Their names are Running H/F 1 through 12. By default, they are reserved for the following:

- Running H/F 1 is reserved for inserting the text that has the Title paragraph tag applied to it.

- Running H/F 2 is reserved for text that has the Heading 1 paragraph tag applied to it.

- Running H/F 3 and 4 are typically used with *marker text*. This is text that isn't visible in the document but can be used in the header or footer (and in other ways). For example, let's say that you have the following heading in your document: *Exploring the Detrimental Effects of Sleeplessness in Rats*. It is possible to link this heading to a variable so it would be displayed in your header, and you'd like to have a header that describes what's on the page. But this heading is too long and you'd rather have your header say: *Sleeplessness in Rats*. Behind the heading, you would insert the marker text that says what you want in the header. The marker wouldn't be visible when you printed the document, but the header would display what you wrote in that marker. You'll learn how to do this soon.

- Running H/F 5-12 use definitions that refer to paragraph tags that you define, such as the autonumber of a paragraph tag.

Here are the building blocks that you can use with the Running Header/Footer variables:

Table 7: Building Blocks for Running Header/Footer Variables

Building Block	Description
<$paratext[paratag]>	Displays the paragraph's text.
<$paranum[paratag]>	Displays the paragraph's autonumber, including any text in the autonumber format.
<$paranumonly[paratag]>	Displays the numeric portion of the autonumber format.
<$paratag[paratag]>	Displays the paragraph's tag.
<$marker1>	Displays the text of a Header/Footer $1 marker.
<$marker2>	Displays the text of a Header/Footer $2 marker.

We've covered a lot of material about system variables in this section. In the next section, you'll learn how to work with variables some more as well as learn how to create your own user variables.

Working with Variables

Let's look first at how to edit system variables. As you learned in the last section, when you want to edit the definition of a system variable, you use the building blocks that are associated with it. For example, if you want to change how the month is displayed, you'll see building blocks in the list such as *<$monthname>* and *<$monthnum>*.

Building blocks are specific to variables. You can use date-related building blocks, for example, only with date-related variables. To edit a system variable, follow these steps:

1. Click **Special > Variables** on the menu bar if the Variables pod isn't already open. (You can also double-click a variable that's

been inserted in your document to open the Variables pod.) If the Variables pod is open already, go to the next step.

2. Select the variable you want to edit from the list of variables, and then click the **Edit** icon. The Edit System Variable panel opens:

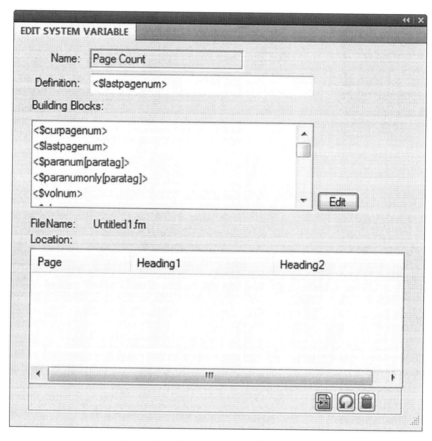

Figure 89: Edit System Variable panel

3. To add a building block to a definition, deselect the definition by clicking where you want to insert the new building block in the definition, and then click a building block you want to add from the Building Blocks list. The building block is added to the definition.

4. Click **Edit** to save your changes.

To see more clearly how this works, modify a date system variable to add the time to it. To do this, follow these steps:

1. Open a new FrameMaker document and place your cursor at the top of the blank page.

2. Click **Special > Variables** on the menu bar and select **Current Date (Long)** from the list of variables.

3. Click **Edit** on the Variables pod. The Edit System Variable panel opens.

4. Notice that the Current Date (Long) system variable is made up of three building blocks: *<$monthname>*, *<$daynum>*, and *<$year>*. Let's add the hour, minute, and second building blocks to the variable. Click after the last character of the last building block in the Definition box.

5. Type a comma after the last character of the last building block, and then click one of the hour building blocks to insert it into the variable. Note that you need to add punctuation and spacing that you would like to appear when the variable text is displayed.

6. After adding the hour building block, insert a colon, add a minute building block, add another colon, and then add a second building block. When you're finished, click **Edit**.

7. On the Variables pod, notice that the definition of the Current Date (Long) variable has changed to what you indicated. If it isn't highlighted already, select it, and then click **Insert** to insert it into your document. The date will be displayed in your document where your cursor was located. If you don't like the way it looks, you can go back to the Variables pod and modify this variable some more.

Creating Marker Text

When we were discussing the Running H/F 3 and 4 variables, I told you about how you use these variables with marker text to display the marker text instead of the actual text in the document. This is a two-part process. First, you need to create the marker text as follows:

1. On your Body Pages, position your cursor on the page where you want to insert marker text. Remember, the marker text won't be visible so you can place it anywhere you like on the page.

2. Click **Special > Marker** on the menu bar. The Marker panel opens:

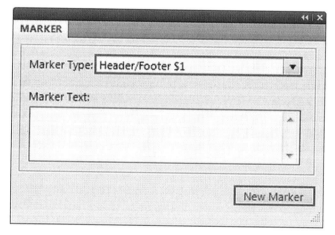

Figure 90:
Marker panel

3. Click the arrow at the right of the Marker Type field and select either **Header/Footer $1** or **Header/Footer $2** from the drop-down list. This can be confusing because you'll be using this text with Running H/F 3 or Running H/F 4 variables. Header/Footer $1 and $2 are the marker identifiers, while Running H/F3 and Running H/F 4 are names of variables.

4. Type the text in the Marker Text field that you'll want to appear in the header or footer of that page when you insert the Running H/F3 or Running H/F4 variable.

5. Click **New Marker**. Your marker will be inserted in your document. If you have the text symbols turned on, you can see where it's located. The marker text symbol looks like a capital *T*.

Next, you need to insert the variable that will use the marker text by doing the following:

1. With your cursor still on the page where your marker is located, click **View > Master Pages** on the menu bar. The Master Page opens that's applied to the Body Page where your cursor is located.

2. Position your cursor in the header or footer area of the Master Page, and then click **Special > Variables** on the menu bar. The Variables pod opens.

3. If it said "Header/Footer $1" in the Marker Type box on the Marker panel when you inserted the marker text, select **Running H/F 3** from the list of variables. If it said "Header/Footer $2" in the Marker Type box on the Marker panel when you inserted the marker text, select **Running H/F 4** from the list of variables.

4. To be certain that your definition is correct, click **Edit**. Just to confuse us a bit more, the building block for the "Header/Footer $1" marker is **<$marker1>** and it should be associated with **Header/Footer $1** marker, which then will be associated with the **Running H/F 3** variable. (That's just the way the application works!) The building block in the Definition field for the Running H/F 3 variable should be <$marker1>. The building block in the Definition field for the Running H/F 4 variable should be <$marker2>.

5. When you're certain that the Running H/F variable is using the correct building block, return to the Variables pod.

6. Be certain the variable is selected, and then click **Insert** to insert the variable into your document. The text in the header on the Master Page should be similar to this: *Running H/F 3.*

7. Return to the Body Pages by clicking **View > Body Pages** on the menu bar. The text that you wrote as your marker text should appear where you inserted the variable on the Master Page.

Moving, Replacing, or Deleting a Variable

When you insert a variable into your document, its value will be displayed at that insertion point. You can move it, replace it with another variable, or delete it within the document by doing one of the following:

*   To copy or move a variable in your text, click to select it, and then click **Edit > Cut**. Move your cursor to where you want to reposition the variable, and then click **Edit > Paste**.

*   To replace a variable in your text, double-click the variable you want to replace. This selects the variable and displays the Variables pod. Double-click the variable on the Variables list that you want to replace the one you selected in your text. The variable you selected in your text is replaced.

*   To delete a variable in your text, select it, and then press the **DELETE** key on your keyboard.

If you change the definition of a variable, as we did with the Current Date (Long) system variable, the definition of that variable will be updated throughout the document, regardless of the type of page it's on. However, the value of that variable won't be changed if the variable is on Body and Reference Pages until you open or print the file. If the variable is on a Master Page, its value will be updated when you save the document. To update the value of a changed variable on the Body or Reference Pages immediately, click **Special >**

Variables on the tool bar to open the Variables pod. Click **Update** on the Variables pod, and then click **OK**.

User Variables

User variables are the ones that you create. Typically, user variables consist of a word or group of words that you use often in your documentation or that may change in future documents. Here's how to create a user variable:

1. Click on the page where you want the variable to appear, and then click **Special > Variables** on the menu bar.

2. Click **Create New User Variable**. The Add/Edit Variable panel opens:

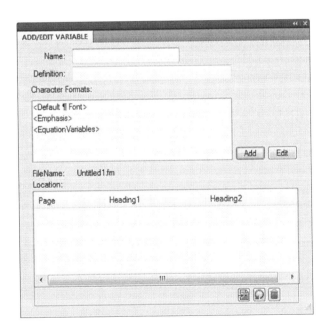

Figure 91: Add/Edit Variable panel

3. Type the name you want to give your variable in the Name field. This is the name that will appear in the list of variables. For practice, type *fm* in the Name field.

   Note: Variable names are case-sensitive, which means that *FM* would be a different variable from *fm*.

4. In the Definition field, type the text that will be inserted into your document when you insert this variable. For your practice user variable, type *Adobe FrameMaker 10*. (You can use up to 255 characters for the definition of your user variables.)

5. You can't use system variable building blocks in your user variables, but you can use character formatting. To format your practice user variable so that it will be italicized, move your cursor to the beginning of the definition (just before the word *Adobe*, and then click **<Emphasis>** in the list of Character Formats.

6. Click **Add**. Your user variable is added to the list of variables. To see how it looks, click it in the variables list, and then click **Insert**. What you defined should be inserted into your document.

Change the Definition of a User Variable

To change the definition of a user variable, open the Variables pod, select the variable you want to change, and then click **Edit**. Make the changes you want to make to the name or definition, and then click **Add.**

Delete a User Variable

- To delete a user variable definition, open the Variables pod, select the variable you want to delete, and then click the **Delete User Variable** icon. If you've used this variable in your text, a message opens asking if you want to convert those instances to editable text. If you do this, the variable in your document is converted to editable text, but the user variable is deleted.

- If you want to delete specific instances of where this variable has been inserted in your document, select the user variable and click **Edit** on the Variables pod. The Edit User Variable panel opens. In the large pane, you'll see a list of the places in your document where this user variable has been inserted. There are three icons at the bottom of the panel. If you select one of the locations where you inserted your user variable and click the first icon, you'll be taken to that location in your document. If you click the second icon, the user variable will be refreshed in your document. If you click the third icon, the text that was inserted by your user variable will be deleted in the text at the location you've selected.

- If you want to delete a user variable directly in your document, select it, and then press the **DELETE** key on your keyboard.

Convert Variables to Text

As mentioned earlier, variables aren't treated like text. Among other things, they aren't checked when you use FrameMaker's spelling checker. To convert a variable to text, follow these steps:

1. Select the variable you want to convert to text.

2. Click **Special > Variables** on the menu bar, and then click **Convert to Text**. The Convert Variables to Text dialog box opens:

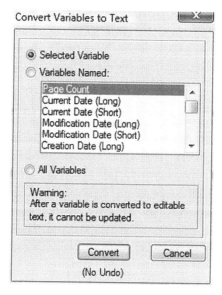

Figure 92: Convert Variables to Text dialog box

3. If you only want to convert the occurrence of this variable you've selected in your document, be certain that the radio button in front of **Selected Variable** is selected.

4. If you want to convert specific types of variables to text, click the radio button in front of **Variables Named**, and then select the variable you want to be converted to text from the list.

5. If you want to convert all variables in your document to text, click the radio button in front of **All Variables**.

6. Click **Convert**.

Creating Dictionary-style Headers

Dictionary-style headers and footers display the range of information on pages. For example, if you have several definitions in your pages and the first definition on the left page is *dog* and the last definition on the right page is *dungeon*, you might want to display the word *dog* in the header of the left page and *dungeon* in the header of the right page so readers know whether the word they're searching for would be on either of those pages.

Using a building block usually displays the first instance of a paragraph tag on a page. To display the last instance of a paragraph tag on a page, you have to use a special building block. To create this, you need to insert a standard Running H/F variable on the left Master Page and then modify it on the right Master Page by following these steps:

1. Open or create a FrameMaker document that has text that you want to use these types of variables with. Be certain that the document has a left Master Page and a right Master Page.

2. Click **View > Master Pages** on the menu bar to display the Master Pages.

3. Place your cursor in the header text box on the left Master Page, and then click **Special > Variables** on the menu bar to display the Variables pod.

4. Select the Running H/F variable you want to use for this header, and then click **Edit**. The Edit System Variable panel opens.

5. If it isn't already in the definition for the Running H/F variable you selected, scroll through the list of building blocks and select **<$paratext[paratag]>**.

6. In the definition, delete the word *paratag* between the brackets in the building block, and then type the name of the paragraph tag that you want FrameMaker to search for in the variable. For example, if you're using Heading1 as the paragraph tag for the words that are defined in your dictionary, your building block would look like this when finished: <$paratext[Heading1]>

   Note: Remember that the names of the paragraph tags are case-sensitive. *Heading1* is different from *heading1*.

7. When you're finished, click **Edit**. This returns you to the Variables pod.

8. Select the variable you just edited in the variables list, and then click the **Insert** icon on the Variables pod to insert the Running H/F variable in the header text frame of the left page.

Next, edit a variable to display the last item on the right-hand page that has a specific paragraph tag applied to it by doing the following:

1. Go to the Master Page for the right page and position your cursor in the header text frame.

2. Since you'll want your text to be aligned on the right side of the page, click the **Right Text Alignment** button on the Formatting toolbar at the top of the screen. (This is displayed as one of four icons indicating four text alignments: left, right, center, and justify.)

3. Click **Special > Variables** on the menu bar to display the Variables pod.

4. Select the Running H/F variable you want to use for this header, and then click **Edit Definition**. The Edit System Variable panel opens.

5. If it isn't already in the definition for the Running H/F variable you selected, scroll through the list of building blocks and select <$paratext[paratag]>.

6. In the definition, delete the word *paratag* between the brackets in the building block, and then type the name of the paragraph tag that you want FrameMaker to search for in the variable. For example, if you're using Heading1 as the paragraph tag for the words that are defined in your dictionary, your building block would look like this when finished: <$paratext[Heading1]>

7. Add a *+,* (plus sign and a comma) between the paragraph tag's name and the first bracket. The plus sign tells FrameMaker to find the *last* paragraph on the page that uses this paragraph tag. Your building block should now look like this:

<$paratext[+, Heading1]>

8. When you're finished, click **Edit**. This returns you to the Variables pod.

9. Highlight the variable you just modified in the variables list.

10. Click the **Insert** icon on the Variables pod to insert the Running H/F variable in the header text frame of the right page.

11. Return to your Body Pages. You should have dictionary-type headers on the pages that have these Master Pages applied to them.

System variables and user variables can save you a great deal of time and help you write your documents with more consistency. Be sure to explore them and experiment with using them in different situations.

Frequently Asked Questions

Q: *Why aren't my system variables updating on my screen?*

A: To update your system variables as they appear on your computer screen, do one of the following:

- If the system variables appear on Master Pages, save the document.
- If the system variables appear on Body or Reference Pages, press **CTRL + l** (lowercase L) to refresh the variable, or save the document and then open it again.
- Manually update the variables by clicking **Update** on the Variables pod.

This page is intentionally left blank.

Conditional Text

Learn how to have multiple versions of the same document—all in the same file. Create conditional text, edit it, delete it, and switch condition tags.

When you're writing documentation, there are times that the documents you're writing are basically the same with small differences. For example, let's say that you're a technical writer for a company that manufactures several different products. These products all have their own user manuals, but while the majority of the information is the same in all of them, there is some product-specific information that needs to be included in each of them too.

Or let's say that you are writing a document that will be used in different formats, such as in online Help files, marketing materials, and a white paper. While the text will be essentially the same in each version, you need to change some of the text to make it "fit" the venue in which it's being presented.

These things and more can be done easily by using FrameMaker's conditional text tools.

Understanding Conditional Text

Conditional text is text that you mark to be used in specific instances. A good example of a document where you might want to use conditional text could be your résumé. Perhaps your basic résumé is the same, but you want two different versions of it to send to different employers. You want both versions to be in the same file. With conditional text, you could enter the text you wanted for both versions of your résumé in the same file and only the version you wanted would be printed.

Another example could be a marketing brochure that will be used for two products. Both of the products have long lists of features, most of them the same for both products. To be consistent, you want both of these brochures to have the same layout and formatting, but there will be different graphics used in each.

By using conditional text tools, you could write the brochure for one of the products, make text, graphics, and tables that are specific to that product conditional, and then add text that is conditional for the other product to the same document. You then could use conditional text controls to display only the text related to one of the products or the other. By doing this, you could use one file to write two documents.

Other uses for conditional text include writing different text for documents that will be published in different ways and writing comments about the document that won't be seen when printed unless you wish them to be seen.

It's important to know that you can make almost anything in your text conditional, including individual characters and words, paragraphs, pages, chapters, graphics, cross-references, tables, and more. To make anything conditional, however, you have to apply a *condition tag* to it.

Condition tags don't hold the information you want to use in your document like AutoText holds information in Microsoft Word.

Instead, condition tags mark the elements they're applied to so it's easy to see which elements you're using at any time. After you've applied condition tags to selected elements in your document, you can use features such as Show/Hide to show the text or hide it.

The name of the condition tag you're using is displayed in the Status bar at the bottom of the window when your cursor is on the conditional text.

Planning Your Conditional Text

When you're considering using conditional text in your document, you need to do a bit of planning. The following questions can help you better determine how to use conditional text in your document:

1. Why do you want to use conditional text in this document? Will you be using the conditional text solely to add comments to the document, or will you use the conditional text to publish different versions of the same document? If the latter, what are the changes that your conditional text will represent for different versions?

2. What text can remain the same in all versions of this documentation (be *unconditional*)? I find that printing out a copy of the documentation and highlighting the portions of the text that I plan to make conditional with a colored marker helps me organize my conditional text better.

3. Can you organize your document so the conditional text is easier to maintain? Or would it make more sense to keep different versions in separate files?

4. Would it make more sense to create user variables that you'd only need to change once and have all instances of that be changed throughout your document than to use condition tags that you have to change?

5. If more than one writer will be working with the text, as with teams of technical writers who often work on the same documents, how will you train the writers to use the conditional text and keep versions from becoming confused?

All of these are important questions that you need to consider when you're thinking of using conditional text in your documents. Conditional text can be a useful tool, but with different ways to accomplish the same result, you should consider all of the pros and cons of using it.

Before you make your final decision, however, let's take a look at how conditional text works.

The Conditional Text Pod

The Conditional Text pod displays a list of condition tags and their attributes in the middle pane. It also includes icons that enable you to apply a selected condition tag, open a dialog box that allows you to create new condition tags, edit existing condition tags, delete tags that you don't want any longer, show or hide condition tags, and refresh the list of condition tags.

To open the Conditional Text pod, click **Special > Conditional Text > Conditional Text** on the menu bar.

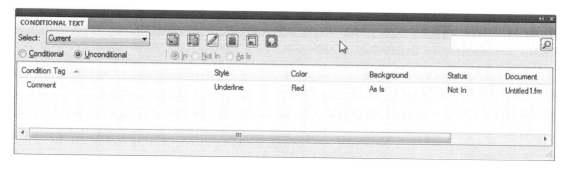

Figure 93: Conditional Text pod

Despite this being called the Conditional Text pod, condition tags can be applied to many elements of your documentation besides text. Condition tags also can be applied to graphics, tables, cross-references, variables, footnotes, and markers.

When you first open the Conditional Text pod, you'll notice that a Comment tag has already been created for you and is listed in the large pane in the middle of the pod. Notice that its style is "underline," its color is "red," its background is "as is," its status is "not in," and the document is the one that you have open. This means that if you use this tag to add a comment to your document, the item you associate with this tag will be underlined and red.

You'll choose the document you want to use with your condition tags from the drop-down list at the end of the Select field at the top of the pod. To the right of that are the icons that you use to apply, create, edit, delete, and show or hide condition tags, and refresh the list of condition tags in the Conditional Text pod. Here's what each of the icons mean:

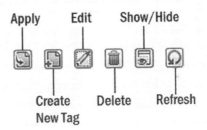

Figure 94: Conditional Text pod icons

Create a Condition Tag

Condition tags add formatting to the elements to which they're applied so you know which condition tag is being used, and they are used to perform other functions such as showing or hiding all of the elements to which they've been applied.

To create a condition tag, follow these steps:

1. Click the **Create** icon on the Conditional Text pod. The Add/Edit Condition Tag panel is displayed:

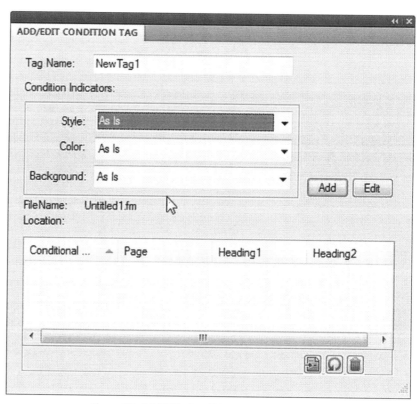

Figure 95: Add/Edit Condition Tag panel

2. The default name "New Tag1" is displayed in the Tag Name field. Highlight the name, delete it, and then type the name you want

to give the text, tables, and/or graphics that you will apply this condition tag to. For an exercise, let's name this condition tag "Green."

3. The Condition Indicators are those properties that will identify which text, tables or graphics have the Green condition tag applied to them. Click the arrow at the end of the Style field, and then choose one of the following from the drop-down list:

- **Overline**
  If chosen, a line will be inserted over the elements to which this condition tag is applied.

- **Strikethrough**
  If chosen, a line will run through the elements to which this condition tag is applied.

- **Underline**
  If chosen, the elements that this condition tag is applied to will be underlined.

- **Double Underline**
  If chosen, a double underline will be inserted under the elements to which this tag is applied.

- **Change Bar**
  A change bar is a vertical line that's inserted in the margin next to where changes are made in the document. If chosen as a style for the condition tag, a vertical line will be inserted in the margin next to the elements to which the tag is applied.

- **Numeric Underline**
  A numeric underline is an underline that's placed a bit farther from the text or other element it's underlining. If this is chosen as a style for the condition tag, a numeric underline will be placed under the element to which this condition tag is applied.

■ **Numeric Underline and Change Bar**
   Choose this option to insert a numeric underline and a change bar under and by the element this tag is applied to.

4. The Color field changes the color of the text to which the condition tag is applied. Click the arrow at the end of the Color field and choose the color you want from the drop-down list.

   The Background field changes the color of the background of the element to which the condition tag is applied. Click the arrow at the end of the Background field and choose the color you want from the drop-down list.

   Note: Select **New Color** from the Color or the Background lists to open the Color Definitions dialog box:

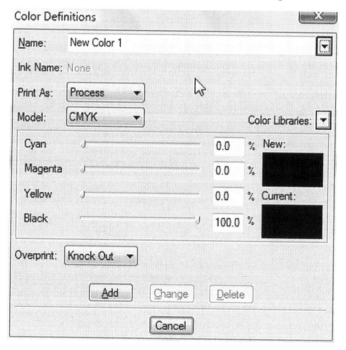

Figure 96: Color Definitions dialog box

Note: You can define colors here that conform to different printing standards and platforms. Explore the Color Libraries in particular.

5. After you've named your condition tag and given it the attributes you want it to give the elements to which it's applied, click **Add**. The name of the condition tag will be added to the Conditional Text pod.

Edit a Condition Tag

To make changes to an existing condition tag, follow these steps:

1. In the Conditional Text pod, select the name of the condition tag that you want to change.

2. Click **Edit**. The Add/Edit Condition Tag panel opens with the name of the condition tag you selected in the Tag Name field:

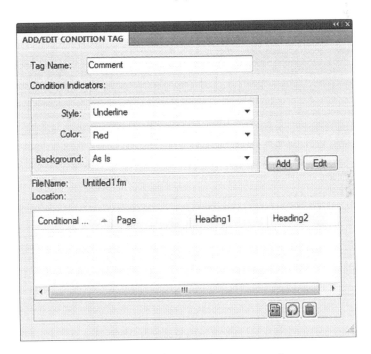

Figure 97: Add/Edit Condition Tag panel

3. Make the changes you want to make to the Condition Indicators.

4. Press **Edit**. The changes you made take effect. Any items you've applied this condition tag to in your document will now reflect the changes you just made.

Apply a Condition Tag

To use the condition tag, you have to apply it to text, tables or graphics in your document by doing the following:

1. Select the text or item in your document that you want to be conditional as follows:

   ■ **Text**
      Highlight the text, and then continue to step 2.

   ■ **Graphics**
      Highlight the frame border or the anchor symbol, and then continue to step 2.

   ■ **Tables**
      Highlight the table anchor, and then continue to step 2.

   ■ **A row in a table**
      Highlight the entire row, and then continue to step 2.

   ■ **Variables**
      Highlight the variables text, and then continue to step 2.

   ■ **Cross-references**
      Highlight the cross-reference text, and then continue to step 2.

   ■ **Markers**
      Highlight the marker text, and then continue to step 2.

2. Open the Conditional Text pod, and then select the name of the condition tag from the list in the large pane of the pod that you want to apply to the selected item.

3. Click the radio button in front of the word **Conditional** at the top of the Conditional Text pod.

4. Click the radio button in front of the word **In** at the top of the Conditional Text pod. Click **Apply**. The item you selected will have the conditions of the condition tag you selected applied to it and the item will be associated with this condition tag.

   For example, if you select some text and follow the steps above after having selected the Comment condition tag in the Conditional Text pod, the text you selected will be red with a line underneath it (per the attributes listed in the Conditional Text pod). If you choose to show all items to which the Comments condition tag have been applied, all items tagged with the Comments condition tag will be shown. See the next section for more information about showing and hiding conditional text.

Remove a Condition Tag from an Item

Let's say that you've applied a condition tag to some text in your document and things change. The text should be included in all versions of this document. It no longer is conditional. How can you remove the condition tag from this one item while retaining the other tagged elements? Here's how:

1. Highlight the element you want to remove the condition tag from.

2. In the Conditional Text pod, click the radio button in front of **Unconditional**.

3. If you want the text to remain in the document, be sure the radio button in front of **In** is selected.

4. Click **Apply**. The condition tag is still listed in the Conditional Text pod, but the item to which it was applied no longer is formatted per that condition tag and it's no longer associated with it.

Show/Hide Conditional Text

The ability to show and hide text, tables, graphics, and other elements is the reason for using condition tags. To show elements tagged with a specific condition tag, follow these steps:

1. With the document open that has conditional text, click the Show/Hide icon on the Conditional Text pod. The Show/Hide Conditional Text panel opens:

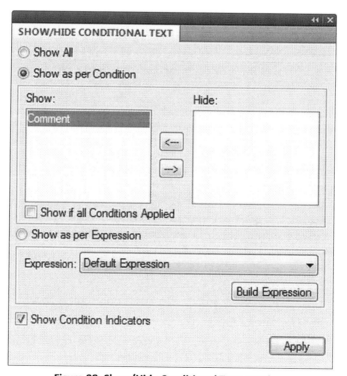

Figure 98: Show/Hide Conditional Text panel

2. If the name of the condition tag whose elements you want to show is listed in the Hide pane, select the name, and then click the arrow button pointing to the Show pane. The name is moved to the Show pane.

3. Click **Apply**. All of the elements tagged with that condition tag are shown in your document.

4. If the name of the condition tag whose elements you want to hide is listed in the Show pane, select the name, and then click the arrow button pointing to the Hide pane. The name is moved to the Hide pane.

5. Click **Apply**. All of the elements tagged with that condition tag are hidden in your document.

Sort Condition Tags

Since you can use several condition tags in your documents, it might be useful to have a way to sort them more quickly. You can do this by using a combination of condition tag names and Boolean operators. Boolean operators are used in search queries to define the relationship between words or groups of words. FrameMaker enables you to use three Boolean operators when building expressions to search for condition tags: AND, OR, and NOT. Here's how these are used in search expressions:

Table 8: Boolean Operators Used to Sort Condition Tags

Boolean operator	Definition
AND	Find tags that contain all of the words used in the expression
OR	Find tags that contain any of the words used in the expression
NOT	Find tags that contain none of the words used in the expression

For example, let's say that you have five condition tags in your document. They are named *Comment, Green, Blue, Red,* and *Yellow*. If you want all of the conditional text associated with both the

Green and Red condition tags to be displayed, you would do the following:

1. On the Show/Hide Conditional Text panel, click the **Build Expression** button. The Manage Conditional Expression dialog box opens:

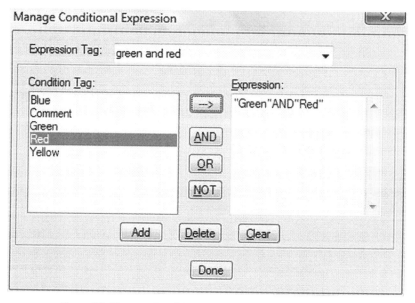

Figure 99: Manage Conditional Expression dialog box

2. Type the name you want to give this expression in the Expression Tag box. In this example, we're calling it "green and red."

3. Select **Green** in the Condition Tag pane, and then click the arrow pointing to the Expression pane. The word *Green* is inserted in the Expression pane.

4. Because we want all of the elements associated with both the green and the red condition tags to be displayed, click the **AND** Boolean operator button. The word *AND* is inserted after the word *Green* in the Expression pane.

5. Select the **Red** condition tag from the Condition Tag pane, and then click the arrow pointing to the Expression pane. The word *Red* is inserted after the word *AND* in the Expression pane.

6. Click **Add** and then **Done**. Notice that the name of this expression tag is displayed in the Expression field of the Show/Hide Conditional Text panel.

7. Click **Apply** on the Show/Hide Conditional Text panel. All of the elements associated with the green and red condition tags will be displayed in your document.

Delete a Condition Tag

To remove a condition tag from your list of condition tags in the Conditional Text pod, follow these steps:

1. Select the condition tag in the Conditional Text pod that you want to delete.

2. Click the **Delete** icon, and then click **OK**.

3. The condition tag is removed from the Conditional Text pod and any item in your document that it was applied to.

4. If the item in your document was tagged with only the condition tag you've deleted, the Delete Condition Tag dialog box opens:

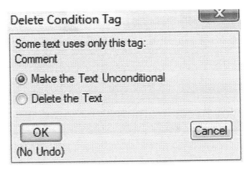

Figure 100: Delete Condition Tag dialog box

5. If you want this item to remain in the document and be unconditional, click the radio button in front of **Make the Text Unconditional.**

6. If you want this item to be deleted, click the radio button in front of **Delete the Text.**

7. After you've made your choice, click **OK.**

Frequently Asked Questions

Q: *I need to use some of the text in my document in two different versions but not in other versions. Do I have to duplicate the text that I need to apply two different condition tags to?*

A: No, you don't have to duplicate the text because you can apply more than one condition tag to the same text. You can identify the elements that have multiple tags applied to them because if you have used different colors of text or background for the different tags, the color is a combination of the different colors.

Q: *Can I simply copy and paste condition tags rather than having to apply them each time I want to use them in the same work session?*

A: Yes, you can copy and paste condition tag settings by following these steps:

1. Place your cursor in the item that has the condition tag applied to it that you want to copy.

2. Click **Edit > Copy Special > Conditional Text Settings** on the menu bar.

3. Highlight the element that you want to apply the condition tag settings to.

4. Click **Edit > Paste** on the menu bar.

Cross-References

Learn how to create cross-references in a single document or to information in other documents; develop cross-reference formats that best suit your style; create "spot" cross-references; convert cross-references to text; and troubleshoot cross-references.

Cross-references are a vital part of many technical documents. They help readers find information they need or that they might be interested in knowing more about. They refer readers to graphics and tables that help them understand complex concepts. And, importantly, they help you avoid repeating information in more than one place. Some typical cross-references might look like these:

- *See Figure 17.5 on page 6.*
- *See Figure 17.5.*
- *See Chapter 10: Troubleshooting on page 216.*
- *Refer to Addendum 3.2.*

Cross-references can be a nightmare to keep up-to-date if you're inserting them manually. As you can see in the examples above, cross-references often include page numbers or numbers that identify the place where you want your readers to look. If, for example, you add a cross-reference to an illustration, most likely you'll reference the figure number in the cross-reference. If you add an illustration in front of the one that you referenced, the figure number changes. If you forget that you added a cross-reference to that illustration several paragraphs before, the number will be incorrect and readers will be confused and perhaps annoyed.

When you insert cross-references using FrameMaker's cross-reference tools, FrameMaker updates the numbers for you if you have to make changes in your document. It also updates text that's included in the referenced material if it's changed.

In addition, when you use FrameMaker's cross-reference tools, the cross-references become hyperlinks if you convert your document to Portable Document Format (PDF) or other online formats.

In this chapter, you'll learn how to insert cross-references to paragraphs and to specific spots within paragraphs (called *spot cross-references*). You'll learn how to work with cross-reference *markers* and how to display the source of a cross-reference, even if the source is in a different document. You'll learn how to create cross-reference formats using *building blocks* and how to update your cross-references manually. Finally, you'll learn how to resolve problems that can occur. Let's get started!

How Cross-References Work

So you can see more clearly how the elements of the cross-references work, let's open a sample document. Click **File > New** to open the New dialog box, and then click the **Explore Standard Templates** button at the bottom of the New dialog box. The Standard Templates dialog box opens:

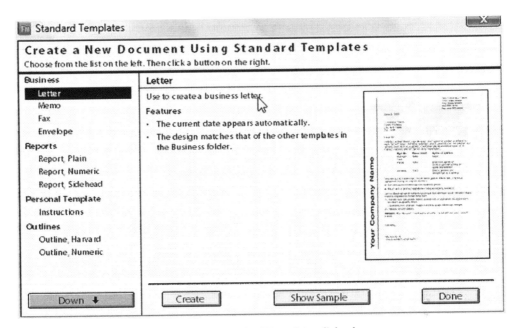

Figure 101: Standard Templates dialog box

On the Standard Templates dialog box, click the **Down** button. Select **Chapter** under the Book heading, and then click **Show sample**. Your page should look like the following:

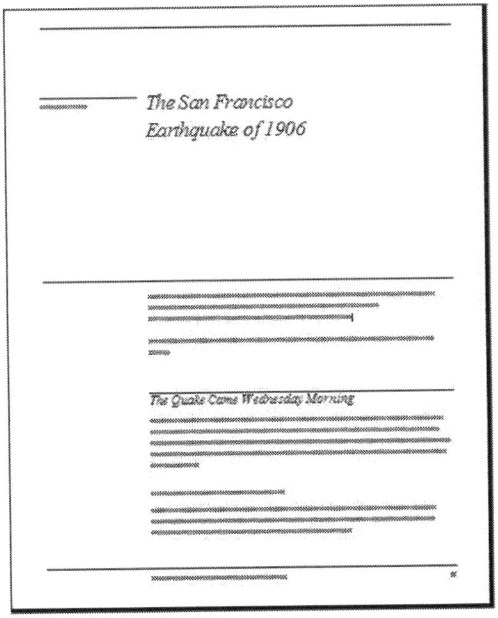

Figure 102: Sample document

Press **ALT + tab** until the Standard Templates dialog box is displayed. Click **Done** to close the Standard Templates dialog box.

The Cross-Reference Panel

Now that we have a document to work with, let's start by looking at the Cross-Reference panel. Click **Special > Cross-Reference** on the menu bar. The Cross-Reference panel opens:

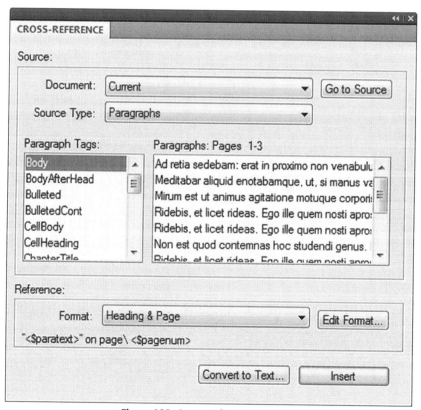

Figure 103: Cross-Reference panel

As you can see, it says *Source* at the top of this panel. The source of your cross-reference is the information that's being referenced.

The first field is the *Document* field. This is where you can designate where the source for this cross-reference is located. Since we're working with only one document, the source information will be located in the *Current* document.

Next to the *Document* field is the *Go to Source* button. When you select a source reference and click **Go to Source**, you'll go directly to that section of your document being cross-referenced.

Below the *Document* field is the *Source Type* field. Click the arrow next to it, and you'll see that two source types are listed: *Paragraph* and *Cross-Reference Markers*. In FrameMaker, you can create cross-references to sources according to the paragraph tag assigned to that text or according to *markers* that you insert in your text.

Inserting a Cross-Reference

Let's start by doing the following to insert a cross-reference in the document you just opened:

1. Save the sample document by clicking **File > Save As** on the menu bar.

2. Navigate to the folder where you want to save this document.

3. In the File name box, type *TestChap1.fm* and click **Save**.

4. Place your cursor at the end of the first paragraph, and type the following: *See*

5. Press the spacebar to add a space after the word *see*, and leave your cursor there.

6. Click **Special > Cross-Reference** on the menu bar to open the Cross-Reference panel.

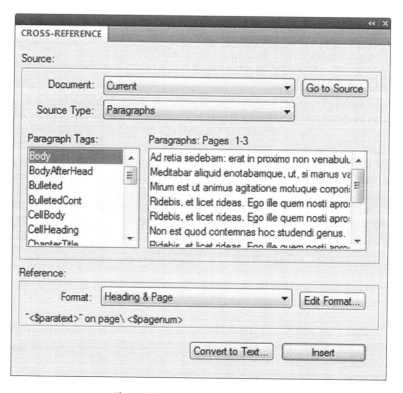

Figure 104: Cross-Reference panel

7. From the Source Type pull-down menu, select **Paragraphs**. This tells FrameMaker that you'll create cross-references to sources using the paragraph tags that are applied to your text.

8. When you select *Paragraph* as the source type of your cross-reference, the *Paragraph Tags* pane opens. This lists all of the paragraph tags that are used in your current document. To the right of that pane is the *Paragraphs* pane, which lists the text associated with the paragraph tags on the left. You select the actual source text that you want to cross-reference from the *Paragraphs* pane.

Note: If you had chosen Cross-Reference Markers as the Source Type, these two panes would have been different. The left pane would list all of the *Marker Types* in the document, and the right pane would have listed the specific markers associated with each marker type. Since all paragraphs in FrameMaker documents have paragraph tags applied to them, cross-references usually use them.

9. From the Paragraph Tags scroll list, select **TableTitle**.

10. From the Paragraphs list, select **TABLE 1: Ridebis et licet rideas**.

11. From the Format pull-down menu under these panes, select **Table Number & Page**.

12. Click **Insert**. The table title and page number are inserted in your text.

13. Type a period to complete the sentence.

In this example, we used a predefined cross-reference format. Since the format is the second element of your cross-references, let's talk more about it.

Cross-Reference Formats

Cross-reference formats are a combination of text and building blocks. We talked about autonumbering building blocks when we discussed paragraph tags and we talked about building blocks that you use with system variables, so by now you know that building blocks are code that tells FrameMaker how to do something.

Cross-reference building blocks tell FrameMaker what to insert for the cross-reference. To format your cross-references, open the Cross-Reference panel by clicking **Special > Cross-Reference** on the menu bar, and then click the **Edit Format** button on the Cross-Reference panel. The Edit Cross-Reference Format dialog box opens:

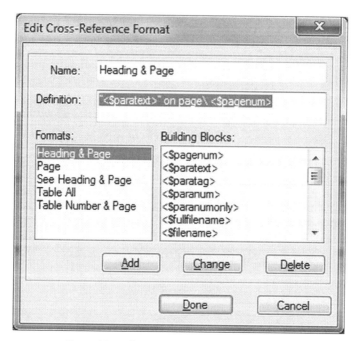

Figure 105: Edit Cross-Reference Format dialog box

At the top of the dialog box, you'll see the name of the cross-reference format that was selected on the Cross-Reference panel. In the Definition field, you'll see the default definition of this cross-reference format. In the Formats pane, different cross-reference formats are listed. To the right of that are the building blocks you can use with the formats. What those building blocks mean is shown in the table on the next page.

As you scroll down the list of building blocks in the Edit Cross-Reference Format dialog box, notice that character tags are listed after the building blocks. You can use these if you want your cross-reference text to be formatted differently from the paragraph in which it's inserted.

Table 9: Building Blocks for Cross-Reference Formats

Building Block	Description
<$pagenum>	Displays the page number of the source.
<$paratext>	Displays the text of the source paragraph, excluding its autonumber if it has one.
<$paratag>	Displays the name of the source's paragraph tag.
<$paranum>	Displays the paragraph number of the source paragraph, including any text in the autonumber format (as in "Figure 1").
<$paranumonly>	Displays only the number of the source paragraph. For example, if the source paragraph is a figure, it displays only the number and not the word "Figure."
<$fullfilename>	Displays the path and the file name of the source.
<$filename>	Displays the file name of the source.
<$volnum>	Displays the volume number of the document that contains the source information.
<$chapnum>	Displays the chapter number of the document that contains the source information.
<$sectionnum>	Displays the section number of the document that contains the source information.
<$subsectionnum>	Displays the subsection number of the document that contains the source information.
<$chaptertitlename>	Displays the name of the chapter title.
<$pagenum[paratag]>	Displays the page number of the information that has the paragraph tag listed in the brackets applied to it. This often is used when you want to refer to the section where the source is located, not just the source.
<$paratext[paratag]>	Used to refer to information that comes before the source. Use this to refer to the section heading instead of the actual source, as in "See Section Three: Troubleshooting," instead of "See Rebooting. "
<$paratag[paratag]>	Displays the paragraph that uses the paragraph tag you specify between the brackets.
<$paranum[paratag]>	Displays the entire autonumber, including text that is a part of the autonumber, of the source paragraph that has the paragraph tag you specify between the brackets.
<$paranumonly[paratag]>	Displays only the autonumber counter of the source paragraph that has the paragraph tag you specify between the brackets.

Creating a Cross-Reference Format

In this section, you'll create a new cross-reference format that will reference a subheading in the sample document you've been working with. This particular format will display the text of a subheading in your document and the page number where this subheading appears. To create this cross-reference format, follow these steps:

1. Return to or open the sample document.

2. Place your cursor at the end of the second paragraph.

3. Click **Special > Cross-Reference** on the menu bar. The Cross-Reference panel opens.

4. Click **Edit Format** on the Cross-Reference panel. The Edit Cross-Reference Format dialog box opens.

5. Notice that the definition is highlighted when you first open the Edit Cross-Reference Format dialog box. For this reason, it's often easier to change the definition first and then name the new format after you've created the definition. To do this, type *See* in the Definition field, and then add a space after the word. The highlighted building blocks in the Definition field should be replaced by the word *See*.

6. Click **<$paratext>** on the Building Blocks list. The <$paratext> building block will be inserted in the Definitions field. As you may recall, the <$paratext> building block tells FrameMaker to display the text of the paragraph.

7. Add a space after the <$paratext> building block in the Definition field, and then type *on page*, adding a space after the word *page*.

8. Click **<$pagenum>** on the Building Blocks list. The <$pagenum> building block will be inserted in the Definitions field, which will tell FrameMaker to insert the page number where this subheading appears.

9. Add a period after the <$pagenum> building block in the Definition field to complete the sentence.

10. Now we'll name this format by selecting the text that's in the Name field, and then pressing **DELETE**.

11. Type *Subhead* in the Name field.

    Note: If you decide to keep this format, it becomes one of the choices in the Format field on the Cross-Reference panel.

12. Click **Add**. Your new format is added to the Formats list. Your settings should look similar to this:

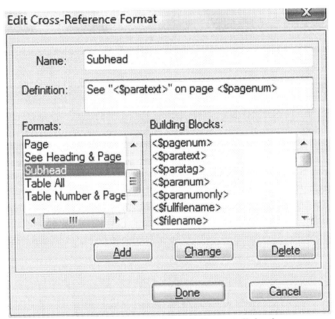

Figure 106: Edit Cross-Reference Format dialog box

13. Click **Done**. The Edit Cross-Reference Format dialog box closes.

Using the Cross-Reference Format

Now that you've defined a new format, you can use it to create a cross-reference. This format is a paragraph tag format, meaning that FrameMaker looks for paragraphs that have the specified tag.

1. With your cursor still at the end of the second paragraph in your document, select **Special > Cross-Reference** on the menu bar to open the Cross-Reference panel if it isn't open.

2. Select **Heading2** from the Paragraph Tags list on the Cross-Reference panel. A list of all of the paragraphs that are tagged with Heading2 appears in the Paragraphs pane.

3. Click the second item listed in the Paragraph pane. It should say **The First Day**.

4. Be sure that *Subhead* is selected in the Format field. If not, click the arrow and select it.

5. Click **Insert**. Your cross-reference will be inserted where you left your cursor in your document.

Changing a Cross-Reference Format

If you decide to change a cross-reference format after you've created it, follow the steps below. In this instance, you'll edit the format so the word *See* won't be inserted in front of the cross-reference entry.

1. To see the changes you make more clearly, place your cursor in front of the cross-reference you inserted in your text and type the words *Go to*, placing a space after the last word.

2. Double-click the cross-reference you inserted. The Cross-Reference panel opens. Notice that the appropriate cross-reference and format are already selected.

3. Click **Edit Format**. The Edit Format dialog box opens.

4. In the Definitions field, delete the word *See*, leaving the rest of the definition intact.

5. Click **Change**, and then click **Done**. The Update Cross-References dialog box opens:

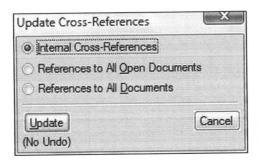

Figure 107: Update Cross-References dialog box

6. Since this cross-reference refers to this one document, be sure that the radio button in front of **Internal Cross-References** is checked, and then click **Update**. Your cross-reference is updated.

Adding a Cross-Reference to Other Files

Now try inserting a cross-reference to another file. To do this, create a second file by doing the following:

1. Save your current document without closing it.

2. Click **File > New > Document** on the menu bar and click **Explore Standard Templates**.

3. On the Standard Templates dialog box, click the **Down** button to see the Book files.

4. Select the **Front Matter** sample file, and then click **Show Sample**.

5. Press **ALT + tab** to navigate back to the Standard Templates dialog box and close it.

6. Back on the Front Matter sample file, highlight the word "Title" on your sample document and type *Great Events of the Twentieth Century* in its place. Notice that the paragraph tag called **TitleBook** is displayed in the Paragraph Formatting bar. This is a paragraph style that is unique to this template and we'll be using it again in a later chapter.

7. Highlight the word "Author" and type *John Smithson* in its place. Notice that the paragraph tag called **AuthorBook** is displayed in the Paragraph Formatting bar.

8. Click **File > Save as**. Name the file *TestFrontMatter.fm*.

Now return to the TestChap1 document and create a new cross-reference format, then insert a cross-reference to the TestFrontMatter document by doing the following:

1. Click **Window > Documents > TestChap1** on the menu bar to return to your first document.

2. Place your cursor after the third paragraph of body text and press **ENTER**.

3. Press the spacebar to add a space, and then type *was written with this in mind* with a period at the end.

4. Place your cursor directly in front of the word *was*, press the spacebar one more time and move your cursor back one space so there's a space between your cursor and the word *was*.

5. Click **Special > Cross-Reference** on the menu bar. The Cross-Reference panel opens.

6. To display only the name of the book, create a Text Only format. Click **Edit Format**. The Edit Cross-Reference Format dialog box opens.

7. Since the text in the Definition field is already highlighted, let's change that first. Select **<$paratext>** from the Building Blocks list.

8. Type *Text Only* in the Name field, and then click **Add**. Your settings should look like the following:

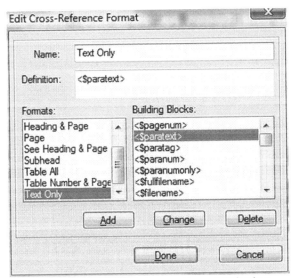

Figure 108: Edit Cross-Reference Format dialog box

9. Click **Done**.

10. Open the Cross-Reference panel again by clicking **Special > Cross-Reference** on the menu bar or selecting it from the panels at the right of the window.

11. Click the arrow at the right of the Document field, and select *TestFrontMatter.fm* from the drop-down list. Notice how the paragraph tags listed change below.

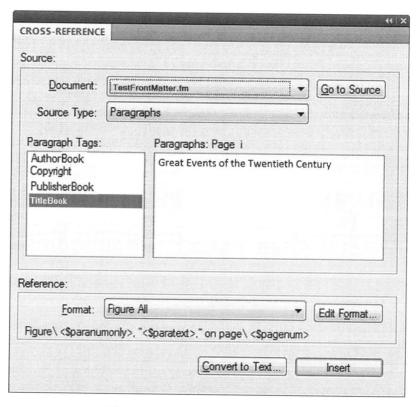

Figure 109: Cross-Reference to another file

12. Select **TitleBook** from the Paragraph Tags scroll list, and then select **Great Events of the Twentieth Century** from the Paragraphs list.

13. If it isn't already selected in the Format box, click the arrow at the right of the box and select **Text Only.**

14. Click **Insert**. The cross-reference appears as text, "Great Events of the Twentieth Century."

Using Character Tags to Format Cross-References

As you can see, you can customize your cross-references by using the building blocks in your formats. You can go even further by using character tags to format the text that's inserted as a cross-reference. To see how this works, modify the Subhead format so that the text of the subhead is italicized, but the remaining text is the same as the rest of the paragraph by doing the following:

1. Open the TestChap1.fm document if you closed it earlier.

2. Double-click the cross-reference you inserted that says *Go to The First Day on page 2*. The Cross-Reference panel opens with the settings for this cross-reference selected.

3. Click **Edit Format**. The Edit Cross-Reference Format dialog box opens.

4. Place your cursor at the beginning of the definition, and then click **<Emphasis>** in the Building Blocks list.

    Note: You'll have to scroll past the building blocks to see the character tags.

5. Because the Emphasis tag italicizes all text to the right of it, you need to insert another tag after the <$paratext> building block so the remaining text won't be italicized. To do this, place your cursor after the <$paratext> building block, and then click **<Default Font>** in the Building Blocks list.

    Note: In the list, there's a paragraph symbol between the words *Default* and *Font* to indicate that this is the default paragraph font.

6. Click **Change**, and then click **Done**. The Update Cross-References dialog box opens.

7. Click **Update** to accept the defaults and update your cross-reference format. Your cross-reference is formatted as you indicated in the definition.

Experiment with different building blocks and character tags. Decide on a style that you like best, and then create cross-reference formats if needed.

Create Spot Cross-References

If the sections in your document are short, using paragraph tags in your cross-references will probably be okay. If you have long sections, however, and the information you want to direct people to read is buried in other text, you'll probably want to create a *spot cross-reference*.

To create a spot cross-reference, you need to insert a *marker* at the exact spot where you want your readers to go. By doing this, the cross-reference displays the correct page number for the location of the material. To create a spot cross-reference, follow these steps:

1. Place your cursor on a line in your TestChap1 document that you want to reference. (Since most of the text is greeked, it doesn't matter what line you place your cursor on.)

2. Click **Special > Marker** on the menu bar. The Marker panel opens:

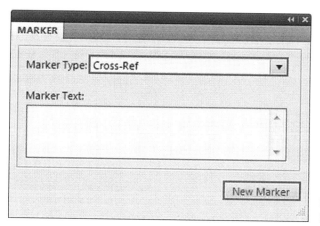

Figure 110:
Marker panel

3. In the Marker Type field, select **Cross-Ref** from the drop-down list.

4. In the Marker Text field, type a short, descriptive label for the marker, such as *test*.

5. Click **New Marker**. If your text symbols are turned on (click **View > Text Symbols** on the menu bar), you'll see the marker symbol in your text. It looks like a *T*.

6. If you're placing the marker in a different document than the one in which the cross-reference will appear, you would leave this document open, and then go to the document in which you want to insert the cross-reference.

7. Place your cursor where you want to insert the cross-reference, and then type the lead-in words you want to use (such as *See*, or *For more information, see*. Be sure to insert a space after the last word). Again, since we are working with a sample document, it doesn't matter where you place your cursor for now. Try to choose a location on a different page than the marker.

8. Leaving your cursor where it is, click **Special > Cross-Reference** on the menu bar. The Cross-Reference panel opens.

9. In the Document field, select the document you're linking to in the drop-down list (in this case, **Current**).

10. In the Source Type field, select **Cross-Reference Markers** from the drop-down list. Notice that the panes below this field change to *Marker Types* and *Cross-Reference Markers*.

11. In the Cross-Reference Markers list (the right pane), select the marker that you created.

    Note: Don't be confused if you see more markers there than you created. When you create a paragraph-based cross-reference, FrameMaker inserts Cross-Ref markers. These will be listed in the Cross-Reference Marker list. You generally can recognize them because they include the paragraph tag name and the text of the paragraph.

12. In the Format field, click a cross-reference format from the drop-down list or create a new one if you don't see any that you like.

13. Click **Insert**. If you don't get the result you expected, check the definition of the format you chose and make changes if needed.

Maintaining and Troubleshooting Cross-References

Cross-references are automatically updated whenever you open, save, or print a file. They're also updated when you update a *book* file. (We'll talk about books in the next chapter.) If you need to update them manually, however, follow these steps:

1. Click **Edit > Update References** on the menu bar. The Update References dialog box opens:

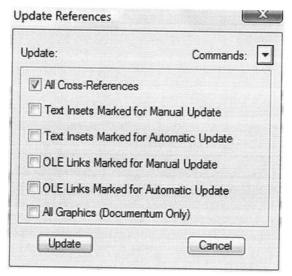

Figure 111: Update References dialog box

2. Be sure there's a checkmark in front of *All Cross-References*, and then click **Update**. All of the cross-references in your document will be updated even if the source is in other documents.

   Note: If any of the cross-references can't be resolved, you'll see an error message. You'll learn how to handle this later in this chapter.

Preventing Cross-References from Updating Automatically

If you never want cross-references to update automatically—perhaps because your document is very large and it takes a lot of time to update the cross-references—follow these steps:

1. With your document open, click **Edit > Update References**. The Update References dialog box opens.

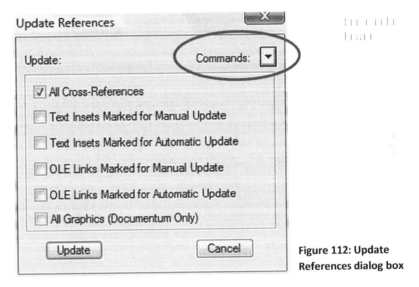

Figure 112: Update References dialog box

2. Click **Commands**, and then select **Suppress Automatic Updating** from the drop-down list.

3. On the Suppress Automatic Reference Updating dialog box, place a checkmark in front of *Suppress Automatic Updating of All Cross-References*, and then click **Set**.

   Note: To reverse this action, follow the steps above. Remove the checkmark in front of *Suppress Automatic Updating of All Cross-References*, and then click **Set**.

4. Close the Update References dialog box when you're returned to it.

Unresolved Cross-References

When cross-references can't be updated automatically, they're called *unresolved cross-references*. This happens most often when your cross-references refer to source information in other files that aren't open. Some common reasons why FrameMaker can't resolve cross-references include:

- The target file uses fonts that aren't installed on your computer.

- A cross-reference marker has been deleted.

- The name of the source file has been changed.

- The location of the source file has been changed.

When FrameMaker can't resolve some cross-references, the Update Unresolved Cross-References dialog box opens, as shown on the next page. You also can open this dialog box by clicking **Edit > Update References**, and then clicking the Commands button and selecting **Update Unresolved Cross-References**.

Figure 113: Update Unresolved Cross-References dialog box

This dialog box provides you with valuable information about where those cross-references are located and how many of them can be found. Let's look at how to fix these problems:

Open all files

First, to prevent FrameMaker from being unable to update cross-references in documents that use fonts that aren't installed on your computer, open all of the files that the current document is linked to before updating your cross-references. The "missing fonts" message prevents FrameMaker from opening the document automatically because you must answer the prompt to allow substituted fonts to be used.

Use the dialog box to find the problem

Now let's say that you have a more complicated problem. You're working on three files. File A contains two cross-references. One of these cross-references is to source information in File B and the other cross-reference is to source information in File C. While working on the document, you change the name of File B to File D, plus you move File C to a different directory.

When you open File A, the Update Unresolved Cross-References dialog box opens and looks like this:

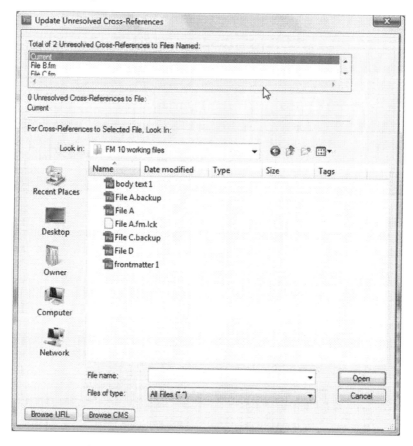

Figure 114: Working with Unresolved Cross-References

The top portion of the window tells you how many unresolved cross-references are in the file you just opened (2).

In the Files Named pane at the top of the dialog box, **Current** is selected, but when you look below the pane, it says there are no unresolved cross-references to the file: Current. This means that none of the unresolved cross-references has a source within the current document.

When you click on File B in the Files Named list at the top of the dialog box, beneath the pane, it says there's one unresolved cross-reference in this file.

When you click on File C in the Files Named list at the top of the dialog box, beneath the pane, it now says there's one unresolved cross-reference in this file.

Now that you know which files have the unresolved cross-references, you can fix them. First, you would click File B and when you remembered that you had changed the name of the file to File D, you could use the file display portion of the dialog box (at the bottom) to navigate to the correct filename. Click File D to display its name in the File Name field, and then click **Open**. When you do this, the Current file will now find its cross-references to the source information using the new path.

Now, to fix the second unresolved cross-reference, you'd click File C. Remembering that you'd moved it to a new directory, you'd navigate to the correct directory in the file display portion of the dialog box, locate the file, and then click **Open**. The Current file should be able to find its cross-references to the source information in this document using the new path. After you take these steps, your unresolved cross-references in File A should be resolved.

Create a List of References

If you can't find all of your unresolved cross-references using the Update Unresolved Cross-References dialog box, you have to take a different approach. Let's say that a cross-reference marker was deleted in one of your files. In cases like this, you have to look at each occurrence of unresolved cross-references to see exactly what the problem is with both the cross-reference and the source information. The easiest way to do this is to create a list of unresolved references by doing the following:

1. Click **Special > List of > References** on the menu bar.

   Note: If you're working on a single file, a message will appear asking if you want to create a stand-alone List of References for this file.

2. When the Set Up List of References dialog box opens, click **Unresolved Cross-Refs** in the *Don't Include* list, and then click the arrow to move it to the *Include References* list.

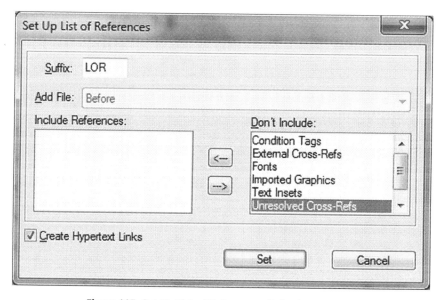

Figure 115: Set Up List of References dialog box

3. Click **Set**. FrameMaker creates a list of unresolved cross-references in a separate document. The name of this document will be the same as your current document plus LOR (List of References). All unresolved cross-references will list the filename, paragraph tag, source content, and page number, making it easier to locate the unresolved source information.

Next, use **Find/Change** to locate unresolved cross-references as follows:

1. Go back to your original document, and then click **Edit > Find/Change** on the menu bar.

2. Click the arrow next to the *Find* field, and then select **Unresolved Cross-Reference** from the list.

3. Click **Find**. FrameMaker moves to the first unresolved cross-reference and displays the same information listed in your List of References you generated.

4. If an unresolved cross-reference is found, double-click it. The Cross-Reference panel opens.

5. If your List of References indicates that this cross-reference was linked to a paragraph tag, click the **Source Type** button and select **Paragraphs**.

6. Select the paragraph tag type indicated in the List of References from the Paragraph Tags list on the Cross-Reference panel.

7. In the Paragraphs list, select the paragraph that matches the source information in the List of References or that appears to be the missing source.

8. Click **Replace**. The link to the source information is re-established.

Convert Cross-References to Text

To avoid the hassle of unresolved cross-references when your document is finished and printed in hard copy, you can convert your cross-references to text. If you do this, they're no longer live links. If you change your mind, you'll have to re-create the cross-references. You can convert single cross-references to text or you can convert all of them by following these steps:

1. Open your FrameMaker document.

2. Click **Special > Cross-Reference** on the menu bar. The Cross-Reference panel opens.

3. Click **Convert to Text**. The Convert Cross-References to Text dialog box opens:

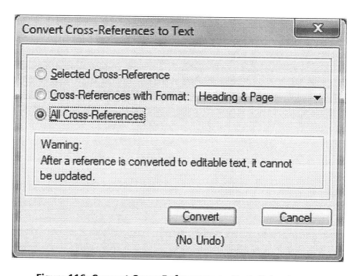

Figure 116: Convert Cross-References to Text dialog box

4. If you want to convert just the selected cross-reference, click the **Selected Cross-Reference** radio button.

5. If you want to convert all cross-references using a specified format, click the **Cross-References with Format** radio button, and then select the format you want to convert to text from the drop-down list.

6. If you want to convert all cross-references in your document to text, click the **All Cross-References** radio button.

7. Click **Convert**. The specified cross-references become regular, editable text that won't be updated automatically.

FrameMaker has several tools to help you maintain and troubleshoot your cross-references—tools that you'll appreciate when you're working on very large documents!

Frequently Asked Questions

Q: *How can I delete cross-reference formats that I no longer use?*

A: To delete cross-reference formats, follow these steps:

1. Click **Special > Cross-Reference** on the menu bar. The Cross-Reference panel opens.

2. Click **Edit Format**. The Edit Cross-Reference Format dialog box opens.

3. In the list at the left, select the format you want to delete, and then click **DELETE**.

4. Click **Done**. If the cross-reference format you're deleting is used in your document, a message appears asking you if you want to convert the cross-references that use this format to text. To delete the cross-reference format and convert it to text, click **OK**. To retain the cross-references that use the format, click **CANCEL**.

This page is intentionally left blank.

Books

Create books and use the book window to add, rearrange, and delete files in your books, number the pages sequentially from file to file in your book, spell check your entire book, search for components, import formats from other files, update your book, and review the book error log.

Writing large documents with regular word processors can be difficult. But large documents are what FrameMaker is best known for, largely because with FrameMaker, you can include several small files into a large file that FrameMaker calls a *book*. By doing this, several people can work on different portions of the same document at the same time, and the chance of document corruption is lessened. The ability to create books is one reason that FrameMaker handles large documents so well.

A book is a special FrameMaker file that groups several files so you can work with them as a single unit or as individual files. When you group your files into a book, you can reformat the pages in all of them by applying new page layouts, paragraph or character tags, cross-reference styles, and more. You can update page numbers and cross-references throughout the entire book, and you can search for and replace text across the entire book. Books also simplify printing.

At the same time, the individual files in the book can be opened and modified—even by different people.

A book file contains the file names of the individual files within it, including not only the documents that you type (such as the chapters and appendixes), but the documents that FrameMaker generates as well (such as the table of contents and index).

You can use books for both small and large documents, but their value really becomes evident when you're working with large documents, especially ones that have thousands of pages and hundreds of individual files as some government documents have.

FrameMaker offers you a great deal of flexibility in designing your books. For example, while you can set up your book so that your pages are numbered sequentially throughout the entire book, you can also set up different numbering systems for individual files within the book.

When you're creating books, FrameMaker opens and scans each file in the book when updating, so updating can take a considerable amount of time. If you build books that are large enough to make this a problem for you, consider opening all of the files within the books manually before updating.

Books are at the heart of FrameMaker's ability to handle large documents. Let's learn more about them now.

Building Books

A FrameMaker book can be made up of one or one thousand individual document files. When you add these to a *book file*, you can work with them individually or as groups of files. You have to create this book file and add each of the individual files to it. The files aren't actually added to this file, though—their file names are just added so there's no duplication of the files. FrameMaker calls this process *book building*. To facilitate book building, put all of the files for your book into one folder. Most   FrameMaker users save each chapter in their documents as separate document files, which are then added individually to the book file. If you have long chapters, you may want to break them into smaller files so FrameMaker can update your book more quickly.

When you build a book, you add the documents you want to a book file. After that, you set up the page numbering for the book, update it, spell-check it, generate your table of contents and index, and update numbering and cross-references throughout your book.

Let's try creating a book file using the *TestChap1* document you used in earlier chapters. To do this, open FrameMaker, and then click **File > Open** on the menu bar. The Open dialog box opens. Navigate to where you saved the *TestChap1.fm* document and open it in FrameMaker. After you've opened the *TestChap1* document, click **File > New > Book** on the menu bar. A message will appear asking if you want to add this document to the book. Click **Yes**. The new book panel opens:

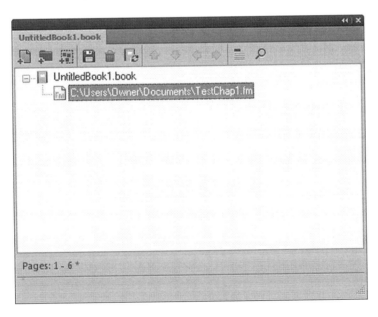

Figure 117: New Book panel

Although it looks simple, there's a lot going on in this panel. First, look at the top of the window. Instead of saying *New Book*, it displays the book filename. In this case, the book filename is *UntitledBook1.book* because you haven't saved and named it yet.

Next, look at the white pane in the middle of the window. Notice that the name of the file you just opened (*TestChap1*) is listed under the book filename in a tree structure. In front of the filename is an icon that indicates this is a FrameMaker document file. When you add a generated file, such as your table of contents or index, you'll notice that the icon in front of that filename will be different.

Immediately beneath the white pane is a line telling you the page number for the selected file. If the file has been modified since the last time you saved it, there will be an asterisk at the end of the line.

Next, look at the icons at the top of the panel:

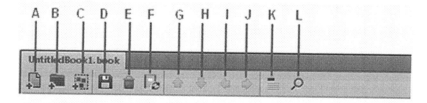

A. Add File
B. Add Folder
C. Add Group
D. Save
E. Delete
F. Update Book
G. Move Up
H. Move Down
I. Move Left
J. Move Right
K. Display Heading Text
L. Find/Change

Figure 118: New Book panel icons

- Click the **Add File** icon to add new files to your book. When you click this, the Add Files to Book dialog box opens.

- The **Add Folder** icon enables you to add a folder to your book. You can use folders to hold documents that you may or may not publish with your book.

- You can group files in books by clicking the **Add Groups** icon.

- To save your book, click the **Save** icon, or click **File > Save Book** or **File > Save Book As** on the menu bar.

- To delete a file in your book, highlight the file name, and then click the **Delete** icon. If you want to delete several files that are listed next to each other in the book window, select them while holding down the **SHIFT** key. If you want to delete several files that aren't listed next to each other in the book window, hold down the **CTRL** key while selecting them. Click **Edit > Delete File from Book** on the menu bar or click the **Delete** icon on the book window. The file or files are removed from your book window. There isn't a confirmation message. Note that when you delete files from your book, you aren't deleting the actual files—you're just deleting their names in your book file.

- If you make changes to your book, such as adding a table of contents or index, or adding cross-references, you'll want to update your book by clicking the **Update Book** icon.

- To move files within the book, highlight the one you want to move, and then use the arrow icons.

- To display the information that begins the first paragraph in the files instead of file names, click the **Display Heading Text** icon.

- To search for elements within your books and possibly make changes, click the **Find/Change** icon.

Add a File to Your Book

Now that you've created your book file, you can add documents to it. When you add a file to your book, FrameMaker adds its name and location to the book file. At the same time, FrameMaker links the file to the book file. Add the TestFrontMatter.fm file to your book by doing the following:

1. Click **File > Save Book As** on the menu bar.

2. In the Save Book dialog box, navigate to the folder where you want to save your book, type *TestBook* in File Name box, and click **Save**. Notice that when the Save Book dialog box closes, the name of your book now is in the banner of the New Book panel.

3. When you're working with a book file, FrameMaker's menu options change as shown in the table below:

Table 10: Menu Bar Options

When Working with a Document	When Working with a Book
File	File
Edit	Edit
Format	Add
View	Format
Special	View
Graphics	CMS
Table	Window
CMS	Help
Window	
Help	

4. To add the *TestFrontMatter1.fm* file to your book, click **Add > Files** on the menu bar or click the **Add File** icon on the books window.

5. Navigate to the folder where you saved your file, select it, and then click **Add**.

6. The file is added to the book file. Don't worry if the files aren't in correct order. You'll learn how to arrange them soon.

You can add non-FrameMaker files to your book, but FrameMaker only includes its own files in your book's pagination. So why would you want to add a non-FrameMaker file to your book? One reason would be to keep track of related files, such as style guidelines or outlines. Another reason would be so you can open the non-FrameMaker files from the book file.

Rearranging the Order of Files

As mentioned earlier, it doesn't matter what order you add files to your book, but if you want your book to print correctly, you have to put the files in the correct order. To rearrange the order of the files in your book, you can 1) select the file you want to move and hold down the left-mouse button while dragging it to where you want it to be located in your book. You'll see a bar that shows you where the file will be positioned. When you've moved the file to the correct location, release the left-mouse button, or 2) select the file you want to move, and then click the arrow icons at the top of the book window to move the file.

Renaming Files

Whenever you rename a file in your book, FrameMaker renames the corresponding file on your computer, and it also updates cross-references and other links in other files in the book. To rename a file in your book, do the following:

1. Open the book window, and then open all of the files in the book by holding down the **SHIFT** key and clicking **File > Open All Files in Book** on the menu bar.

Note: Opening all of the files speeds up the process of updating the book and ensures that all files are updated.

2. Select the file to rename from the list in the book window.

3. Click **Edit > Rename file** on the menu bar or right-click the filename and select **Rename** from the menu that is displayed. The name is highlighted and has a box around it.

4. Type the new name, and then press **ENTER**. FrameMaker will display a message telling you what's happening and asking you to confirm this action. Click **OK** to proceed.

5. A second message will be displayed telling you again what's happening and that you can't undo this action. Click **OK** to proceed. FrameMaker scans all files in the book and updates them with the new name.

Adding Page Numbers to Your Book

By default, FrameMaker uses numeric (Arabic) page numbers (*1, 2, 3 . . .*) starting with page 1, but you can choose a different numbering style. All Body Pages in each file will use the same numbering style, but you can use different styles from file to file in your book. For example, you may want to use Roman numerals for your front matter pages and Arabic numbers for the remainder of the document.

Use the Numbering Properties dialog box to set volume, chapter, page, paragraph, footnote, and table footnote values. You can use volume and chapter numbers to create page numbers that incorporate the volume or chapter numbers (such as 1.2.1, which would indicate volume one, chapter two, page one).

The Numbering Properties Dialog Box

To look at the Numbering Properties dialog box, open the book window, select the first document in the book window, and then click **Format > Document > Numbering** on the menu bar. The Numbering Properties dialog box opens.

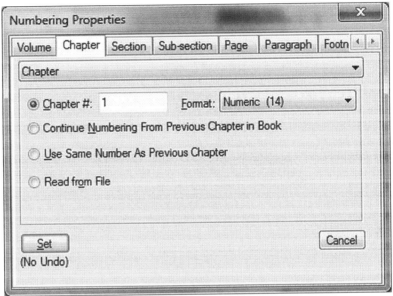

Figure 119: Numbering Properties dialog box

1. To specify volume, chapter, section, or subsection numbers, click the appropriate tab on the Numbering Properties dialog box. (The drop-down list immediately below the tab names is another way to move from tab to tab.)

2. To specify a volume, chapter, section, or subsection number, click the radio button in front of *Volume #, Chapter #, Section #,* or *Subsection #,* (depending on which tab you're looking at), and then choose a numbering style from the **Format** drop-down list.

3. If you want your numbering to continue from a previous file in your book, click the radio button in front of *Continue Numbering From Previous (File/Chapter/Section/Subsection) in Book.*

4. If you want to use the same number as the previous file in your book, click the radio button in front of *Use Same Number As Previous (File/Chapter/Section/Subsection).*

5. If your book file is open, you'll have the option to *Read from File*. Clicking the radio button in front of this option tells FrameMaker to use the numbering value specified in the document you've highlighted in the book file.

6. If you chose more than one file in your book window, you'll have the option to choose *As Is* as your numbering style.

7. When you're finished, click **Set**.

There are three options for numbering your pages on the **Page** tab on the Numbering Properties dialog box: *First Page #, Continue Numbering from Previous Page in Book*, and *Read from File*. To define the page numbers in your book, follow these steps:

1. Select the **Page** tab.

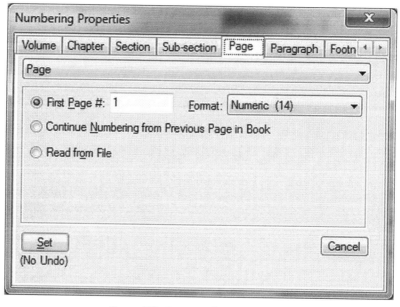

Figure 120: Page numbering tab

2. If you want to specify the starting page number, click the radio button in front of *First Page #*, type the number you want to

start with, and then select the format from the drop-down menu.

3. If you want the page numbering to continue from the previous document, click the radio button in front of *Continue Numbering from Previous Page in Book*.

4. If you want the page numbering to use the numbering value specified in the document you selected, click the radio button in front of *Read from File*.

Paragraph Numbering

You might want to use paragraph numbering in certain types of documents. The **Paragraph** tab allows you to specify whether you want autonumbering of paragraphs to continue or restart from one file to the next. If you select *Restart Paragraph Numbering*, your paragraph numbering starts from zero at the beginning of the document file you selected. If you choose *Continue Numbering from Previous Paragraph in Book*, the paragraph numbers in the selected document will continue from the previous document file.

Footnote Numbering

You also can set up your footnote number system from the Numbering Properties dialog box. After clicking the **Footnote** tab, you can designate footnote numbers to run sequentially for each document file by selecting the radio button in front of *First Footnote #*, and then selecting the format you want to use. Restart footnote numbers on each page by selecting the radio button in front of *Start Over on Each Page,* and then selecting the format you want to use. Or you can designate footnote numbers to run sequentially throughout the entire document by selecting the radio button in front of *Continue Numbering from Previous Footnote in Book*.

Table Footnotes

Table footnotes are a little different from the other numbering properties. You can only designate the format you want to use. Table footnotes (footnotes that are created for text within a table) always restart for each new table.

Setting up Page Numbering

You'll probably use only a few of these options in your daily work. For example, you'll probably set most of your files to continue page numbering from the previous file. To set this up, follow these steps:

1. Open the book file you want to work with, and then open all of the files within it.

2. On your book window, select all of the files in the book that you want included in this numbering system.

3. Open the Numbering Properties dialog box by clicking **Format > Document > Numbering** on the menu bar.

4. Click the Page tab, and then click the radio button in front of **Continue Numbering from Previous Page in Book**.

5. Click **Set**.

6. Select the document in your book window that will be printed first in this particular numbering scheme, and then display the Page tab again.

7. Click the radio button in front of First Page #, and type **1**.

8. In the Format drop-down list, select **Numeric**.

9. Click **Set** and update your book.

To apply this to the Body Pages of your test book file, follow these steps:

1. Select the TestChap1.fm file in your Test book file.

2. Open the Numbering Properties dialog box by clicking **Format > Document > Numbering** on the menu bar.

3. Click the Page tab. Since this will be the first chapter in your book, start your page numbering here. Click the radio button in front of **First Page Number**.

4. If "1" isn't already in the box following this, type it in that box.

5. In the Format field, if **Numeric** isn't already displayed, click the arrow at the end of the field and select it from the list.

6. Click **Set**.

Later, you'll add another chapter file to the book, and then you'll add page numbers to it at that time.

Advanced Maintenance and Troubleshooting Books

You can do many things with your books that you may have thought you could only do at a document level. For example, you can spell-check your entire book at one time, find or change items in all of the documents in your book, even change the format of files throughout your book. As you learn how to do the following things in your books, remember that you also can do these things in your individual documents as well.

Spell-Checking Your Book

FrameMaker has powerful spell-checking capabilities. Automatic spell-checking (new in version 10) is turned on by default. If you want to turn off automatic spell-checking, or if automatic spell-checking gets turned off by accident and you want to turn it back on, click **File > Preferences > General** to open the Preferences dialog box that you reviewed in Chapter 1. When the automatic spell-checking is turned on, words that aren't in FrameMaker's dictionary will be underlined with red wavy lines as you type. Possible punctuation errors will be underlined with wavy green lines. You can spell-check all of the files in your book by following these steps:

1. After you've opened your book file, open all of the files in it.

2. Click **Edit > Spelling Checker** on the menu bar. The Spelling Checker panel opens:

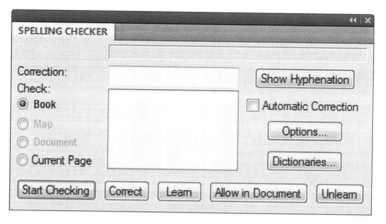

Figure 121: Spelling Checker panel

3. Notice that under the word *Check* on the left, there are four options. Be sure the **Book** radio button is selected if you want to spell-check your entire book.

4. Click the **Options** button on the right to open the Spelling Checker Options dialog box. This is where you can specify different things you want FrameMaker to check, such as repeated words, unusual hyphenation and capitalization, two characters in a row, "straight" quotation marks instead of the more modern curved quotation marks, extra spaces between letters or sentences, etc. Note that you also can select items that you want FrameMaker to ignore when performing a spell-check, such as single-character words (such as "a" and "I"), words that contain characters you indicate in this document box, and more.

Note: Professionally formatted documents that use a proportional typeface such as Arial or Times Roman should only have one space between sentences. If you're accustomed to adding two spaces between sentences, be sure to use the option to delete extra spaces between sentences on the Spelling Checker Options dialog box.

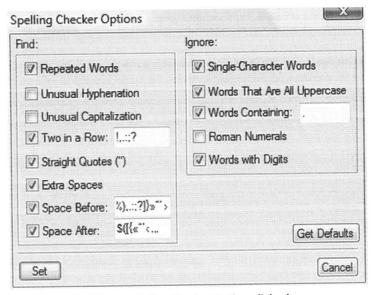

Figure 122: Spelling Checker Options dialog box

5. When you're finished specifying the items you want FrameMaker to check for, click **Set** to return to the Spelling Checker dialog box.

6. Click **Start Checking**. When FrameMaker comes across a word that it doesn't recognize while you have the Spelling Checker dialog box open, the word will have a wavy red line under it and the word is displayed in the **Misspelling** text box with the most probable correction listed in the **Correction** text box. Under the **Correction** text box, you'll see other possible words that you might use.

Note: If you don't have the Spelling Checking dialog box open and see either a red or green wavy line under some text, right-click on the word or punctuation to see the options for correcting or accepting the possible errors.

7. Look at the buttons at the bottom of the dialog box.

- If you choose **Correct**, the word that's in the **Correction** text box will replace the misspelled word.

- If you choose **Learn**, FrameMaker adds the word that it thought was misspelled to the dictionary.

- If you choose **Allow in Document**, FrameMaker will allow this spelling in the current document but will show it as a misspelled word in other documents.

- If you click **Unlearn**, FrameMaker removes the spelling in the **Correction** text box from the dictionary.

Find/Change

There may be times when you want to search through all of the files in your book to find something and perhaps change it. To do this, you'll use FrameMaker's Find/Change option. An important addition to the Find/Change panel in version 10 is the capability to search for paragraph, character, and table format overrides. Use the Find/Change panel as follows:

1. Open your book file, and then open all of the files.

2. Click **Edit > Find/Change** on the menu bar. The Find/Change panel opens:

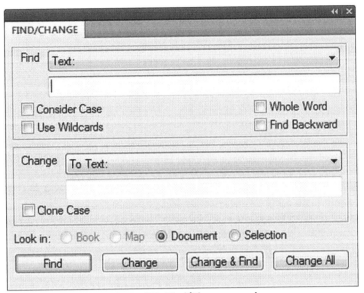

Figure 123: Find/Change panel

3. *Text* is the default when you first open this dialog box, but if you click the arrow at the end of the **Find** field, you'll see that you can search for many other things as well. If you're looking for a certain word or phrase, type the word or phrase that you want to find in your document in the blank box under this field.

4. Select any of the options under the **Find** field that are applicable:

   - Click **Consider Case** if you want your search to be case-sensitive.

   - Click **Whole Word** if you only want FrameMaker to find whole words that match what you typed.

   - Click **Use Wildcards** if you aren't certain of the spelling and want to use wildcards such as asterisks.

   - Click **Find Backward** if you want FrameMaker to search backward from where your cursor is located.

5. In the **Change** field, select whether you want to change the word above to text or something else, and then type what you want this changed to in the blank text box next to this. Select **Clone**

Case if you want FrameMaker to use the same case as the word that's being replaced.

6. Be sure you have the radio button in front of *Book* selected if you want FrameMaker to search all of the files in your book. Then click one of the following:

  ▪ Click **Find** to find the first occurrence of the item or word but not replace it.

  ▪ Click **Change** to find the item or word and change it to what you designated in the Change field.

  ▪ Click **Change & Find** to find the item or word and change it to what you've designated, and then continue searching without you clicking the Find button.

  ▪ Click **Change All** to change all without stopping on individual instances.

Import Formatting

Sometimes, books hold document files that have different formatting (such as paragraph tags that are formatted differently in some of the documents). To have the formatting the same in all of your documents (such as using the same typeface for the Body Text and Heading tags), you can go through each document in your book and make the formatting changes manually, or you can change the formatting throughout your book by doing the following:

1. Open your book file and locate the document that has the formatting you want all of the documents to have.

2. Note the name of that document, and then open the documents to which you want to import the first document's formats.

3. With your cursor in a document that you want to import the formats to, click **File > Import > Formats** on the menu bar. The Import Formats dialog box opens:

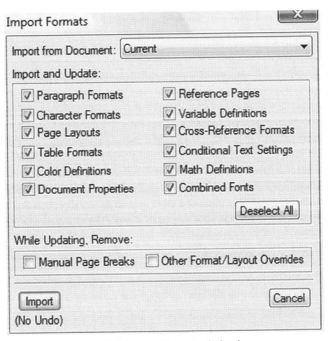

Figure 124: Import Formats dialog box

4. Click the arrow at the end of the *Import from Document* field and select the document from which you're importing formats.

5. In the Import and Update section of the dialog box, select what you want to import.

6. When you're finished, click **Import**.

7. Repeat this for all documents that you want to import formats to. Be sure to save all of the documents that you've changed so the formatting will be updated.

Update Your Book

After you set up your book file and establish your numbering properties, update the files in your book by doing the following:

1. Click **Edit > Update Book** on the menu bar or click **Update Book** on the book window. The Update Book dialog box opens:

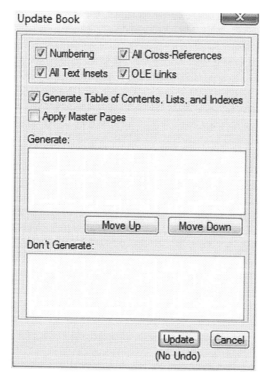

Figure 125: Update Book dialog box

2. Select what you want to update, and then click **Update**.

    Note: We'll talk in the next chapter about updating generated files, so don't worry about this for now.

3. Be sure to save all of the files that you've updated or your updates will be lost.

Book Error Log

Working with books goes smoothly most of the time. But you might run into the occasional problem. Most of the time, problems are reported on the *Book Error Log*, a window that opens with a report of error messages whenever there are problems with a book.

Some of these error messages contain hyperlinks that you can click to take you to the source of the problem. Note, however, that book logs are not stored. If you close the Book Error Log, thinking that you can come back to it later, it will be lost. If I don't have time to correct the errors in the Book Error Log, I take a screen shot of it or I click **CTRL + a** to select all and paste it in a blank document so I can resolve the problems later. Here are a few of the problems you might have when updating:

- **Unresolved Cross Refs**. All files that contain unresolved cross-references will be listed in the Book Error Log. You'll need to correct these by using the process we discussed in the last chapter, and then update your book again.

- **Inconsistent Numbering Properties**. This message appears when the numbering properties in the document are different from the numbering properties in the book, such as page numbers. To correct this, be certain that your numbering properties within a specific document aren't conflicting with the numbering properties in the book file.

- **Couldn't Open File**. This error message generally appears when FrameMaker can't open a file because it uses fonts that aren't installed on your computer. To correct this error, open all of the files in your book before updating it.

- **File Is in Use**. If another user has opened any of the files in your book, FrameMaker will display the machine name or user name that's using the file (it will be *locked*). If you open all of your book files before updating, you'll see the message saying the file is in use at that time. To correct this error, ask the other user to close the file so you can update the book.

- **Read/Write Permissions**. Since FrameMaker needs to read the files it updates, you must have read permission to access the files. Additionally, you'll need to have write permission on the files to save the updates. If you receive a message saying you don't have read/write permissions, be sure that you have read/write permissions for all of the files in your book. If you're trying to update a view-only document, press **ESC, SHIFT + f + l (lowercase "L") + k** to unlock the file. (Press and release the ESC key, and then hold down the SHIFT key while pressing and holding down the f, l, and k keys.)

FrameMaker might report other problems in the Book Error Log, but these are the most common. To minimize errors, always remember to do two things:

- Keep all of the document files for your book in the same folder.

- Open all of the files in your book before you update, spell-check, search, or perform other actions. FrameMaker will prompt you if it can't open a file when you're opening them individually, but it won't prompt you if it can't open a file while trying to update your book.

Frequently Asked Questions

Q: *How can I select more than one file at a time to add to my book file?*

A: To add several files at once to your book file, press **CTRL** while you're selecting them, and then click **Add** on the Book panel. The files will be added to your book file.

Q: *Are there shortcut keys I can use to open and close all of the files in a book?*

A: Yes, FrameMaker provides shortcut keys to open, save, and close all of the files in your book at one time.

  - To open all files in a book, press **ESC, f, SHIFT+O.** (Press and release the ESC key, then press and release the f key, then press SHIFT while pressing O.)

- To save all files in a book, press **ESC, f, SHIFT+S.** (Press and release the ESC key, then press and release the f key, then press SHIFT while pressing S.)

- To close all files in a book, press **ESC, f, SHIFT+C.** (Press and release the ESC key, then press and release the f key, then press SHIFT while pressing C.)

This page is intentionally left blank.

Tables of Contents

Give your documents and books a more professional look and make them easier to use by generating a table of contents for them. Learn how to use tags to determine what is included in your table of contents, format it, and develop a table of contents template on your reference pages that you can use in other documents and books.

When you look at a technical document for the first time, where do you look first? If you're like most people, you look at the table of contents. You want to know what's in the document and how it's organized. Tables of contents provide you with a brief outline of the document. They help you find the information you need more quickly and skip the information that you don't need.

In the last chapter, you learned how to build a book and add document files to it. In this chapter, you'll learn how to create tables of contents for books and stand-alone documents.

Tables of contents are generated files. *Generated* means that FrameMaker creates (generates) your table of contents from paragraph tags or marker text in your documents. If you make changes in your document and generate your table of contents or list again, FrameMaker automatically updates the information. That means you don't have to worry about messing up your table of contents if you add new chapters or sections that need to be included in your table of contents. When you generate your table of contents, FrameMaker will update it for you.

Adding a table of contents to a document or a book involves four steps:

1. You have to prepare your document so that FrameMaker can generate a table of contents from it.

2. You have to define what you want in your table of contents.

3. You have to generate the table of contents.

4. You have to format the table of contents.

A table of contents is usually generated from the headings and subheadings in your document. To generate your table of contents, you'll specify which paragraph tags (such as Heading1 or Heading2) FrameMaker will use to build your table of contents. FrameMaker will search for those paragraph tags, and then display the text that's associated with them in your table of contents along with the numbers of the pages upon which they appear.

FrameMaker can create tables of figures, illustrations, or tables in the same manner. These elements should have captions or titles. When you're setting up these tables, you'll specify the paragraph tags FrameMaker will search for, and then FrameMaker will display the text that's associated with these paragraph tags and the page numbers upon which they appear.

One FrameMaker feature that's especially useful is its ability to create a table of contents from several different documents that are included in a book. It doesn't matter if your book has one document file or 100 document files. FrameMaker will scan them all and generate your table of contents for you.

While FrameMaker generates your table of contents and other lists quickly and easily, you have to do some work to prepare your documents first. In this section, you'll learn how to set up your documents to generate tables of contents as well as how to format and update them. Let's get started.

Preparing Your Documents

Tables of contents are generated from documents called *source documents*, which you probably remember is just another name that FrameMaker uses to describe the documents you're working with. To avoid problems when you're generating your table of contents, you need to prepare your source document by doing three things:

- First, use paragraph tags in a manner that's consistent with what you want to see in your table of contents. For example, if you want all of your first-level headings to be included, use the Heading1 paragraph tag for all of them.

- Second, you must make sure that there isn't more text included in the heading than you want in your table of contents and that you don't break your headings into two lines with paragraph returns.

- Third, be sure that you haven't applied paragraph tags that would be included in your table of contents to blank lines. In general, don't press **ENTER** to create blank lines above or below text as this could cause problems in your table of contents

Defining and Generating Your Table of Contents

After you've prepared your source document, you're ready to define what FrameMaker will use to generate your table of contents. You can generate tables of contents for books or for stand-alone documents. Let's first generate a table of contents for a book using the book file you created in the last chapter.

1. Open the *test.book* file in FrameMaker, and then open all of the document files in the book window.

2. In the book window, select the file that's next to where you want the generated file to appear. It doesn't matter if the selected file is before or after the table of contents, because you'll have an opportunity in the next few steps to designate its position. In this case, select the *TestChap1.fm* file.

3. To prevent FrameMaker from adding a phantom chapter (unique to the sample document we're using), scroll to the last two pages in the *TestChap1.fm* file and check to see if there's a line that says *Chapter 1*. If you see this and there isn't any text below this, place your cursor on that line and change the paragraph tag to *Body* on the task bar.

4. Click **File > Save** on the menu bar to save the change.

5. Click **Window > Document** on the menu bar, and then click the book file name to return to the book window.

6. Click the book window, and then click **Add > Table of Contents** on the menu bar. The Set Up Table of Contents dialog box opens:

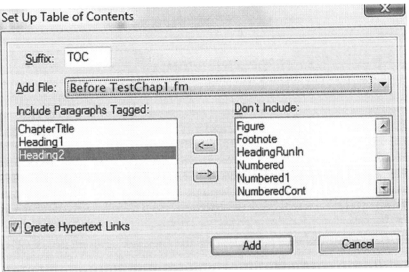

Figure 126: Set Up Table of Contents dialog box

7. In the Add File field, select whether the table of contents will appear before or after the file you selected in the book file. In this case, we want the table of contents to be inserted before the *TestChap1.fm* file.

8. Select the paragraph tags in the right pane that you want FrameMaker to search for when generating your table of contents, and then click the arrow that points to the Include Paragraphs Tagged pane. In this case, select **ChapterTitle**, **Heading1**, and **Heading2**, and move them to the Include Paragraph Tagged pane.

9. To link each entry in your table of contents to its source (making it easy to click the entry in the table of contents and jump to the source), click the checkbox in front of **Create Hypertext Links**.

10. Click **Add**. The Update Book dialog box opens:

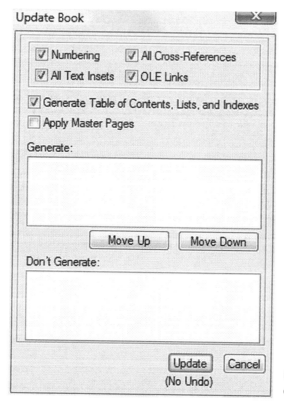

Figure 127: Update Book
dialog box

11. Make sure there's a checkmark in front of Generate Table of Contents, Lists, and Indexes.

12. Click **Update**. FrameMaker generates the table of contents. Notice that FrameMaker gives it a name that's based on the book's filename, in this case *TestTOC*. If you rename your book and leave the generated names with the default filenames, FrameMaker will change their filenames in the book but not on your computer. If you rename the generated file instead of accepting the default name, renaming the book won't rename the generated file.

13. Double-click *testTOC.fm* in the book window. The test table of contents opens. It should look similar to this:

```
The San Francisco Earthquake of 1906 1
The Quake Came Wednesday Morning 1
The Flames Followed Soon After 1
Surrender Is Complete 2
The First Day 2
```

Figure 128: Generated table of contents

14. You'll soon learn how to format this so it looks better, but for now, click **File > Save as** on the menu bar and save the *TestTOC.fm* file in the same folder as your book file.

Formatting Your Table of Contents

To format your table of contents, you need to do some work on both your Body and Reference Pages. Formatting generated files takes some time and work, and frankly, I think this is one of the more difficult things you have to do in FrameMaker. The good news is that you only need to do it once. After you've formatted your table of contents, you can use it as a template for other documents or books. Start with formatting the text on the Body Page as follows:

1. If you closed your test TOC.fm file after you saved it in the previous instructions, open it now.

2. Click in the first line of your table of contents.

3. Look at the Tag Name box on the Paragraph Formatting toolbar at the top of the window and notice that the name of the paragraph tag that's applied to this line is *ChapterTitleTOC*. (You may need to click the arrow to drop the list of paragraph tags to see the complete name). If you move to the lines below, you'll see that the paragraph tag names in the Tag Name box change to Heading1TOC and Heading2TOC. FrameMaker generates these special TOC paragraph tags when it generates the table of contents.

4. Place your cursor in the first line again, and then open the Paragraph Designer by clicking **Format > Paragraphs > Designer** on the menu bar.

5. Click the **Basic** properties tab and click the arrow at the end of the Above Pgf field. Select **2 Lines** from the pull-down list.

6. Click **Update All**. If you see a message saying that some of the paragraphs have overrides, click **Remove Overrides**.

7. Click the **Default Font** tab, change the Weight to **Bold**, and then click **Update All**.

8. We want the chapter numbers to be shown in the table of contents, so click the **Numbering** tab. Place a checkmark in front of Autonumber Format, and then in the box below type *Chapter <n+>: .*

   Note: Be sure to include the colon at the end of what you type. Also, please note that you can't use the <$chapnum> building block here because FrameMaker will pick up the chapter number of the current file only.

9. Click **Update All**. The words *Chapter 1:* should be inserted in front of the text on the first line.

10. Place your cursor in the second line. This paragraph uses the Heading1TOC tag. Click the **Basic** properties tab, and then click the arrow at the end of the Above Pgf field. Select **1 Line** from the pull-down menu.

11. In the *First* box under Indents, type **0.3**, and then type **0.3** in the *Left* box.

12. Click **Update All**. If you see a message saying that some of the paragraphs have overrides, click **Remove Overrides**.

13. Place your cursor in the third line. This paragraph uses the Heading2TOC tag. While still on the **Basic** properties tab, type **0.5** in the First box under Indents, and then type **0.5** in the Left box.

14. Click **Update All.** If you see a message saying that some of the paragraphs have overrides, click **Remove Overrides**.

15. Save your document.

Adding Tabs and Tab Leaders

It's looking better, but it still doesn't look like a table of contents. Now we need to add tabs and tab leaders as follows:

1. Leave the Paragraph Designer open.

2. Move your cursor to the end of the first line of your table of contents, immediately behind the number 6 in the date 1906. This will be in front of the page number 1.

3. Click the **Edit** button on the Basic properties tab. The Edit Tab Stop dialog box opens:

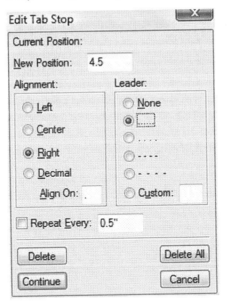

Figure 129: Edit Tab Stop dialog box

4. In the New Position box, type *4.5*.

5. In the Alignment area, select **Right**.

6. In the Leader area, select a leader style.

7. Click **Continue**.

8. In the Paragraph Designer, click **Update All**. You won't see any results yet, but we'll fix that soon.

9. Repeat the steps above to add a right tab just like this one to the Heading1TOC and Heading2TOC paragraph formats.

10. Close the Paragraph Designer.

Now we'll modify the TOC Reference page so your table of contents will be consistent even if you add more documents to your book.

Modifying the TOC Reference Page

Earlier, we discussed how Reference Pages hold boilerplate graphics that you can use throughout a document and how FrameMaker automatically generates Reference Pages when you open a new document.

Reference Pages are used for more, though. You can use them to control what information is included in the paragraphs that are generated in your table of contents and how those paragraphs will be formatted.

Within your Reference Pages, you need to locate the one that contains the TOC reference flow. To do this, place your cursor on the table of contents page, and then open your Reference Pages by clicking **View > Reference Pages**. Scroll to the last Reference Page and click on it.

IMPORTANT: *Be sure that it says* **Flow: TOC** *in the Status bar at the bottom of the window displaying the reference pages.*

You may have a Reference Page that says it's the Table of Contents Specification page, but when you place your cursor on it, the words **Flow: TOC** don't appear in the Status bar at the bottom of the screen. **This is NOT the right page!** These specifications have to do with hyperlinking, so ignore this page and continue scrolling through the Reference Pages until you find the one that displays the TOC flow message in the Status bar. This is the one that you want.

When you've found the correct Reference Page, you'll modify the TOC flow reference page by doing the following:

1. Place your cursor between the <$paratext> and the <$pagenum> building blocks in the following line:

   Chapter 1 <$paratext> <$paranum>.

2. Delete the space between the building blocks, and press **TAB**.

3. Repeat the steps above for Heading1TOC and Heading2TOC. (Place your cursor in the lines and look at the Status bar to see what paragraph tag is being used.) Your TOC Reference Page should look similar to this:

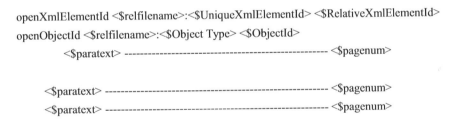

openXmlElementId <$relfilename>:<$UniqueXmlElementId> <$RelativeXmlElementId>
openObjectId <$relfilename>:<$Object Type> <$ObjectId>
    <$paratext> --- <$pagenum>

    <$paratext> --- <$pagenum>
    <$paratext> -- <$pagenum>

Figure 130: Completed TOC Reference Page

4. Select **View > Body Pages**, and then save your document.

You won't see the changes until you regenerate your table of contents. Before we do that, let's add a title to the page by doing the following:

1. Click outside of the text frame of your Table of Contents Body Page to deselect it, and then click at the beginning of the first

paragraph. Because *Chapter 1* is generated automatically, you will have to place your cursor behind these words.

2. Type *Table of Contents*, and then press **ENTER**. Your chapter number will change, but don't worry about that. It will be corrected soon.

3. Place your cursor in the Table of Contents title line, and then apply the TitleBook paragraph tag.

   Note: The TitleBook paragraph tag was added when you added the TestFrontMatter file to your book in Chapter 9. If you don't see this paragraph tag, import it from that file as described in Lesson 10.

4. Save your document.

Because you added the specifications for the formatting of your table of contents on your Reference Pages, when you add more chapters to your document, the formatting should be consistent. To see your formatting, update your table of contents as follows:

1. Click the book window to make it active.

2. Click **Edit > Update Book** on the menu bar. The Update Book dialog box opens.

3. Click **Update**. FrameMaker updates your table of contents. Your table of contents should now look like this:

Table of Contents

Chapter 1: The San Francisco Earthquake of 1906........................1

The Quake Came Wednesday Morning............................1

The Flames Followed Soon After................................1

Surrender Is Complete..2

The First Day...2

Figure 131: Formatted Table of Contents

Adding More to Your Book's Table of Contents

To learn how to do more things with your table of contents and your book files, let's add another document to your book. Here's how:

1. Close all of your files by holding down the **SHIFT** key while clicking **File > Close All Files** on the menu bar.
2. Click **File > New > Document** on the menu bar.
3. Click **Explore Standard Templates.**
4. Scroll down to the Book samples, and click **Chapter**.
5. Click **Show Sample**. This is the same document that we saved earlier as *TestChap1.fm*.
6. Click **File > Save As** and save this latest version in the same folder as the other book files, calling it *TestChap2.fm*.
7. Go back to the Standard Templates dialog box and click **Done** to close it.

8. Go back to the *TestChap2.fm* document. So you can see the difference in the two chapters, change the chapter title and headings as follows:

   - Chapter title—The Great War

   - First Heading1 (*The Quake Came Wednesday Morning*)—A Call to Patriotism

   - First Heading2 (*The Flames Followed Soon After*)—A Nation at Odds

   - Second Heading1 (*Surrender Is Complete*)—Going Into the Fray

   - Second Heading2 (*The First Day*)—Those Who Were Left Behind

9. As with the *TestChap1.fm* document, scroll to the end of the document, and place your cursor on the line that says *Chapter 1*. Click the Body paragraph tag in the Paragraph Formatting toolbar at the top of the window so you won't have a phantom chapter in your table of contents.

10. Click **File > Save** to save your changes.

Now add the *TestChap2.fm* file to your book by opening the test book window and then clicking the **Add** icon. Locate the *TestChap2.fm* file and click **Add**. The *TestChap2.fm* document file is added to your book. If necessary, drag the file name in the book pane so that *TestChap2* follows *TestChap1*.

Save your book, and then update your table of contents by clicking **Edit > Update Book** while your cursor is anywhere in the book window. Click the **Update** button.

Double-click the *TestTOC.fm* filename so you can see how your table of contents has been updated.

Adding Page Numbers

It's looking pretty good, but there's a problem. Look at the page numbers. The page numbers for Chapter 2 start at page 1. FrameMaker doesn't number pages consecutively until you do the following:

1. Return to your TestBook window.

2. Select **TestChap2.fm** in the book window, and then click the right button on your mouse to open the context menu for this window.

3. Click **Numbering** on the context menu. The Numbering Properties dialog box opens. (You also can click **Format > Document > Numbering** if you wish.)

4. You probably recall this dialog box from our discussion of it in the last chapter. In this chapter, you're going to fix the pagination of your book so the pages will be numbered consecutively from Chapter 1 to Chapter 2.

5. Click the **Page** tab of the Numbering Properties dialog box.

6. Click **Continue Numbering From Previous Page in Book**, and then click **Set**.

7. Whenever you make changes to your book, it's a good idea to update it and see if you're achieving what you want. So with your cursor in the book window, click **Edit > Update Book**, and then click the **Update** button. Look at your *TestTOC.fm* document to see how the page numbers have changed.

Adding Page Numbers to Your Table of Contents Pages

You may have noticed that while there are page numbers in your table of contents, there aren't any page numbers on your table of contents pages. Let's add them by doing the following:

1. Open your *TestTOC.fm* document if it isn't already open.

2. With your cursor on the TestTOC document, click **View > Master Pages** on the menu bar.

3. Scroll to the First Master Page.

4. Click **Graphics > Tools** to display the Tools palette.

5. Click the **Text Frame** icon on the Tools palette.

6. Draw a text frame at the bottom of the First Master Page where you want the footer to be.

7. As soon as you release the mouse button, the Add New Text Frame dialog box opens.

8. Click **Background Text**, and then click **Add**.

9. Place your cursor in the text box you just drew, and then click the **Text Alignment** button on the formatting bar at the top of the window.

10. Select **Right**.

11. Insert a page number variable by clicking **Special > Variable** on the menu bar and selecting **Current Page Number**.

12. Click **Insert**.

13. Repeat these steps for the other Master Pages, moving the cursor to the right side of the text box for the right-hand page and leaving it at the left side of the text box for the left-hand page.

14. Click **View > Body Pages** on the menu bar.

15. Click anywhere on the first page of your table of contents.

16. Apply the First Master Page to the first page of your table of contents by clicking **Format > Page Layout > Master Page Usage.** When the Master Page Usage dialog box opens, click the radio button in front of **Custom**, and then select **First** from the drop-down list to the right. Click **Apply**.

17. To change the page numbers to lowercase Roman numerals and specify what page number to start with, click **Format > Document > Numbering**, and then click the **Page** tab.

18. Click the radio button in front of *First Page #*, and then select the lowercase Roman numerals from the Format dropdown list.

19. Click **Set**. Your table of contents should now have page numbers that are lowercase Roman numerals.

Now you have a professional-looking table of contents that you can update as you add more files to your book. Go ahead and save all the files in the book.

Other Types of Generated Lists

While tables of content are one of the most common types of lists you'll generate, you also can generate several other types of lists in FrameMaker. For example, you can generate lists of figures, tables, paragraphs, markers, and references.

All generated files have unique suffixes. These suffixes are used for the file names, the paragraph tags in the generated file, and the Reference Page flow tag. The suffix for your table of contents file was TOC, and the file name was a combination of the book name and the suffix—*testTOC.fm*. The paragraph tags that were applied to the text in your table of contents also carried the TOC suffix, and the Reference Page upon which the table of contents flow was located was named *TOC*. These suffixes provide an easy way to organize elements that are common to specific generated files.

The suffixes that FrameMaker adds to different types of generated files are listed in the table below:

Table 11: Generated File Suffixes

Generated File Type	Suffix
Alphabetic List of Paragraphs	APL
Alphabetic List of Markers	AML
List of Figures	LOF
List of Markers	LOM
List of Paragraphs	LOP
List of References	LOR
List of Tables	LOT
Table of Contents	TOC

Using Your TOC Template in Other Documents

Do you remember earlier when I told you that you could use the formatting you create for your table of contents (or other types of lists) as a template for other books? Here's how you do it:

1. Be sure to use the same paragraph tag names in your new book as you did in your old one.

2. Add the table of contents document file that you want to use as your template to your new book file.

3. Rename it to match the name of the new book file.

4. After you've renamed it, delete it from the list of files in the book window. Its Reference Page (with the template you built) will still be in the book's directory, but the old TOC file will be deleted from your book.

5. While still in the book window, add a table of contents file in the usual manner (clicking **Add > Table of Contents** on the menu bar).

6. Click **Update**. FrameMaker automatically uses the template on your Reference Pages to format the new table of contents file.

Frequently Asked Questions

Q: *Why do I have some empty entries in my table of contents?*

A: This is a problem that occurs when you use blank paragraphs to add space between paragraphs. If the blank paragraph uses a paragraph tag that's used in generating the table of contents, you'll end up with empty entries in your table of contents. To correct this problem, go to the source document, delete the blank paragraphs, and then use the space above and space below settings in the Paragraph Designer to get the spaces that you want.

Q: *I've written a single document and want to create a table of contents for it. How can I do this?*

A: FrameMaker calls this a stand-alone table of contents. To create this, open your document, and then click **Special > Table of Contents** on the menu bar. Generate your table of contents as normal. Whenever you want to update your table of contents, click **Special > Table of Contents** on the menu bar again.

This page is intentionally left blank.

Indexes

Learn how to determine the text that you want to include in your index, mark it, generate and format your index, and create subentries and See references.

Where do readers turn first when they need to find information in a hurry? Studies show that readers look first at your document's index to find the answers they're seeking, especially in long documents. In fact, indexes are the most widely read section of any technical document.

Indexes, like tables of contents, are generated files. Because you can't generate the file from paragraph tags as you can with tables of contents, you need to insert *index markers* in your text. This is a time-consuming task.

After you've inserted the markers, FrameMaker will alphabetize your entries, insert group headings (such as *A*, *B*, and so forth), consolidate identical entries into a single entry with multiple page numbers, place subentries under their parent entries, and insert the correct page number for each entry, based on the location of the marker.

Great indexes are works of art. To write a good index, you need to have knowledge of indexing conventions, attention to detail, and an understanding of how people look for information.

In this chapter, you'll learn how to insert index markers, generate indexes, and format them. We'll discuss adding main index entries and how to edit and delete them. You'll also learn how to create subentries and more. In addition, we'll review some of the conventions of indexing that you need to know to create indexes that are easy-to-use and complete.

Indexing is an exacting task. When you're planning your documentation project, allow the same amount of time to write your index as you would any other chapter. If possible, avoid doing it in a hurry or as a last-minute thought. The earlier in your writing process that you begin to plan your index, the easier it will be to write it.

What to Index

Indexing is more difficult than it looks. Before you start writing an index, you'll have to answer several questions.

First, you need to decide whether you should index your document. Some people say that any technical document longer than 30 pages needs an index. Other experts say that documents with 20 pages or more require indexes. Still others say that technical documents with more than 10 pages need indexes.

In short, there aren't any specific rules about when a document must have an index. The need for an index depends more on how technical the information is and how readers will use the document. If your document has a large amount of technical information that readers need to find quickly, index it.

Second, you need to decide how many entries your index should have. Again, there aren't any specific guidelines about the size of an index. Some large documents that aren't very technical might have small indexes. Smaller documents that use many technical terms might have large indexes.

As with other aspects of technical writing, analyze what your readers need. Professional indexers tell us that an average index should comprise about 2% of the total number of pages in your document. If your document has many terms and concepts, your index may run to more than 5% to 6% of your total number of pages. Decide before you start marking index entries whether you need a large, detailed index or if a smaller, less detailed one is sufficient. Making this decision will save you time and give you a clearer idea of what you want to index.

Third, you have to decide what to include in your index. Consider how educated your readers are, how familiar they are with the product, and how they'll use your documentation. The less education and knowledge your readers have, the more you need to include in your index. Plus, if your readers are unfamiliar with the subject, you must be creative in providing **multiple points of access** to the information in your document.

Providing multiple points of access means including different words or different ways for readers to look up information in your index. For example, if you're indexing a medical document for lay readers, you may have a listing for *abdominal pain* with *stomachache* as a subentry. However, some of your readers may look for *stomachache* first without thinking about looking for *abdominal pain*.

So, you'll want to provide your readers with multiple points of access. Add *stomachache* as a main index entry (to list under *S* in your index) and also as a subentry of *abdominal pain*.

When deciding what to include in your index, put yourself in your readers' shoes. Imagine yourself needing to find information in your document. What would you need to look up? Here are some ideas of things to index to help you begin:

- Chapter or section headings
- Table, figure, and diagram captions

- Examples
- Warnings and caution notices
- Names of organizations and places
- Names of people
- Names of other books or manuals mentioned in the text
- Main topics and important concepts
- Tasks
- Features of a product
- Functions, commands, and parameters
- Menu options
- Keyboard shortcuts
- Items in tables and figures
- Screen messages
- Information in appendixes

Use words that you think people will look up. For example, if you're indexing a procedure and the heading for that procedure says, "Performing a systems check," your readers probably won't look for an index entry under *P* (for *performing*). Instead, they'll probably look for *systems check, performing*.

As a rule, create index entries that are specific, not general. Read your index when you're finished. See if any entries are confusing or if they don't provide information that tells readers what they can expect to find on that page.

Index Cross-References

Cross-references in your index guide readers to related information and can be extremely helpful. Here are some guidelines for using cross-references in your index:

- Cross-references in your index must lead to additional information, not the same information indexed under another heading.
- Entries that have no page numbers associated with them and only have a *See* reference under them are called *blind entries*. If

you create a blind entry, be sure that you aren't directing readers to another blind entry through the reference.

- The words *See* and *See also* should be italicized. If the words that follow are italicized (such as a book title), you might want to use a font that isn't italic for the words *See* and *See also* to distinguish them from the rest of the cross-reference.

- You can use cross-references to include generic references to a type of heading rather than specific headings. For example, you might write the following: abrasion, *See also skin disorders*. Cross-references of this type are completely italicized.

Tips for Creating Your Index

Since indexing requires manual work, you can save time by creating a list of words you may want to include in your index as you write your document. Some technical writers open a second document as they write and copy words that they think they'll want to put in their indexes into the second document. Other writers keep a notepad next to their keyboard and write down possible index entries.

Creating lists like these can give you a head start on indexing. Additionally, creating lists of possible index entries can help you identify problems in your document, such as inconsistently used terminology.

Your index's usefulness reflects how much thought you put into it. Plan it carefully. Think of many possible ways your readers will look for information. Be sure that your index is accurate and concise—that it will be a useful tool for your reader.

FrameMaker's Index Markers

When you create an index with FrameMaker, you must insert index markers in your text to identify what you want included in your index. You also need to create an index file, just as you did when you created a table of contents.

Most of the time, you'll probably create indexes for several documents that you're compiling into a book, but you can also create an index for a single file. This is called a *stand-alone* index. In this section, you'll learn how to create a stand-alone index for a single document, and then we'll discuss how to create an index for a book file with several document files.

The document or book that the index is generated from is called the source document. You need to mark index entries in the source document manually, but fortunately, it isn't that difficult to do with FrameMaker. Let's use another sample document as our source document, and then mark index entries as follows:

1. Click **File > New** on the menu bar.

2. Click the **Explore Sample Documents** button.

3. On the Standard Templates dialog box, click **Report, Sidehead** under the Reports heading.

4. Click **Show Sample** to open the side head report sample, and then close the Standard Templates dialog box.

5. Highlight the word *Quake* in the first heading.

6. Select **Special > Marker** on the menu bar. The Marker panel opens with the word you highlighted in the Marker Text box. Check to be sure that *Index* is displayed in the Marker Type field, and then click **New Marker**.

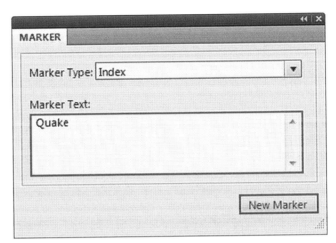

Figure 132:
Marker panel

7. Continue marking index entries in this document by highlighting them. After the text appears in the Marker, click **New Marker**. Repeat until you've marked all of the main index entries that you want to be displayed in your index. If the Marker panel closes after you make each entry, place your cursor on the Marker tab, and then hold down the left-mouse button while moving the panel to another location. Once the panel is away from the other panels, it should stay open while you mark your entries.

8. When you're finished, close the Marker panel by clicking the arrows or the **X** at the upper-right corner of the box.

9. Save your document.

Generate Your Index

After you've marked your index entries, you can generate your index and see what it looks like by following these steps:

1. With the document open, click **Special > Standard Index** on the menu bar. A message is displayed that asks if you want to create a stand-alone index.

2. Click **Yes** to create a stand-alone index. The Set Up Standard Index dialog box opens:

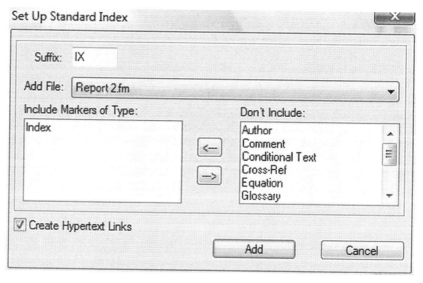

Figure 133: Set Up Standard Index dialog box

3. In the Add File drop-down list, choose whether you want the index before or after the file you're indexing. The default is *after*.

   Note: This option is grayed out because *after* is the only choice for a stand-alone index.

4. Make sure that *Index* is the only marker listed under Include Markers of Type. If *Index* isn't included, locate the marker in the Don't Include list, and double-click it.

5. Click **Set**. FrameMaker will generate your index in a separate file. It probably isn't formatted as you'd like, but don't worry—we'll take care of that soon.

Adding to the Index

If you decide to add more to your index, do the following:

1. Return to the source document and select **Special > Marker** on the menu bar. The Marker panel opens.

2. Be sure that *Index* is selected from the Marker Type pull-down menu.

3. Highlight the words you want to mark, and then click the Marker panel. The words you highlighted should now appear in the Marker Text field of the Marker panel.

4. Click **New Marker**.

   Note: Whenever you want to view the contents of a marker, turn on the Text Symbols setting by clicking **View > Text Symbols**. When you insert a marker, FrameMaker places a symbol that looks like a capital *T* in the text. If you select the marker symbol while the Marker panel is open, the contents of the marker are displayed in the Marker panel.

5. After you insert an index marker for the last index entry you want to add, close the Marker panel and save your document.

6. To update your index, select **Special > Standard Index** on the menu bar.

7. Click **Yes** to create a stand-alone index. The Set Up Standard Index dialog box appears.

8. Be sure that *Index* is the only marker listed under Include Markers of Type. If *Index* isn't included, locate the marker in the Don't Include list, and double-click it.

9. Be sure there's a checkmark in front of *Create Hypertext Links*.

10. Click **Set**. FrameMaker generates your index.

Those are the basic steps for generating a simple index. If you were creating an index for a book instead of a single document file, you would follow much the same steps. The primary differences are that you would open the book file, insert your index markers in each of your document files, save each of them after you've marked your index entries, click the file that will be immediately before or after the index in the book window, and then select **Add > Standard Index** on the menu bar. The Set Up Standard Index dialog box would open. After you clicked **Add**, the index you're creating would be shown in the generated files list of the Update Book dialog box. You then would make sure there's a checkmark in front of Generate Table of Contents, Lists, and Indexes, and then click **Update**.

If you're indexing a book and add more entries to it after you've created your index, you can update the index by clicking **Special > Standard Index** on the menu bar and then clicking **No** when asked if you want to create a stand-alone index. The Set Up Standard Index dialog box opens, and after you click **Add**, the Update Book dialog box opens. Click **Update** to update your book's index.

As you can see, creating an index takes a bit of work, but FrameMaker makes it relatively easy. In the next section, you'll learn how to refine your index by adding subentries and formatting it.

Adding Index Subentries

It's simple to insert index markers in your text and generate an index. Usually, however, you'll want to include subentries, cross-references, ranges of pages, and such.

To do this, you'll use building blocks and commands. You'll enter these into the Marker Text pane of the Marker panel when you're inserting your index markers. For example, if you want to create a subentry for a listing in your index, you type the primary entry, add a colon, and then add what you want for the subentry. To give you some practice, open the document you indexed in the last section, and add a subentry to some of your index entries by doing the following:

1. If it isn't already open, open the source document that you used to generate an index in the previous section.

2. Click **Special > Marker** on the menu bar. The Marker panel opens.

3. Highlight a word that you'd like to be a subentry in your index. The word will be displayed in the Marker panel.

4. Place your cursor in front of the word in the Marker Text pane, and then type the word you want to use as the main index entry with a colon behind it. For example, if you wanted the words *Disaster Plans* to be a subentry of the main index entry *Quake*, you'd highlight the words *Disaster Plans*, and then type *Quake:* in front of it. Note that the colon after the first word tells FrameMaker that the words that come after the colon are a subentry. It should now look like this:

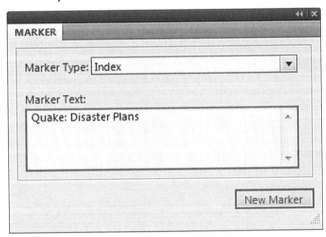

**Figure 134:
Marker text
with subentry**

5. Click **New Marker**.

6. Close the Marker panel and save your document.

7. To see if FrameMaker has added the subentry to your index, regenerate your index by clicking **Special > Standard Index** on the menu bar, and then clicking **Yes** to create a stand-alone index. The Set Up Standard Index dialog box opens.

8. Be sure that *Index* is the only marker listed under Include Markers of Type and that there's a checkmark in front of *Create Hypertext Links*.

9. Click **Set**. FrameMaker generates your index.

10. If you're satisfied with your index, save your files.

Indexing a Range of Pages

When the topic of the entry covers several pages, you'll need to add an index entry that covers a range of pages. To do this, you'll use two building blocks in your Marker Text description as follows:

1. Open your source document and locate a range of pages you'd like to index.

2. Place your cursor anywhere in the first paragraph of that section.

3. Click **Special > Marker** on the menu bar. The Marker panel opens.

4. Be sure that *Index* is selected as the Marker Type.

5. In the Marker Text pane, type *<$startrange>* followed by the word you want to appear in your index. You have to type the building block.

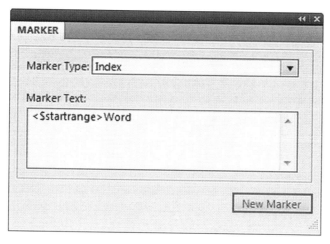

Figure 135: Marker text with the start of a range of pages defined

6. Click **New Marker**.

7. Scroll to the end of the range of pages and place your cursor anywhere in the last paragraph of that section.

8. In the Marker Text pane, type *<$endrange>* followed by the name of the word you want to appear in the index. This must be the same word you used in the startrange marker.

9. Click **New Marker**.

10. Close the Marker panel, save your document, and regenerate your index. If you're satisfied, save your files.

Adding *See* References

When you're indexing a document, you'll probably use what are called *See* references. These entries point readers to another entry for more information. You'll insert these references like other index markers, but you need to suppress the page numbers. To do this, you'll add a building block in the Marker Text definition as follows:

1. Place your cursor anywhere in the document. Since we're creating a marker for an entry that won't have a page number, it doesn't matter where you place it.

2. Click **Special > Marker** on the menu bar. The Marker panel opens.

3. In the Marker panel, type *<$nopage>*, and then type the index entry you want to appear, followed by a comma and the word *See* followed by the index entry you want your readers to go to. For example, if you think your readers will search for *"Home Loans,"* and you want them to go to the Loan Division entry, you'd type *<$nopage>Home Loans, See Loan Division*.

4. Don't click **New Marker** yet, because you'll want to italicize the word *see* in the index entry. To do that, place your cursor in front of the word *See*, and then type *<Emphasis>*. This adds the character marker that italicizes everything that comes after it.

5. If you only want the word *See* to be italicized, place your cursor immediately behind the word *See* and type *<Default Para Font>*. This character tag returns the text that follows the word *See* to the default paragraph font. Your marker text should look like this:

<$nopage>Home Loans, <Emphasis>See<Default Para Font> Loan Division

6. Click **New Marker**.

7. Close the Marker panel, save your document and regenerate your index.

8. If you're satisfied, save your files.

Formatting Your Index

You probably noticed that your index needs to be formatted. Typically, you'll format your index in FrameMaker after inserting the index markers and generating the index. To format your index, follow these steps:

1. Open your index file.

2. Place your cursor in the first line of your index under the single letter identifying the group. It should be tagged *Level1IX*.

3. Open the Paragraph Designer.

4. On the Basic properties tab, click the arrow at the Above Pgf field, and select **1 Line**.

5. Click **Update All**.

6. If you want to change the typeface for your index entries, click the Default Font properties tab and make the changes you want.

7. Click **Update All** when you're finished.

Add a title to the page and format it so it has a two-column layout by doing the following:

1. Place your cursor in front of the first letter in your index and press **ENTER**.

2. Move your cursor up to the first line, type *Index,* and then apply the paragraph tag you want to the word or create a new paragraph tag to apply to it.

3. Your title should be centered on the page, so go to the Pagination properties tab after you apply the paragraph tag and click the radio button in front of **Across All Columns** in the Format section. Click **Update All** after you make the change. When you're finished, close the Paragraph Designer.

4. To give your index a two-column layout, keep your cursor on the same page, and then click **Format > Page Layout > Column Layout**. The Column Layout dialog box opens:

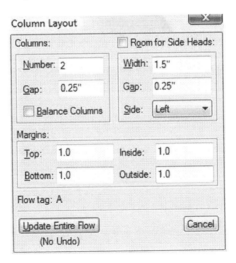

Figure 136: Column Layout dialog box

5. In the Number field in the Columns area, type *2*, and then click **Update Entire Flow**. Your index now should have two columns on the page.

Editing Your Index

Your index is looking good, but what happens if you want to change some of the entries? Here's how to edit your index:

1. Open your index document.

2. Turn on the text symbols by clicking **View > Text Symbols** on the menu bar.

3. Click **Special > Marker** to display the Marker panel.

4. Look for the index markers in the index entries. Index markers look like capital *T's*.

5. To go to an index tag in the source document, hold down **CTRL** and **ALT**, move the mouse pointer over the index marker in the index entry, and when the pointer turns into a hand, click the mouse. FrameMaker will go to the file that contains the index tag you want to change. When you open the Marker panel, the index entry is displayed in the Marker Text pane.

6. Make your changes in the Marker Text pane, and then click **Edit Marker**.

7. Regenerate your index and save it with your changes.

Frequently Asked Questions

Q: *I generated my index, but some of the entries for page ranges have two question marks. How can I fix this?*

A: This occurs when FrameMaker can only find one of the two markers it needs to define the range. Check the marker text for the marker to make sure that it includes both the <$startrange> and <$endrange> building blocks. If you see both of these building blocks, check to be sure that the spelling, punctuation, and capitalization of the marker text is exactly the same for both building blocks and that the <$startrange> building block appears in the first marker and that the <$endrange> building block appears in the second marker.

Q: *How can I delete an index marker?*

A: To delete an index marker, follow these steps:

1. Open your index document.

2. Turn on the text symbols by clicking **View > Text Symbols** on the menu bar.

3. Click **Special > Marker** to display the Marker panel.

4. Look for the index markers in the index entries. Index markers look like capital *T's*.

5. To go to an index tag in the source document, hold down **CTRL** and **ALT**, move the mouse pointer over the index marker in the index entry, and when the pointer turns into a hand, click the left-mouse button. FrameMaker will go to the file that contains the index tag you want to change. When you open the Marker panel, the index entry is displayed in the Marker Text pane.

6. Click **Delete Marker**.

7. Regenerate your index and save it with your changes.

Q: *Can I use FrameMaker's Find/Change feature to locate markers in my text?*

A: Yes. To do this, follow these steps:

1. Open the source document, and then click **Edit > Find/Change** on the menu bar.

2. Click the arrow next to the Find field and select **Any Marker**, **Marker of Type**, or **Marker Text** from the drop-down menu.

3. If you know what marker you're looking for, type the marker type or marker text in the text box under the Find field.

4. Click **Find**. FrameMaker moves to the first marker that matches your description.

Publishing

Learn how to publish your documents in three different ways —on a printer that's connected to your computer, as a Portable Document Format (PDF) file, or in HTML format for online publishing.

With FrameMaker, you have more publishing options than you have with many other applications. For example, you can print your documents on the printer that's connected to your computer or save them as Portable Document Format (PDF) files that most people can read on their computers. You also can print them as PostScript files or save them in HyperText Markup Language (HTML) or a number of other formats.

The flexibility that you have when publishing your FrameMaker documents allows more people to read them on more types of devices. For example, if you publish your document as a PDF, all people with Acrobat Reader on their computers can read your document—whether they're using a PC or a Macintosh computer. You can even configure your PDF files so your readers can save them and read them on small-screen devices, such as eBook readers.

In this chapter, we'll talk about the three most common ways authors publish their FrameMaker documents: on their own printers, as PDF files, or as HTML files.

As you'll learn, even if you're just printing your document to the printer connected to your computer, FrameMaker gives you powerful options to make the job easier. From your FrameMaker screen, you'll be able to control which pages to print, how to order the pages when printing, and special options you can use to make them print more quickly. FrameMaker even allows you to print the registration marks on your pages if you set up your print job for color separations at the printer.

If you decide to publish your document as a PDF, you'll find equally powerful features here. From being able to designate bookmarks within your PDF file to creating hyperlinks from one PDF document to another, FrameMaker will help you manage your documentation better and make it more useful for your readers.

Publishing your document as HTML enables you to post your document quickly on your company's intranet or Web site. Here too, you'll find that FrameMaker gives you many options for controlling the look of your finished document.

As you go through the steps for printing a document on a printer, compare FrameMaker's features with those of your favorite word-processing application. Notice the similarities and differences. This exercise will help you grasp the concepts of printing with FrameMaker more quickly.

Let's start by looking at how to print a FrameMaker document on the printer that's connected to your computer.

Printing Your FrameMaker Documents

You have several options when you're printing your FrameMaker documents. In addition to normal print options, such as printing an entire document or a range of pages within the document, you also can print registration marks (handy if you're having your document printed professionally) and create special files called PostScript files that are used for professional printing.

To print a single document (not a book), follow these steps:

1. Open the document you want to print.

2. Click **File >Print Setup** on the menu bar. The Print Setup dialog box opens:

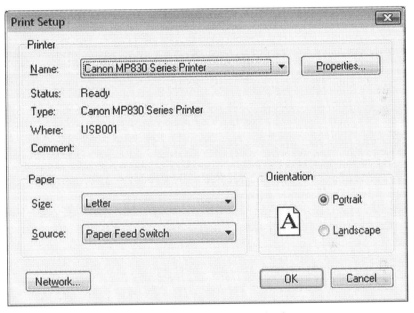

Figure 137: Print Setup dialog box

3. If the name of the printer you're using isn't already displayed in the Name field, click the arrow at the end of the field and select your printer from the drop-down list.

4. Click **Properties** to open the dialog box that shows the properties for the printer you're using. These vary by the manufacturer of your printer but can include some helpful options, such as printing watermarks (such as "Draft" or "Confidential," for example) on all of your pages, and much

more. Since these options are different for different printers, take a few minutes and see what's available for you.

5. After you've reviewed the properties for your computer, click **OK** to return to the Print Setup dialog box and close it.

6. Click **File > Print** on the menu bar to open the Print Document dialog box.

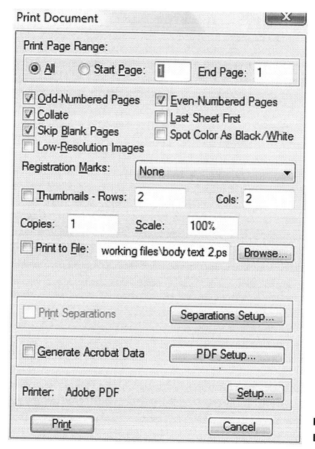

Figure 138: Print Document dialog box

7. Take a moment and study this dialog box. Notice that you have many options for printing your document. You can print all of the pages in it or only the pages you select. If you have a checkmark in front of *Collate* and you're printing more than one copy of your document, FrameMaker will print one complete copy before printing the next copy. If you want to print your

document more quickly (for example, if you're printing a copy to proofread), place a checkmark in front of *Low-Resolution Images* and your images will be printed as gray boxes (in Windows). If you want to print the registration and crop marks on your pages, you can choose either *Western* or *Tombo* (Japanese).

If you want to print small representations of your pages on one page (called *thumbnails*), enter the number of page images you want to print vertically on the page in the *Rows* field and the number of page images you want to print horizontally across the page in the *Cols* field.

Note: There's one important "gotcha" that you should know: If you've turned off graphics earlier in the View Options dialog box when you were looking at your grid lines, your graphics won't appear in the printed document.

8. After you've reviewed all of the choices on the Print Document dialog box and made your selections, click **Print**.

Printing a Book

When you print a book, you'll need to follow these extra steps:

1. Open your book file. As you've done before, it's a good idea to open all of the files in your book before proceeding.

2. Specify what you want to print by doing one of the following:

   ■ To print the entire book, click **File > Print Book** on the menu bar. The Print Book dialog box opens. This dialog box is identical to the Print Document dialog box above. The only thing that's different is the name at the top of the dialog box.

   ■ To print selected files in a book, press **CTRL** on your keyboard, and then select the files you want in the book window. After you've selected them, click **File > Print Selected Files** on the menu bar. The Print Selected Files in Book dialog box opens. This, too, is identical to the Print Document dialog box.

3. Choose the options that you want from either of these dialog boxes, and then click **Print** to print your document or files.

Changing Printers

When you're printing a document, you may need to change the printer. Notice that FrameMaker displays the name of the printer it will use at the bottom of the print dialog boxes. This will usually be your default printer. If you need to print your document on another printer, click the **Setup** button next to the printer's name on the print dialog boxes. The Print Setup dialog box opens just as it would if you clicked **File > Print Setup** on the menu bar.

Troubleshooting Printing

If your document doesn't print, check the following:

- Be sure there isn't a checkmark in front of the **Print to File** field on the Print dialog box.

- If your document is very large or has many graphics, it may take some time for the document to start printing. Check the print job dialog box for your printer (click **Start > Printers** on the desktop of your computer and select the printer you're using) to see if the document is still spooling before trying to print again.

- Make sure there isn't a problem with your printer, such as a paper jam or an empty paper tray.

FrameMaker offers you a wide range of options for printing your documents. Experiment with the print options so you'll be comfortable using them and know what works best for you.

Creating PDF Files

Portable Document Format (PDF) files are read by a program called *Acrobat Reader*, a free download from Adobe, Inc. You convert the file with *Acrobat Distiller*, which is a component of Adobe's Acrobat application that's included in FrameMaker.

There are many advantages to publishing your documents this way. A PDF file is a self-contained cross-platform document, meaning that your document will look the same on the screen and in print regardless of what kind of computer or printer someone is using and regardless of the software package used to create it. Additionally, PDF files contain all of the formatting of the original document, including fonts and images, but they're highly compressed, allowing you to download large documents more efficiently.

Finally, converting your document to PDF makes it available to more readers. If your readers have access to computers, they can open PDF files with any computer that has Acrobat Reader installed, thereby eliminating the need to have FrameMaker installed on their computers. Readers can search through PDF files for the information they need and writers can update PDF files more quickly than they can print new documentation.

Starting with FrameMaker version 7.1, converting your document to PDF became easier than ever in FrameMaker. In previous versions of FrameMaker, you had to configure the Acrobat Distiller before you saved a FrameMaker document as a PDF file. In FrameMaker 7.1 and later versions, you create your PDF files at the same time that you save them. To convert your document to PDF when using FrameMaker 7.1 and later versions, follow these steps:

1. Open the document you want to convert to PDF, and then click **File > Save As PDF** on the menu bar. The Save Document dialog box opens.

2. Click **Save**. If you've previously saved your document as a FrameMaker document (with an .fm extension), a message will appear asking if you're sure that you want to save it as a PDF. Click **Yes**. The PDF Setup dialog box opens:

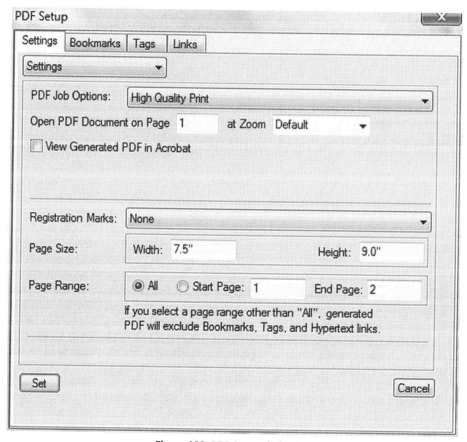

Figure 139: PDF Setup dialog box

3. Choose the options you want on the PDF Setup dialog box.

Note: Your options may be different from the ones discussed here if your version of FrameMaker is using a different version of Acrobat Distiller.

Notice that there are four tabs on this dialog box. Let's take a closer look at each of them now.

Settings Tab

The Settings tab is where you define the settings for your published document.

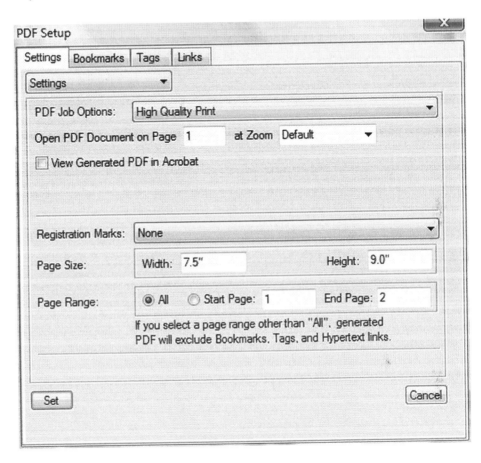

Figure 140: Settings tab

The settings are as follows:

- **PDF Job Options**
  In the PDF Job Options field, you have different options for publishing your PDF. These options may vary, depending on the version of Acrobat Distiller installed with FrameMaker. Common options are:

- High Quality Print
- PDFA1b 2005 CMYK
- PDFA1b 2005 RGB
- Press Quality
- Smallest File Size
- Standard
- Standard (1)

- **Open PDF Document on Page**
  This field enables you to specify what page will be displayed when readers first open the PDF file.

- **At Zoom**
  This option works with the one above. When readers open the page you specify, it will open at the size you choose from the drop-down menu.

- **View Generated PDF in Acrobat**
  If you place a checkmark in front of this, your document will open as a PDF in Acrobat Reader after it's saved.

- **Generate PDF for Review Only**
  This is a new feature with FrameMaker 10 that enables you to import comments made on your PDF documents by reviewers directly into your documents if there's a checkmark in front of this.

- **Registration Marks**
  These are the marks that printers would use to align pages for printing. You can choose *None, Western*, or *Tombo* (Japanese style).

- **Page Size**
  This is where you change the default page size if you wish.

- **Page Range**
  In this field, select **All** if you want to print all of the pages in your document as a PDF or select specific pages to print.

- **Convert CMYK to RGB**
  CMYK stands for Cyan, Magenta, Yellow, and Black. This is the color model used in 4-color printing, such as commercial full-color magazines. *RGB* stands for Red, Green, and Blue. This is the color model usually used to display colors on a computer. If your document will be viewed primarily on a computer, place a checkmark in front of this.

Bookmarks Tab

Bookmarks are placeholders that make it easy for your readers to navigate from one section of a PDF document to another. To set your bookmarks, click the Bookmarks tab on the PDF Setup dialog box.

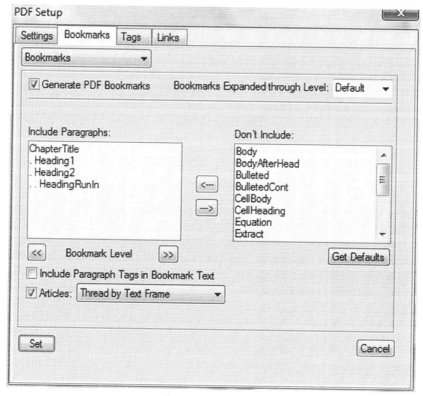

Figure 141: Bookmarks tab

The settings are as follows:

- **Generate PDF Bookmarks**
  Place a checkmark in front of the *Generate PDF Bookmarks* field if you want FrameMaker to generate bookmarks in the published PDF document.

- **Bookmarks Expanded through Level**
  This field defines how many levels of bookmarks appear expanded in the exported PDF file.

- **Include Paragraphs/Don't Include panes**
  Select the paragraph tags in the Don't Include pane that contain text you want converted to bookmarks, and then click the arrow button to move them to the Include Paragraphs pane.

- **Bookmark Level**
  To change the level of a specific bookmark, select the paragraph tag name in the *Include Paragraphs* pane, and then either promote or demote the level by clicking the arrow buttons at the beginning and end of the *Bookmark Level* field.

- **Include Paragraph Tags in Bookmark Text**
  Sometimes when you're proofreading a document, you might want to see which paragraph tags are associated with the final bookmarks. If you want to do this, click the box in front of the *Include Paragraph Tags in Bookmark Text* field. Be sure to deselect this before you publish your final version.

- **Articles**
  This field is where you define how readers will view the bookmarked material. This is called *article threading*. If you want the reading order to follow the order that your cursor would move if you were scrolling down the page, choose **Thread by Column** from the drop-down menu. This is the setting you should use when you have multiple columns in your document.

  If you want the reading order of all articles to go from text frame to text frame, choose **Thread by Text Frame** from the drop-down menu. This setting is most appropriate when your document has a single column.

Tags Tab

Adding tags to your PDF file ensures that your readers can view your document on a wider variety of devices, such as eBook readers and other small-screen devices. Tagged PDF files convert text into formats that readers can view on these devices. This is something that you may not need to use very often. If you do need this, you would place a checkmark in the Generate Tagged PDF field on this tab, and then indicate what paragraphs you want to include by moving the tags from the Don't Include pane to the Include Paragraphs pane.

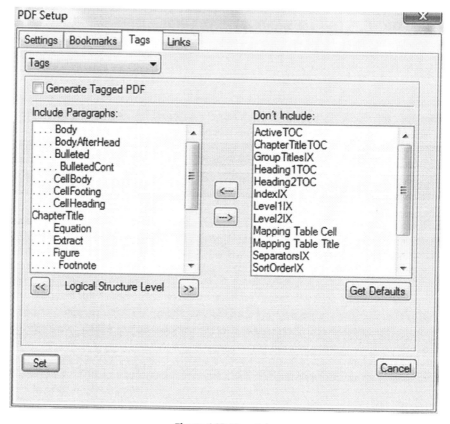

Figure 142: Tags tab

Links Tab

This tab enables you to create hyperlinks from one PDF file to another.

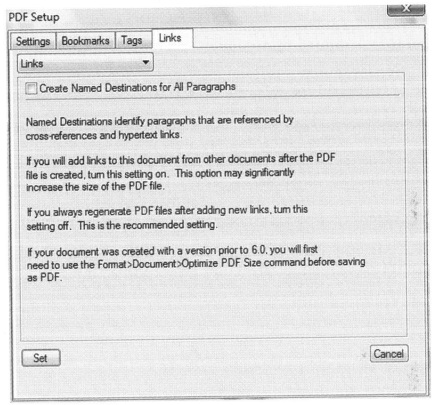

Figure 143: Links tab

You have three choices:

- Place a checkmark in front of *Create Named Destinations for All Paragraphs* to identify paragraphs that are referenced by cross-references or hyperlinks.
- Click **Set** to create the hyperlinks.
- Click **Cancel** to leave the tab without setting hyperlinks in your PDF file.

Because creating named destinations increases the size of your PDF file, you should avoid using this feature if possible.

After you've specified what options you want for your PDF file, click **Set** and FrameMaker will generate your file.

Experiment with converting some of the documents we used in previous chapters to PDF. It's easy to do and there are many advantages to publishing your documents as PDF.

Publishing as HTML

Converting your document to HTML allows you to publish your document on your company's intranet or Web site. Authors often use HyperText Markup Language (HTML) to create the documents that they publish in this manner. FrameMaker offers a number of ways to create these types of files. In this section, we'll look at the easiest way to create your HTML files by using FrameMaker's Save As feature. Creating HTML files this way generally is reserved for quick conversions of short documents. Using this method, however, doesn't allow you to control the appearance of the output, so you need to edit your documents carefully when you convert them using this method.

When you convert your files to HTML, FrameMaker uses mapping settings that are stored on the Reference Pages of your document. If you're creating an HTML file, the conversion settings are stored on the Reference Pages called *HTML* and *HTML (cont)*.

To save your document as HTML, follow these steps:

1. Open the document that you want to convert.

2. Click **File > Save As** on the menu bar. The Save Document dialog box opens.

3. In the File name field, type the name of the output file with the extension .htm or .html.

4. In the Save as type field, click the arrow at the end of the box, and then click **HTML (*htm).**

5. Click **Save**. If you see a message asking if you're sure you want to save the file in this format, click **Yes**. If you see any messages saying that a paragraph tag isn't in your catalog and asking if you want to add it, click **Yes**. FrameMaker will save your document as an HTML file.

The steps are much the same if you save a book as an HTML file. However, FrameMaker won't automatically save the document files as separate documents in the HTML file. To save a book as an HTML file, follow these steps:

1. Open the book file you want to save as HTML.

2. Click **File > Save as** on the menu bar and select HTML as the *Save as type*.

3. In the File name field, type the name of the output file with the extension .htm or .html.

4. Click **Save**. If you see a message asking if you are sure you want to save the file in this format, click **Yes**. If you see any messages saying that a paragraph tag isn't in your catalog and asking if you want to add it, click **Yes**. FrameMaker will save your book as an HTML file.

To view your HTML file, open it in your Web browser or open Windows Explore by right-clicking the Start button on your desktop, click **Explore**, and then locate the file. When you double-click the file name, the file will open in your Web browser.

Adding Hyperlinks

When you save your document as HTML, cross-reference links within your document become hyperlinks. If you want to create additional hyperlinks in your FrameMaker documents, apply them as follows, and then save your document again as HTML:

1. Open your document in FrameMaker, and then select the text that you want to be an active hyperlink.

2. Click **Special > Hypertext** on the menu bar. The Hypertext panel opens:

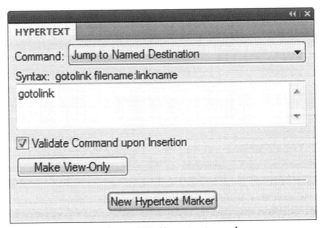

Figure 144: Hypertext panel

3. Select the appropriate option from the Command pull-down menu. For example, select *Go to URL*.

4. In the pane below the Command field, type the syntax for the link, such as *http://www.nonamebank.com/*.

5. Click **New Hypertext Marker**. FrameMaker will insert the hyperlink into your document. When you save your document as HTML, this link becomes active.

Making Changes to HTML Documents

Let's say that when you open your HTML document, you decide that you want to make some formatting changes. You can make some changes to your document by using the HTML Setup panel as follows:

1. Open the file that you're converting to HTML. Make sure the Reference Pages aren't displayed because this can cause file corruption.

2. Click **File > Utilities > HTML Setup** on the menu bar. The HTML Setup panel opens:

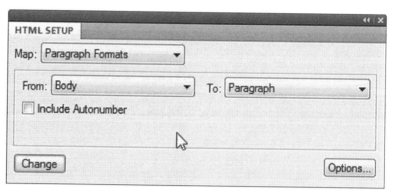

Figure 145: HTML Setup dialog box

3. In the Map field, click the arrow at the end of the box and select **Paragraph Formats** if it isn't already displayed in the box (this is the default).

4. The drop-down menu in the *From* field lists the paragraph tags in your document. To change the mappings (how these tags will be displayed in HTML), select a paragraph tag in the *From* field, and then select the mapping you want for it from the *To* drop-down menu.

   If you click a line of text in your document while the HTML Setup panel is open, the name of the paragraph tag is displayed in the From field and the default mapping for that tag is displayed in the To field. Most of the time, you'll probably accept the default. For those that you want to change, here's a guide:

   - **Heading** (Auto Level)
     Use this for headings in your document. Heading levels are determined by a mapping table on the Reference Pages.

   - **Paragraph**
     Use this for body text in your document.

   - **Preformatted Text**
     Use this for monospace text, such as code examples.

   - **Address**
     Use this for address blocks.

- **Block Quote**
  Use this to indent a quote in your HTML document.

- **List Item**
  Use this for paragraphs that have bulleted or numbered lists.

- **List Item (Continued)**
  Use this for lists that are continued to a different page

- **Data Term**
  Use this when you're listing terms.

- **Data Definition**
  Use this when you're writing a definition.

- **Data Definition (Continued)**
  Use this to continue a paragraph in a definition.

- **Throw Away**
  Use this for paragraph that you want to delete from text in your HTML output.

5. As you modify the mappings of paragraph styles, you may notice that some mappings have additional options, such as *Start New* when you select the Headings mapping. Here's a guide to what options are available and when you would use them:

  - **Include Autonumber**
    This can be applied to all styles. If this is checked, the paragraph's autonumber is included with the output. If this isn't checked, paragraph autonumbering will be discarded.

  - **Start New, Linked Web Page**
    This can be applied to Heading (Auto Level) mapping styles. If this is checked, the selected paragraph tag starts a new Web page.

  - **List will be in a bulleted/numbered list field**
    This can be applied to the List Item and List Item

(Continued) mapping styles. This tells you that when you select this mapping style, FrameMaker automatically sets a bulleted or numbered list for list items.

- **Nest List at Depth field**
  This can be applied to the List Item and List Item (Continued) mapping styles. When you selected the corresponding mapping style, this allows you to set the indentation level of the list item.

6. When you're finished making changes, click **Change**, and then re-save your document as an HTML file.

Setting Up Character Tag Mappings

In addition to mapping your paragraph tags in the HTML Setup panel, you can set up character tag mappings. This works the same as with the paragraph tag mappings. With the file open that you want to convert to HTML, open the HTML Setup panel, and then select **Character Formats** from the Map drop-down list.

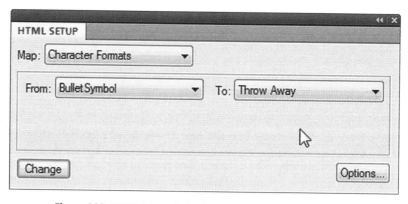

Figure 146: HTML Setup dialog box to map Character formats

The From drop-down menu then will include all of the character tags that are in your document. Select a character tag from the drop-down menu, and then go to the To field and select the mapping you want for it. Your options are as follows:

- **Blink (Netscape)**
  Use this when you want your text to blink after being converted to HTML.

- **Citation**
  Use this to create inline citations or quotes.

- **Code**
  This converts the text to a monospace font and often is used to format programming commands in text.

- **Definition**
  Use this for inline definitions.

- **Emphasis**
  Use this for emphasized text.

- **Keyboard**
  Use this for text that you want people to type, such as code.

- **Language (Intl)**

- **Sample**
  This is another monospace typeface.

- **Short quotation (Intl.)**
  Use this for inline quotes.

- **Span** (CSS)
  Use this to reference formatting that is in a Cascading Style Sheet (CSS) file.

- **Strong Emphasis**
  Use this when you want to emphasize something very strongly.

- **Typewriter**
  This changes the text to a monospace typeface.

- **Variable**
  Use this for text that contains variables in programming code.

- **Plain Text**
  This produces text that doesn't have any additional formatting.

- **Throw Away**
  Use this to for text that has character tags applied to it, but you want to eliminate from your online document.

Mapping Cross-References

Since cross-references usually refer to page numbers in a document, they become meaningless in HTML output. When you save your document as an HTML file, these cross-references typically are mapped by default to a cross-reference conversion macro called *See also* that changes the page-number references to paragraph references and also changes the cross-references to hyperlinks.

If you want to change these mappings, make sure that your Reference Pages aren't displayed in the original document, and then open the HTML Setup panel. This time, however, select **Cross-Reference Formats** from the drop-down menu in the Map field.

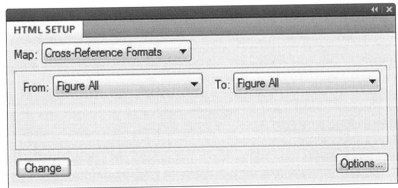

Figure 147: HTML Setup with mapping for Cross-Reference Formats

Notice that now a list of the cross-reference formats appears in the drop-down menu in the From field. For each cross-reference format, select one of the following cross-reference mapping styles from the To drop-down list:

- **Figure All**
  When you associate this with a cross-reference format, it displays the figure number and title in the HTML output.

- **Figure Number**
  When you associate this with a cross-reference format, it displays only the figure number in the HTML output.

- **Heading**
  This will display the paragraph text only and is appropriate for many online references.

- **See Also**
  This displays the paragraph text with the word *See* in front of it.

- **Table All**
  This displays the table number and title.

- **Table Number**
  This displays only the table number.

- **Original Cross-Reference Format**
  This processes the cross-reference without changing the format.

- **Throw Away**
  This eliminates the cross-reference from the converted file.

As with the other procedures, when you've finished making your changes, click **Change**, close the HTML Setup panel, and then save your document as an HTML file.

Converting Graphics

Finally, you need to be concerned about how your graphics will display in your HTML output. You can convert the graphics in your document to one of three formats: GIF, JPEG, or PNG. To specify how FrameMaker will convert your graphics, follow these steps:

1. With your document open and your Reference Pages not displayed, click **File > Utilities > HTML**. The HTML Setup panel box opens.

2. Click **Options**. The HTML Options dialog box opens:

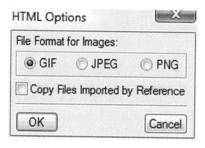

Figure 148: HTML Options dialog box

3. Choose which format you want for your graphics in the File Format for Images area of the dialog box.

4. If you've imported your graphics by reference and want to copy them in your document, place a checkmark in front of **Copy Files**

Imported by Reference. This makes sense because your referenced files may not be accessible on the Internet.

5. Click **OK**, and then close all dialog boxes and panels and save your document as an HTML file.

As you become more proficient with FrameMaker, you'll probably find that the options offered on the HTML Setup dialog box will be all you need to create great-looking HTML output.

Frequently Asked Questions

Q: *When I convert my documents to PDF, the extra space around the boundaries and registration marks are eliminated. How can I prevent this from happening?*

A: Acrobat Distiller does this automatically when it converts your file to PDF. To prevent this from happening, increase the page size in the PDF Setup dialog box and uncheck the Generate Acrobat Data option in the print dialog box as follows:

1. Open the Print dialog box, and then click **Western** or **Tombo** in the Registration Marks drop-down list.

2. Click **PDF Setup**. The PDF Setup dialog box opens.

3. Click the **Settings** tab, and then click the type of registration marks you want from the Registration Marks drop-down list.

4. In the Page Size section, add an inch or so to the height and width of the page.

This page is intentionally left blank.

Templates

Learn the basics of creating templates that enable you to create the same types of documents more easily and consistently.

Templates help you be more productive and create your documentation more easily. If you use templates, you won't have to reconstruct the formatting when you create new documents of the same type. If you want certain text or graphics to be in a specific type of document, you can put these in your template and never have to worry again about finding these things when you create a new document. They'll already be there when you open a new document based on this template.

Finally, templates help teams of writers create documents that have the same look and feel. This is especially useful when you have several writers working on the same documentation. Not only do templates make it easier for all writers to produce documentation that looks the same, templates also help less experienced writers be more productive more quickly.

Templates sometimes get a bad rap. People often think that a template is going to take away their creativity and force them to follow a format that they may not like.

While this may be true to a certain extent, there are many positives to using templates. First, templates help many people create documents or sections of a document that have the same look and feel. Readers won't be distracted by different ideas about formatting a document.

Second, templates take a while to create, but when they're done, they can save writers a great deal of time.

But what is a template? Templates provide a pattern for the type of document being written. Templates generally have defined paragraph tags that establish what typefaces and fonts will be used in the document, cross-reference formats for authors to use, and pre-set margins and line spacings. Templates also can include the information to be displayed in the headers and footers, how your tables of contents and indexes will be formatted, and more. Templates also can already contain the following:

- Graphics and text that you want to appear in all documents of this type. (This is called *boilerplate*. A good example of boilerplate is a legal notice.)
- Design elements, such as borders and columns
- Master Pages that can be applied to different types of pages.

A good template should make it easier for people to write the text for the document. This means that a template maker needs to be able to foresee many different ways that an author might need to format text in documents of this type. For example, someone might need to insert a worksheet or graphic on a page that has a landscape orientation while the other pages in the document have a portrait orientation. If individual authors had to create the Master Page to accommodate this type of orientation, there could be as many variations of the landscape page as there are authors writing the documentation. This is something that you want to avoid, so you would include a landscape Master Page that people could use if needed.

In FrameMaker, documents can be templates. This means that if you have a document that you think is well-formatted and has many elements that you want in a document of this type, you can save that document in the Templates folder as you did in Chapter 1.

When you open a template, you should save your document with a different name so the template itself remains the same as it was before you opened it. This helps ensure that future documents based on a particular template will have all of the elements needed to write those documents.

If you want to use the same information or graphics in each document of a certain type, you can save it in your template so that it's already there when you start a new document based upon that template.

Many students ask how to create templates. You create them by doing the things you've already learned how to do here, such as setting page sizes and orientation, creating paragraph and character tags, creating table formats, etc. The first templates you make probably will be relatively simple. As you learn more about FrameMaker's capabilities, your templates will become more and more sophisticated and complex. Even after you become an expert FrameMaker template maker, however, the idea of creating a template can be daunting. Let's see if we can make it seem easier.

Planning a New Template

Before you start developing a new template, you should always check the templates that have already been developed by FrameMaker. You'll find these by clicking **File > New > Document** on the menu bar. When the New dialog box opens, be sure that *Templates* is displayed in the Look in box. If so, the large pane in the middle of the dialog box will display the folders that hold the templates that are installed on your computer. See if there is one that you can modify to suit your needs. It's far easier and quicker to "tweak" an existing template than to start one from scratch.

If you don't see anything that will meet your needs, you may need to create a new template. It's easier to create a template if you have a clear picture of what you need. Here are some questions you need to answer:

1. What type of documents will be written using this template? Will they be instructional documents, manuals, quick reference guides, books, etc.?

2. Who will be the audience for these documents? Employees? Students? Managers? Professionals in a specific community? Young people who respond better to documents with many colorful graphics? Older people who appreciate documents that use larger type and lots of white space?

3. Why will people read the documents that will be written using this template? Will they be reading these documents to learn how to do specific tasks (and thereby need step-by-step instructions, lots of graphics, and special formats for cautions, warnings, and notes)? Will the documents written using this template be published commercially and therefore need to follow more commercial formatting standards? Try to be as specific as possible about why people will be reading the documents based on the template you're creating.

4. What conditions will readers be in when they read documents based on your template? Will they likely be reading those documents in low-light conditions? If so, they will appreciate larger type and more white space. Will they be using the documents based on this template in small spaces, such as a Customer Service Representative with only a few inches of desk space? If so, you should scale down the page size so it will fit more easily on the end users' desks.

5. Who will use your template? Are the writers highly skilled in using FrameMaker or are they inexperienced? The level of experience the writers have with FrameMaker will affect the complexity of the template you develop. If there's a range of

skills amongst the writers (from inexperienced to highly experienced), opt to design the template for the least-experienced writers so everyone can be more productive right away.

6. Are there any special formatting guidelines that you should follow? For example, do you have to use certain page numbering styles or place certain elements in the headers and footers? Do you have to use certain typefaces in your document?

7. In addition to the right and left Master Pages that can be created when you open a new document in FrameMaker, what other types of Master Pages do you need in your template? Will you need a Master Page for the cover of the document? Different Master Pages for the front matter? A different Master Page for the first page of sections or chapters? If most of your pages will have a portrait orientation, is there a chance that some writers may need to add some pages with landscape orientation? Even if it's a remote possibility, it's best to try to think of all of the different types of pages writers may create when they are writing documents based on your template, and then create Master Pages that they can apply as needed.

8. What kinds of heading styles will you use in your document? Will headings be outline numbered or plain? Will you use sideheads? Is it likely that there will be certain words in the documents based on your template that need to be formatted differently than other text (such as examples of lines of code)?

9. How will the documents based on this template be published? Will they be printed on paper, as PDFs, online, or another format?

10. Will documents based on this template be translated into other languages?

Character and Paragraph Tags

When you're developing character and paragraph tags to be used with your templates, look first at the tags that have already been created. See if you can use them as they are, or use them with some small modifications. It's generally easier to modify character and paragraph tags than to create new ones.

When you build the catalogs for your character and paragraph tags for your template, don't forget that you can include only the tags you want people to use in documents based on your template. This is one way that you can help authors be more consistent in how they create their documents.

Some common paragraph tags that you'll probably create for your templates include the following:

- Body text
- Headings (different levels)
- Bulleted lists
- Numbered lists
- Lettered lists
- Indented lists of the types above
- Notes, cautions, warnings, and footnotes
- Figure and table labels
- Table Headings and titles
- Table text
- Cover page titles
- Chapter titles
- Headers
- Footers
- Page numbers
- Callouts
- Comments

Some typical character tags that you can create for your templates may include the following:

- Bold emphasis
- Small caps
- Superscript
- Subscript
- Code (using a monospace typeface)
- Special bullet styles
- Colors
- Tags that incorporate graphics (such as a note graphic for a note paragraph)

You may not use all of these tags in your templates, or you may use tags that aren't listed here. These simply are ideas to help you get started.

Controlling Pagination with Paragraph Tags

As you learned when we reviewed the properties of the Pagination tab of the Paragraph Designer, you can set the pagination properties when creating your paragraph tags as follows:

- **Next Pgf**
  The paragraph to which this property is applied will stay with the paragraph following it. This is a good property to use for heading paragraph tags because it will prevent the heading from being separated from the text that is related to it.

- **Previous Pgf**
  The paragraph to which this property is applied will stay with the paragraph preceding it. If you use this property and the paragraph breaks to a new page, it will pull the paragraph preceding it to the new page too.

- **Widow/Orphan Lines**
  If you apply this property to your paragraph tag, you can set how many lines in a paragraph can be left at the bottom or top of a page when the page breaks in the paragraph. This is a good setting to apply to your body paragraph tags.

Experiment with the settings on this tab and see what will work best for the type of document template you're creating.

Paragraph and Character Tag Names

The names you give your tags also are very important in helping the people who use your templates. We talked briefly about giving your tags names in Chapter 3, but when you're developing templates that other people will use, you have to give even more thought to the names of your paragraph tags in particular.

There are two logical ways you can name your paragraph tags: You can name them according to their physical characteristics or you can name them according to the functions they serve in your document.

For example, you can name a paragraph tag *10ptArial*, which is a good description of the physical characteristics of the text to which this tag might be applied. Or you can name the same paragraph tag *BodyText*, which is a good description to indicate that you intend the text to which this tag is applied to function as body text in the document.

If we name our paragraph tags according to the function rather than appearance, it will be easier for the people using our templates to understand how we want the tags to be used.

A second advantage to naming tags according to function is that this method tends to group paragraph tags that are used in similar ways. For example, if you name your heading paragraph tags *Heading1, Heading2, Heading3*, etc., they will be grouped together in the Paragraph Catalog and therefore will be easier to find than if you had named them *18ptTRBF, 14ptCALITAL, 10ptBulBT*, etc.

Here are some other tips about naming tags that can save you time and make your templates more efficient:

- In addition to giving your tags names that describe their functions as much as possible, try to give them generic names so you can easily add them to other templates that you build. You can change the name of a tag, of course, but you'll save steps if you name a tag *BlockText* rather than *ProposalBlockText*. (By the way, using the same tag names for the same functions in different templates also helps writers learn how to use different templates more quickly and make fewer mistakes in formatting.)

- If your template will be used primarily to format documents converted from another application (for example, Microsoft Word), use tag names that are used by the other applications. For example, Microsoft Word's paragraph styles are very similar to FrameMaker's paragraph tags.

- Similarly, if your FrameMaker documents will be converted to HTML, XML, etc., give your tags names that are commonly used in those environments.

- Because FrameMaker's tag names are case sensitive, set standards for naming conventions. Decide when you will capitalize tag names and use underscores. Also, remember that even though FrameMaker allows you to use spaces in your tag names, it's recommended that you try to avoid that as much as possible.

Cross-Reference Formats

As you learned in the chapter about creating cross-references, you can develop formats to use when inserting cross-references, such as *"See X on page X,"* *"Go to X,"* etc.

By including pre-built formats for cross-references in your templates, you will help writers save time and be more consistent in their writing, especially if they are working in teams or on documents that are rewritten over time.

To determine what formats to create, first check to see if your company has a style guide that includes information about the preferred way to word cross-references. If your company's style guide doesn't mention this (or if your company doesn't have a style guide), review documents that have been written in the past at your company and see if there is a certain style that you like.

When you're developing cross-reference formats, try to think of the different formats writers will need. You might want to develop cross-reference formats that can be used for references to the following:

- Chapters
- Appendices
- Headings
- Figures
- Tables
- Footnotes

Here are some tips for creating useful cross-reference formats:

- It's generally better to create short cross-reference formats than long ones. For example, you could create one that says, "If you want additional information, please see XXXX on page X," or you could create one that says, "See XXXX on page X." If a writer has problems with space or lines breaking across pages, the shorter cross-reference format will be appreciated.

- Use character tags in your cross-reference formats to ensure that the text will be formatted correctly.

- Include simple cross-reference formats as well as more complex ones. For example, cross-reference formats that say, "See page X" or "Go to page X" can be some of the most useful ones for the people using your template.

Tables

When developing templates, it's easy to forget to provide formats for the tables writers might use in their documents.

As you know, tables organize information into rows and columns by category and type. They simplify access to information and can accurately present many quantitative values at one time.

The people using your templates probably will use tables when they need to do the following:

- Present a large amount of detailed information in a small space

- Support detailed, item-to-item comparisons

- Show individual data values precisely

- Simplify access to individual data values.

In addition to rows and columns, tables can contain the following parts:

- Column headings

- Column spanners

- Field spanners

- Stubs

- Stub heads

- Row headings

Column Headings

Column headings are placed in the row above the actual data fields. They label dependent variables, while row headings label independent variables. Column headings should describe all members of the column below them and be unique to that column. Capitalize column headings in the same manner as the table title.

The standard practice is to center one-line column headings and left-justify longer column headings, but you can change that if you wish. Just be consistent. Avoid diagonal headings as much as possible. If a heading is a lead-in phrase completed by the table entry (as in "if/then" tables), end the column heading with an ellipsis.

Column Spanners

Column spanners are headings that label two or more column heads. They also are called *decked heads*. Include column spanners only in horizontally ruled tables. Here is an example of column spanners:

	Flow		Pressure		
	Specified	Actual	Specified	Actual	← Column Spanners / ← Column Headers

Field Spanners

Field spanners are placed in the body of the table in the cells below the column headings and to the right of the row headings. Field spanners cut across all columns of the field and contain a heading that applies to all items below them. Field spanners are also called *cut-in heads*. Here's an example of a table with a field spanner:

	Flow		Pressure		
	Specified	Actual	Specified	Actual	
	Model 8712				← Field
					Spanner

The top field spanner should be placed immediately below the column headings, never above. Don't use a single field spanner in a table and do not extend any field spanner into the stub column (the column at the farthest-left side of the table). Since field spanners essentially start the table all over again for another category of data, repeat the stub headings beneath each field spanner.

Consider using field spanners when you have separate tables, each with the same column headings and stub headings. Field spanners enable people to compare the information in these tables more easily.

Stubs

The stub is the left-most column of a table. It lists the items about which information is provided in the columns to the right.

The stub heading is the title of the stub column. It describes the row headings listed in the stub, as in the following example:

Property Variables	Flow		Pressure	
	Specified	Actual	Specified	Actual
Model 8712				

Stub Heading →

Row Headings

Row headings describe independent variables or categories. They should clearly and concisely label the rows of the table, be unique, and apply to all items in the row. Row headings should be short and left-justified. Capitalize the first word, proper nouns, and proper adjectives only. Do not place a period at the end of row headings.

General Rules about Tables

Some general things to keep in mind when you're designing table formats and paragraph styles are the following:

- Spell out all titles, labels, and notes. Abbreviate only where necessary. If you must abbreviate, only use common abbreviations, such as those for units of measurement.

- Express numbers in the same format. If you use decimal points in a table, use the same number of decimal points in all numbers in that table.

- In long columns of numbers, consider inserting a blank line every five to ten rows to make it easier for your readers to follow.

- If your tables will be scanned, design column and row headings for scanning by using a sans serif typeface in a size that will scan well.

Color

Companies often have specific colors that they use to brand themselves. You can add color to paragraph and character tags, graphical elements, lines, etc. to make the documents based on your template more interesting.

FrameMaker enables you to use different color models and libraries to create the colors you want in your document. To determine which is best for your project, follow these guidelines:

- If the documents written using your template will mostly be read online, use the RGB (Red, Green, Blue) or HLS (Hue, Lightness, Saturation) color model.

- If the documents written using your template will mostly be printed by commercial printers, use the CMYK (Cyan, Magenta, Yellow, and Black) color model.

- If the documents written using your template will mostly be printed by commercial printers, contact the printer and find out what color library (Crayon, Pantone, DIC, etc.) he or she uses and the color your company is using from that library.

You can easily add colors to FrameMaker's color catalog that match your company's colors by doing the following:

1. While working in your template, click **View > Color > Definitions** on the menu bar. The Color Definitions dialog box opens.

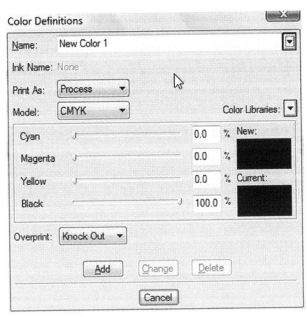

Figure 149: Color Definitions Dialog box

2. Type a name for the color in the Name box.
3. Select how the color will be printed by clicking the arrow at the Print As field. Your options are:

   - Tint
   - Spot
   - Process
   - Don't Print

4. If you will be publishing your document online or printing it from a local printer, select the color model you want to use, and then define the color to achieve what you want by moving the sliders

beneath the Model field (changes with the model chosen). Click **Add** to create the new color.

5. If a commercial printer will be printing the documents based on your template, click the arrow button next to Color Libraries to select the color library your printer uses. Locate the color your printer said he or she uses, select it, and then click **Done**.

A Checklist for Building Templates

Here are things to consider when building templates. You may not need to do all of these things in your template.

☐ Check to see if there is an existing template or document that you can base your template on.

☐ Set up the Right and Left Master Pages if your template will be double-sided.

☐ Determine the need for custom Master Pages (such as pages for the first page of chapters, landscape pages for large graphics, etc.) and create them.

☐ Set up the way the pages will be numbered.

☐ Add headers, footers, background text, and/or graphics to Master Pages.

☐ Define the Document Properties, including numbering, footnotes, text options, PDF setup, etc.

☐ Create paragraph and character tags. Delete tags in the catalogs that won't be used in documents based on this template.

☐ Create table formats. Delete formats in the catalog that won't be used in documents based on this template.

☐ Create custom colors.

☐ Create cross-reference formats. Delete formats that won't be used in documents based on this template.

☐ Create tags and settings for conditional text. Delete formats that won't be used in documents based on this template.

☐ Create user variables.

☐ Create equation definitions if needed.

☐ Define File and View Preferences.

☐ Save any graphics on the Reference Pages you want to appear in notes, warnings, cautions, or for other uses.

☐ Create a style guide for your template.

☐ Test the template, and then ask users to test it too.

☐ Distribute the template.

The Envelope Template

The easiest way to learn how to create templates is to look at what you already have on your computer. FrameMaker includes a number of templates for you to use. They're listed in the large pane on the New dialog box. You also can learn more about some of them by looking at the Standard Templates dialog box.

FrameMaker's envelope template is a good one to look at first because it only has a few components.

Let's take a closer look at this template by doing the following:

1. Click **File > New > Document** on the menu bar to open the New dialog box.

2. Be sure that **Templates** is listed in the Look in box, and then double-click the Business folder in the large pane in the middle of the dialog box.

Figure 150: New dialog box with Business folder selected

3. Double-click the Envelope file to open a document based on this template.

Figure 151: New dialog box with Envelope template selected

The most obvious thing about the Envelope document is its size. If your rulers are turned on (**View > Rulers**), you'll see that the envelope is 9.5 inches wide (24.13 cm) and a little more than 4 inches tall (10 cm). Since the rulers don't tell you exactly how tall this document is, click **Format > Page Layout > Page Size**. The Page Size dialog box opens with the exact measurements of the envelope noted.

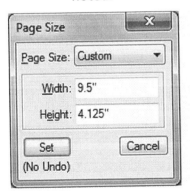

Figure 152: Page size of the envelope in inches and centimeters

Next, look at the area where there is text. To be sure that you're looking at the Body Page, click **View** on the menu bar and make sure there's a checkmark in front of Body Pages.

Try to place your cursor on the line that says, "Your Company Name." You won't be able to do so. That's because those words and the lines following it, plus the graphics behind the words are in a ***background frame***. We talked about background frames in Chapter 2 when we talked about header and footer frames that are placed on Master Pages. As you may recall, you can only add or modify text in these frames while you're looking at the Master Pages. Let's look at the Master Page for this template now by clicking **View > Master Pages** on the menu bar.

Hold down the CTRL key and click on different boxes you see on the Master Page. There are four text frames and one anchored frame on this page as follows. (I've outlined the different frames and labeled them to make it easier for you to see them):

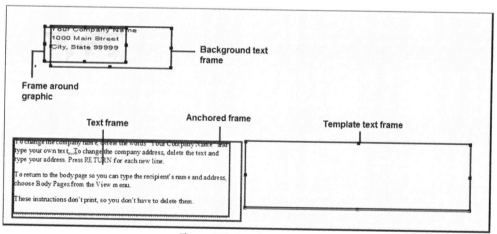

Figure 153: Envelope Master Page

Select each of these and examine them a bit. For example, if you select the frame around the graphic (hold down your CTRL key while clicking until you find the frame), and then open the Object Properties dialog box (**Graphics > Object Properties** on the menu bar), you'll discover that the graphic behind the return address actually is composed of several individual graphics that have been grouped and that the very light gray color actually is 5 percent black tint.

When you select the text frame that's inside of the anchored frame, you'll see that it isn't linked to any text flow. If you select the anchored frame, you'll see that its anchoring position is outside of any text frame, meaning that it isn't a part of any text flow. Because of this, the designer of the template was able to write instructions for changing the text in the background frame that holds the company's return address and know that those instructions wouldn't appear on the Body Page.

If you don't remember the difference between background frames and template text frames, you can review them in Chapter 2. Basically, template text frames are the ones that you type in on the Body Pages and the background frames are the ones that you type In on the Master Pages so that information will be displayed on all of the Body Pages to which those Master Pages are applied. You designate whether a frame is going to be a background frame or a template frame after you draw it with the Text Frame tool from the Tools palette. After you draw the frame, the Add New Text Frame dialog box opens and you select whether this frame will be a background frame or a template frame. One of the traits of a template frame is that when you first open the document, your cursor will already be on the first line of the document.

Take a few moments to examine the Master and Body Pages of this template. Check the paragraph tags that are used and become familiar with how the graphic was created. After you've finished, close the envelope document without saving it, and then create a template based on this one by doing the following:

1. Click **File > New > Document** on the menu bar.
2. Select **Custom** for the page size.
3. When the Custom Blank Paper dialog box opens, enter the dimensions of the envelope template you're creating.

4. Take what you learned by examining the existing envelope template and create an envelope template for yourself or your company. If possible, design your template for envelopes of different sizes. Try incorporating some graphics with text running over them. Be sure to place your template text frame where you want people who use this template to type the name and address of the parties to whom they are sending this envelope.

Don't limit yourself to the envelope template. Explore the other templates that FrameMaker has included for unstructured documents. Look at the different details of them and then see if you can figure out why certain things were done. Take note of features that you think you would like to use in templates that you create. Check the Standard Templates dialog box and see if there are any notes there about the templates you're examining. Modify any of the templates that you want to use for your personal use. Save your templates in the Templates folder so they'll be displayed when you open the New dialog box, or save them in a different folder, and then navigate to the folder you chose when you open the New dialog box. The choice is yours!

This page is intentionally left blank.

This page is intentionally left blank.

Afterword

This concludes this introduction to the basics of FrameMaker 10 for Windows. There's much more that you can learn, and the more skilled you become, the more your skills will be in demand. You see, while FrameMaker is the "gold standard" for technical writers, people who know how to use it and use it well are rare. Those who take the time to learn its complexities and can show their expertise in using it are in demand by many large companies and government agencies.

When you run into a problem using FrameMaker, be sure to check the Help files. People often forget to look there first! FrameMaker's Help files are set up a little differently than you may be accustomed to seeing. I find the Index useful for finding out more about a topic. When you click a subject, you'll find that FrameMaker provides a lot of information about it plus steps for completing tasks and links to related subjects.

Whatever you do, don't become discouraged when you're learning to use FrameMaker. It has a steep learning curve, and it will take time for you to become proficient with it. If you're having trouble performing a certain task, sometimes the best thing to do is to close the document without saving it, reopen it, and then try again. Most of all, try not to overcomplicate FrameMaker. Many of its features and procedures are much simpler than they appear when you first try them.

I hope this information on FrameMaker has been helpful and that this book helps you in your career!

Janet

This page is intentionally left blank.

Appendix A: Glossary

baseline
The imaginary or real line upon which most letters "sit."

boilerplate
Text, graphics, or other information that is used, usually verbatim, in all documents of the same type. Legal notices are a good example of boilerplate.

Boolean operators
The logic that Boolean operators are based on was developed by George Boole in the mid-1800s. He identified several "gates" that could be used to sort information. These gates and related elements of the logic form the basis for much that we do with computers today. When you're sorting FrameMaker's condition tags, you can use three of these "gates" (called operators): AND, OR, and NOT.

building block
Codes that are used to enable FrameMaker to insert specified types of text, such as dates in variables, page numbers and text references in cross-references, and numbering schemes in autonumbered text.

change bar
A vertical line that's placed in the margin where changes are made when you're in the editing mode.

character tag
A set of formatting characteristics that are set and given a name that are applied to a single word or a few words within a paragraph without changing the formatting of the rest of the paragraph. *Emphasis* is an example of a character tag.

CMYK

Cyan, Magenta, Yellow, and Black. This is the color model used in 4-color printing, such as commercial magazines.

collate

The process of assembling pages in the correct order in printed documentation. Can be used to indicate the order in which pages will be printed on a printer that's attached to the computer.

DITA

Darwin Information Typing Architecture. This is a method of creating "information-type" modules that can be used in different delivery methods. This is an XML-based architecture style of documentation.

double-sided

Printed on both sides of the page. Also called *duplexing.*

feather

A feature that first adds space between paragraphs, up to a limit that you preset, and then adds more space between lines, up to another preset limit. FrameMaker doesn't feather the text in a text frame in which text runs around graphics.

fixed-width type

This means that the space allotted on the page for letters is the same for all letters. "Skinny" letters, such as "i" and "l" are given the same amount of space as "fat" letters such as "M" and "W." *See also proportional type.*

font

In professional typography circles, a font is part of a typeface with specific characteristics, such as boldface, italic, or size of the typeface. Today, the word "font" often is used to mean the same thing as "typeface."

FrameImage	This is a format for imported raster images for all three platforms you could use in early FrameMaker versions. The format saves a copy of the image and adds to the size of the file. It's rarely used today.
gravity	A feature that makes objects be attracted to each other.
handles	Small boxes that are displayed around an object or frame when you select it.
HTML	*Hyper Text Markup Language*. The programming language used to create many Web pages.
HTTP	*HyperText Transfer Protocol*. A networking protocol that enables information to be distributed across the World Wide Web. (WWW).
kern	The process of adjusting the space between letters in proportional typefaces. When kerning is turned on, "skinny" letters have less space allotted to them on the page than "fat" letters. This results in a more professional looking document.
landscape	A document that is wider across the top and bottom than it is long across the sides.
leading	Pronounced *ledding*. A measure of the vertical space between lines. It's measured from the baseline of one line to the baseline of the next line.

mapping Defining how elements in one version of FrameMaker output will be displayed in other versions of output. A good example is mapping how formatting characteristics in printed FrameMaker documents will be displayed in HTML versions of the same document.

MIF *Maker Interchange Format.* A group of ASCII statements that create a text file that includes all of the text, graphics, formatting, and layout elements that Adobe® FrameMaker® understands. This format allows FrameMaker and other applications to exchange information while preserving graphics, document content, and format and is often used to save files in earlier versions of FrameMaker so they can be opened in later versions.

orphan A printing term for the first line of a paragraph isolated at the bottom of a page.

overline A line that's placed over the text.

override Formatting that you manually apply that is different from and overrides the defined settings.

panels Modified dialog boxes that can be docked in your workspace. A part of the new user interface introduced in FrameMaker 9.

paragraph tag A set of formatting characteristics that are defined and given a name so they can be applied at one time to paragraphs in documents.

PDF   *Portable Document Format.* A file format developed in 1993 by Adobe Systems Inc. to enable users to view documents independently of application, hardware, or operating system used to create it.

Pgf   *Paragraph.*

pods   Modified dialog boxes that can be docked in your workspace. A part of the new user interface introduced in FrameMaker 9.

portrait   A document that is longer along the sides than it is wide across the top and bottom.

poster   The image that is displayed in your document to indicate a SWF media file.

proportional type   Typefaces that adjust the amount of space around letters to the width of those letters. Most typefaces are proportional. *See also fixed-width type.*

RGB   *Red, Green, and Blue.* This is the color model usually used to display colors on a computer.

Rubi text   Small characters that appear above regular text in Asian text.

run-in head   A heading that starts on the same line as the first line of a paragraph and is a part of that paragraph.

screen tip

A message that appears when you move your mouse over an element on your screen. The message usually tells you what that element is or how to use it.

side head

A heading that is inserted in a left column on a page with its associated text being added in the adjacent right column.

strikethrough

A line that is placed through the text.

tags

Sets of formatting characteristics that you use to change the look of your text.

template

A pattern for the type of document being written. Templates generally have defined paragraph tags that establish what typefaces and fonts will be used in the document, cross-reference formats for authors to use, and preset margins and line spacings. Templates also can include the information to be displayed in the headers and footers, how your tables of content and indexes will be formatted, and more.

typeface

A typeface is a set of letters, characters, punctuation marks, and symbols that have a similar design. Some popular typefaces include Arial, Helvetica, Times Roman, and Verdana. Today, the word "font" is often used interchangeably with the word "typeface." This is incorrect by typography definitions. *See font.*

UI

User Interface. Traditionally, user interface has referred to the way users interact with machinery. Today, more and more, the term is used in the same manner as graphical user interface (GUI) to describe the screens that users use to interact with computers.

UNIX
An operating system (OS) developed in the late 1960s at Bell Labs. There are many variations of this OS. UNIX operating systems are used in servers, workstations, and mobile devices.

WebDAV
Web-based Distributed Authoring and Versioning. A protocol that enables people to read and write documents on the World Wide Web (WWW). It provides a framework for people to create, change, and move documents on a server.

widow
A printing term for a single word or a few words at the end of a paragraph that are printed at the top of the next page.

WYSIWYG
What You See Is What You Get.

This page is intentionally left blank.

Appendix B: A Short History of FrameMaker

In the 1980s, a mathematics student named Charles Corfield wrote a WYSIWYG (*What You See Is What You Get*) document editor to be used on Sun 2 workstations. Until that time, such software didn't exist to be run on a UNIX platform. A salesman for Sun Microsystems saw the prototype version of FrameMaker and asked Corfield if Sun could use it for demonstration software on their workstations. Since Sun lacked commercial applications to showcase its workstations' graphics capabilities during those early days, FrameMaker received plenty of exposure in the UNIX workstation arena.

Steve Kirsch, who had started and sold a successful company called Mouse Systems, thought FrameMaker had potential in the marketplace. Kirsch contacted Corfield, and along with David Murray and Vickie Blakeslee, the four started the Frame Technology Corporation.

FrameMaker was a popular technical writing tool on the UNIX platform, and the company was an early success. Desktop publishing was becoming popular with Macintosh users around this time, so the company developed a version of FrameMaker to run on the Mac.

Several companies began producing UNIX workstations in the early 1990s, and all of the new entries to the marketplace wanted FrameMaker on their machines. Frame Technology Corporation received funding from numerous companies to produce an Original Equipment Manufacturer (OEM) version of FrameMaker for their UNIX boxes. At the height of its popularity, FrameMaker ran on more than 13 different versions of UNIX.

The company later developed a version of FrameMaker for Microsoft Windows. Interestingly, this was when the company began to lose money. When its market focus was professional users writing large, highly technical publications, FrameMaker could charge up to $2,500 for each license. To compete with other desktop publishing applications that ran on Windows, however, FrameMaker had to drop its price to $500. The program was too difficult for the average home computer user, however, and the price drop for the Windows version undermined FrameMaker's established customer base of non-Windows users.

In the 1990s, the company was sold to Adobe Systems, which once again positioned FrameMaker as a tool for professional technical writers. The strategy worked, and FrameMaker regained its popularity. Today, it's widely used by technical writers around the world.

Appendix C: Picas and Points

Picas (pronounced *pie-kuhs*) and points are units of measurement used in typography. They were developed by the printing industry to provide a more precise way of measuring typographical elements (typefaces, formatting layouts, etc.) than other methods of measurement.

In the United States, a pica is $1/6^{th}$ of an inch (0.166033 inch), or it may be easier to remember that there are six picas in a United States inch.

There are two other interpretations of a pica. One is the French pica of 12 Didot points (also called cicero) that is about 0.177 inch; and the other is a computer pica that is 0.166 inch.

Just to keep us on our toes, there's one other use of the word "pica" in reference to typographic measurements: When you're talking about typewriters (not computers or typesetting conventions), the word "pica" is meant to denote a size of characters that equals 10 characters per line (horizontal) inch. Since we're not talking about typewriters here, this definition is provided simply for interest.

You may be more familiar with points than picas. Points are the smallest unit of measurement in typography. We often use points to define how wide a line will be (as in 1pt. line) or the size of the typeface font we want to use and the distance between lines of type (as in 12pt. Times Roman with 13pt. leading, written as 12/13 Times Roman).

A point equals $1/12^{th}$ of a pica; therefore, there are 72 points in a United States inch.

This page is intentionally left blank.

Appendix D: Add Menu Options

This appendix lists the menu options for the Add menu of unstructured FrameMaker's book view. The Add menu is not included in the document-view menu. The options are listed in alphabetical order with shortcut keys (if applicable) and descriptions. Codes are as follows:

UB = Unstructured, Book view

<u>Shortcut keys</u>:

- Keys that are pressed one at a time are separated with commas.
- Keys that are pressed together are connected with a plus (+) sign.

Table 12: Add Menu Options and Shortcut Keys

CODE	Name	Navigation	Description
UB	FILES	Add > Files (ESC, f, f)	Opens the Add Files to Book dialog box. You also can add files to your book from the book window.
UB	FOLDER	Add > Folder	Adds a folder to your book file. You also can add folders to your book from the book window. Rename an added folder by right-clicking on it and the selecting **Rename** from the context menu.
UB	GROUP	Add > Group	Adds a group to your book file. You also can add a group to your book by pressing the Add Group icon on the book window. Rename an added group by right-clicking on it and the selecting **Rename** from the context menu.
UB	TABLE OF CONTENTS	Add > Table of Contents (ESC, t, o, c)	Opens the Set Up Table of Contents dialog box.
UB	LIST OF	Add > List of	Opens a submenu that lists several options of other types of lists that you can generate, such as figures, tables, paragraphs, markers, and references.
UB	Standard Index	Add > Standard Index	Opens the Set Up Standard Index dialog box.
UB	Index of	Add > Index of	Opens a submenu that lists several options for specific types of indices that you can generate, such as authors, subjects, markers, and references.

This page is intentionally left blank.

Appendix E: CMS Menu Options

This appendix lists the menu options for the CMS menu of unstructured FrameMaker's document or book views. The options are listed in alphabetical order with shortcut keys (if applicable) and descriptions. Codes are as follows:

UD = Unstructured, Document view

UB = Unstructured, Book view

Shortcut keys:

- Keys that are pressed one at a time are separated with commas.
- Keys that are pressed together are connected with a plus (+) sign.

Table 13: CMS Menu Options and Shortcut Keys

CODE	Name	Navigation	Description
UD UB	CONNECTION MANAGER	CMS > Connection Manager	Opens the Connection Manager dialog box where you set up connections to Documentum or SharePoint.
UD UB	OPEN REPOSITORY	CMS > Open Repository	Opens the Repository Manager dialog box where you can type a search term in the first text box, select the repository you want to search, and then click the first icon to the right to conduct a basic search of the repository. To conduct an advanced search, select the repository you want to search, and then click the icon to the right of the one you selected above. The appropriate search dialog box for the repository you selected will be displayed. The two icons to the right of select repository box will 1) close the connection (the minus sign) or 2) open the Connection Manager dialog box so you can add a new connection (the plus sign). When you've chosen a repository, its files will be displayed in a tree structure in the large pane. The icons at the top of this pane, from left to right, are 1) Check out a selected item, 2) Check in a selected item, 3) Cancel, or 4) Delete a selected item.
UD UB	SET PREFERENCES	CMS > Preferences	Opens the CMS Preferences dialog box where you can set your preferences for uploading files and other options related to Documentum.

CODE	Name	Navigation	Description
UD UB	UPLOAD ACTIVE DOCUMENT UPLOAD ACTIVE BOOK	CMS > Upload Active Document CMS > Upload Active Book	Choose this option after selecting the repository you want to upload your document to in the Repository Manager dialog box to upload an open or closed file to the repository. You also can upload folders to the repository.

Appendix F: Edit Menu Options

This appendix lists the menu options for the Edit menu of unstructured FrameMaker's document and book views. The options are listed in alphabetical order with shortcut keys (if applicable) and descriptions. Codes are as follows:

UD = Unstructured, Document view

UB = Unstructured, Book view

Shortcut keys:

- Keys that are pressed one at a time are separated with commas.
- Keys that are pressed together are connected with a plus (+) sign.

Table 14: Edit Menu Options and Shortcut Keys

CODE	Name	Navigation	Description
UD UB	CLEAR	Edit > Clear (ESC, e, b)	Clears the items you've selected.
UD UB	COPY	Edit > Copy (CTRL + c) (ESC, e, c) (CTRL + INSERT)	Copies the item or items that have been selected and places them on your computer's Clipboard until you cut or copy something else in your document.
UD	COPY SPECIAL	Edit > Copy Special Attribute values (ESC, e, y, a) Paragraph format (ESC, e, y, p) Character Format (ESC, e, y, c) Conditional Text Setting (ESC, e, y, d) Table Col. Width (ESC, e, y, w)	Note that this menu option has a submenu: Paragraph Formatting, Character Formatting, Conditional Text Setting, and Table Column Width. By placing your cursor in any of these items, and then clicking **Edit > Copy Special** on your menu bar and selecting the element you're copying from, the formatting or settings attached to the element you've selected will be copied so you can apply them to other elements in your document by positioning your cursor in that element or highlighting it, and then clicking **Edit > Paste** on the menu bar.
UD UB	CUT	Edit > Cut (CTRL + x) (ESC, e, x) (SHIFT + DELETE)	Cuts the item or items that have been selected and places them on your computer's Clipboard until you cut or copy something else in your document.

CODE	Name	Navigation	Description
UB	DELETE	Edit > Delete (ESC, f, x)	Deletes the book file your cursor is on when you select this option.
UD UB	FIND NEXT	Edit > Find Next (CTRL + SHIFT + f) (ESC, e, I, f)	Enables you to find the next instance of the element you're looking for. Note that you also can use the Find button or one of the other buttons on the Find/Change panel.
UD UB	FIND/CHANGE	Edit > Find/Change (CTRL + f) (ESC, e, f)	Opens the Find/Change panel where you can search for (find) an impressive number of elements in your document. Be sure that you've selected the option you want in the Look in section of the panel.
UD UB	HISTORY	Edit > History (CTRL+ k)	Opens the History panel that displays the actions you've performed. If you click once on an action listed on the History panel, that action will be repeated at the location where your cursor is positioned. If you click twice on that action on the History panel, the action will be undone.
UD	LINKS	Edit > Links (ESC, e, k)	Opens the Links dialog box.
UD UB	PASTE	Edit > Paste (CTRL + v) (ESC, e, p) (SHIFT + INSERT)	Pastes items you have copied or cut from your document where your cursor is located.
UD	PASTE SPECIAL	Edit > Paste Special (CTRL + SHIFT + v)	Opens the Paste Special dialog box where you can choose from different file formats to insert as native FrameMaker content, paste the items on the Clipboard into your FrameMaker document as a link, or choose to indicate the items as an icon in your document. Paste Special is often used when inserting some text from Microsoft Word documents into FrameMaker documents. By using the Paste Special command, the text is then editable.
UD UB	REDO	Edit > Redo (SHIFT + CTRL + z)	Redoes the action you just performed. Note that when action has undone, this menu option also displays what that action was. For example, if you import a file and want to undo that action, when you click Edit > Undo on the menu bar, this option will say, "Undo Import File." If you then decide that you want to redo that import, this menu option will say, "Redo Import File."

CODE	Name	Navigation	Description
UB	RENAME	Edit > Rename (F2)	Enables you to rename the file that your cursor is on when you select this option. After selecting this option, the name of the file will be highlighted and a box will be around it. Start typing the new name.
UD	REPEAT	Edit > Repeat (F6)	This can be very handy if you need to repeat an action several times in a row. For example, if you have typed some text and need to repeat it, move your cursor to where you want the text to be display and then click Edit > Repeat on the menu bar or press F6.
UB	SELECT	Edit > Select Select All (CTRL + A) (ESC, e, a) Generated Files (ESC, e, SHIFT+a, SHIFT+g) Nongenerated Files (ESC, e, SHIFT+a, SHIFT+n) FrameMaker Files (ESC, e, SHIFT+a, SHIFT+f) Excluded Components (ESC, e, SHIFT+a, SHIFT+e) Non-excluded Components (ESC, e, SHIFT+n, SHIFT+e) Chapter Components (ESC, c, l) Section Components (ESC, s, l) Subsection Components (ESC, s, s, l)	Enables you to select all of the files in your book, or select only files of a specified type.

CODE	Name	Navigation	Description
UD	SELECT ALL IN FLOW	Edit > Select All in Flow (CTRL + a) (ESC, e, a)	Selects everything in the text flow in which your cursor is located.
UB	SET UP GENERATED FILE	Edit > Set Up Generated File (ESC, f, d)	Opens the Set Up Generated File dialog box when it isn't grayed out.
UD UB	SPELLING CHECKER	Edit > Spelling Checker (ESC, e, s)	Opens the Spelling Checker panel. Be sure to check out the options you can apply to your spell check operation by clicking the Options button.
UB	SUPPRESS AUTOMATIC REFERENCE UPDATING	Edit > Suppress Automatic Reference Updating (ESC, e, SHIFT + s)	Suppresses the automatic updating of cross-references and text insets when opening all files in the book.
UD	TEXT INSERT PROPERTIES	Edit > Text Insert Properties (ESC, e, i)	If you import a document created in another application (for example, Microsoft Word) into your FrameMaker document, it will be imported as a text insert that you can't edit. Whenever you try to put your cursor in the imported text, the entire frame around the imported text is highlighted. To see the properties of the text insert and, if you wish, convert it to FrameMaker format, choose this menu option to open the Text Insert Properties panel.
UD	THESAURUS	Edit > Thesaurus (ESC, e, t)	Opens the Thesaurus Look Up dialog box where you can type a word and synonyms will be displayed. If you highlight a word and then select this option, synonyms for the word you have highlighted are displayed.
UD UB	UNDO	Edit > Undo (CTRL + z) (ESC, e, u)	Undoes the action you just performed. For example, if you import a file and want to undo that action, when you click Edit > Undo on the menu bar, this option will say "Undo Import File."
UB	UPDATE BOOK	Edit > Update Book (ESC, e, Shift+u) (ESC, f, g)	Opens the Update Book dialog box where you can update generated files, cross-references, etc. in your book.
UD	UPDATE REFERENCES	Edit > Update References (ESC, e, SHIFT+u)	Opens the Update References dialog box where you can update cross-references, text inserts, OLE links, and graphics (Documentum).

Appendix G: File Menu Options

This appendix lists the menu options for the File menu (ALT, f) of unstructured FrameMaker's document and book views. The options are listed in alphabetical order with shortcut keys (if applicable) and descriptions. Codes are as follows:

UD = Unstructured, Document view

UB = Unstructured, Book view

Shortcut keys:

- Keys that are pressed one at a time are separated with commas.
- Keys that are pressed together are connected with a plus (+) sign.

Table 15: File Menu Options and Shortcut Keys

CODE	Name	Navigation	Description
UD	ADOBE CAPTIVATE	File > Adobe Captivate	Opens Adobe Captivate if it's loaded on your computer.
UD	ADOBE PHOTOSHOP	File > Launch Photoshop	Opens Adobe Photoshop if it's loaded on your computer.
UD	ALERT STRINGS	File > Preferences > Alert Strings	Opens the Alert Strings dialog box that enables you to turn on or off the warnings displayed when you undo or redo an action, FrameMaker detects unresolved cross-references, when you are opening an "old release" document, and the file contains unavailable fonts.
UD	CHARACTER PALETTE	File > Utilities > Character Palette	Opens the Character palette to insert special characters in your document. Note that you can change the typeface used. To close the palette, click an area away from it.
UD	CHOOSE SCRIPT	File > Script > Run	Opens the Choose Script dialog box to enable you to navigate to the folder where you have stored your scripts.
UD	CLOSE	File > Close (CTRL + w) (CTRL + F4) (ESC, f, c) (ESC, f, q	Closes an open document.

CODE	Name	Navigation	Description
UB	CLOSE BOOK	File > Close Book (CTRL + w) (ESC, f, c)	Closes an open book and the document files associated with it.
UD	COMPARE DOCUMENTS	File > Utilities > Compare Documents (ESC, f, t, c)	Use this to compare two documents. Both documents must be open. If you click the Options button, the Comparison Options dialog box opens where you can define options you want to be compared.
UD	CREATE AND APPLY FORMATS	File > Utilities > Create and Apply Formats (ESC, f, t, f)	Use this to create a custom catalog of paragraph tags by doing the following: Delete all paragraph tags in the paragraph catalog. Open the Create and Apply Formats dialog box. Press Continue. All paragraph tags used in the document are added back to the catalog. This is useful when you're creating custom templates.
UD	DOCUMENT REPORTS	File > Utilities > Document Reports (ESC, f, t, r)	This dialog box counts the number of Asian characters or the number of words in your document, depending on which you choose.
UD	EXTENDSCRIPT TOOKKIT (ESTK)	File > Script > New Script	ExtendScript TookKit (ESTK) is a development and debugging utility used to create and debug scripts.
UD	EXIT	File > Exit (ALT + F4)	This closes all documents and the FrameMaker application. If you have unsaved changes in any open documents when you select this option, a message will be displayed asking if you want to save your changes.
UD	FILE INFO	File > File Info	When you choose this option, the File Info dialog box opens where you can enter the author names, keywords, copyright information, and other information about the document being written.
UD	HEX INPUT	File > Utilities > Hex Input (Windows Key + h)	When you place your cursor on some text and select this option, the Hex Input palette is displayed. From this palette, you can select a Unicode character to add to your text.
UD	HTML SETUP	File > Utilities > HTML Setup (ESC, f, t, h)	When you choose this option, the HTML Setup panel opens. This is where you define how paragraph, character, and cross-reference formats will be "translated" to HTML. If you click the Options button on the HTML Setup panel, the HTML Options dialog box opens.

CODE	Name	Navigation	Description
UD	IMPORT	File > Import > File (ESC, f, i, f)	When you select this option, the Import dialog box opens. Use this dialog box to import graphics and other types of files. Be sure to note the two buttons at the bottom of the screen: **Import by Reference** and **Copy into Document.** If you import the file by reference, the actual graphic or text is not inserted into your document. Instead, a link to it is inserted. This helps keep the size of the file smaller, but can be a problem if the file being imported by reference is moved to another location. If you copy the file into the document, a copy of it is made and inserted in your document. This will make your file size larger, but will give you a second copy of the graphic or other file.
UD	IMPORT FORMATS	File > Import > Formats (ESC, f, i, o)	When you choose this option, the Import Formats dialog box opens. Use this dialog box to import paragraph formats, character formats, table formats and more from other documents, thereby saving yourself a great deal of time. Select the document from which you want to import the formats in the Import from Document field (the document you want to import from must be open), and then place checkmarks in front of all formats you want to import.
UD	IMPORT OBJECT	File > Import > Object (ESC, f, i, b)	When you choose this option, the Insert Object dialog box opens. Use this dialog box to insert a file from another application as an object in the current document, or to create a new file as an object from another application to insert in the current document. This enables you to make changes to the inserted object in the application it was created in.
UD	IMPORT PDF COMMENTS	File > Import > PDF Comments	The first time you use this option, a window will be displayed that tells you the requirements for importing PDF comments. You have the option to start importing the comments and also to suppress this message from being displayed again.
UD	INTERFACE PREFERENCES	File > Preferences > Interface	This opens the Interface Preferences dialog box. Select the ways you want to view panels, documents, and composite documents on this dialog box. Also, you can define how you want to see tool tips, how bright you want dialog boxes to be, and if you want icons to be grayscale.

CODE	Name	Navigation	Description
UD	LOCATION CRITERIA	File > Preferences > Pods Location Criteria	If you're working in unstructured FrameMaker, use this dialog box to specify paragraph tags that should be used to identify what location should be displayed in pods.
UD UB	NEW DOCUMENT	File > New > Document (CTRL + n) (ESC, f, n)	This opens the New dialog box. Use this to open a new blank document (portrait, landscape, or custom), open a document based on a template, to browse the Internet for documents or templates (Browse URL), browse a connection management system (Browse CMS), and explore examples of documents developed from existing standard and structured templates.
UD UB	NEW BOOK	File > New > Book (ESC, f, SHIFT+ n)	This opens a new book window in FrameMaker.
UD UB	OPEN	File > Open (Ctrl + o) (ESC, f, o)	Use this dialog box to open existing documents.
UB	OPEN ALL BOOK FILES	(ESC, f, SHIFT+ o)	This is a keyboard shortcut that opens all of the files in a book when the book view is displayed.
UD	PREFERENCES	File > Preferences > General Preferences (ESC, f, Shift + p)	This dialog box enables you to set your auto-save options, and several other options.
UD	PRINT DOCUMENT	File > Print (CTRL + p) (ESC, f, p)	This dialog box enables you to define your print settings. Note that if you're printing a PDF document, you need to click the PDF Setup button to open the PDF Setup dialog box. You also can setup your printer from the Print Document dialog box by clicking the Setup button to the right of the printer field. Finally, you can setup how you want separations to be handled (if you're printing separations) by clicking the Separations Setup button.
UD	PRINT SETUP	File > Print Setup (CTRL+ SHIFT + p)	On this dialog box, you select the printer you want to use, review information displayed here about that printer, and select the paper size, orientation, and source. After you've selected the printer you want to use, if you click the Properties button, a dialog box will open with more information about that printer. The dialog box that opens if you choose Adobe PDF as the printer is especially useful.
UD	PUBLISH	File > Publish	

CODE	Name	Navigation	Description
UD	RECENT FILES	File > Recent Files	Displays a list of files you've worked on recently.
UD	ROBOSCREEN CAPTURE	File > Launch RoboScreenCapture	Use this to capture screen shots and manipulate them.
UD	SAVE AS REVIEW PDF	File > Save as Review PDF	
UD UB	SAVE DOCUMENT OR SAVE BOOK	File > Save (CTRL + s) (ESC, f, s) File > Save as (ESC, f, a) File > Save as PDF (ESC, f, w, p) File > Save as XML (ESC, f, w, x)	Use this dialog box to save new documents, save previously saved documents, save previously saved documents with a new name, or save a document as a PDF or other format.
UD	SCRIPT LIBRARY	File > Script > Catalog	Opens up as a panel on the right-side of the screen. You can add your favorite scripts, remove scripts from your list of favorites, and set scripts to AutoRun.
UD	SEND	File > Send (ESC, f, m)	Opens a window from your operating system so you can send the file via email.

This page is intentionally left blank.

Appendix H: Format Menu Options

This appendix lists the menu options for the Format menu of unstructured FrameMaker's document and book views. The options are listed in alphabetical order with shortcut keys (if applicable) and descriptions. Codes are as follows:

UD = Unstructured, Document view

UB = Unstructured, Book view

<u>Shortcut keys:</u>

- Keys that are pressed one at a time are separated with commas.
- Keys that are pressed together are connected with a plus (+) sign.

Table 16: Format Menu Options and Shortcut Keys

CODE	Name	Navigation	Description
UD UB	APPLY MASTER PAGES	Format > Page Layout > Apply Master Pages	Applies designated Master Pages to Body Pages.
UD UB	CHANGE BARS	Format > Document > Change Bars (ESC, o, b)	Opens the Change Bar Properties dialog box where you can set the properties for the change bars that will be displayed if activated during review processes.
UD	CHARACTER CATALOG	Format > Characters > Catalog (ESC, o, c, c)	Opens the Character Catalog.
UD	CHARACTER DESIGNER	Format > Characters > Designer (CTRL + d) (ESC, o, c, d)	Opens the Character Designer.
UD UB	COLUMN LAYOUT	Format > Page Layout > Column Layout (ESC, o, c, l)	Opens the Column Layout dialog box where you can set the number of columns you want, the gap between the columns, width of columns, page margins, sideheads, and more.
UD	CONNECT TEXT FRAMES	Format > Customize Layout > Connect Text Frames (ESC, Shift+c, Shift+c)	Use this when you're on a Body Page to connect two text frames.

CODE	Name	Navigation	Description
UD	CUSTOMIZE TEXT FRAME	Format > Customize Layout > Customize Text Frame (ESC, o, c, f)	Opens the Customize Text Frame dialog box where you can set attributes of the text frame your cursor is currently located in. Note that you can change the number of columns and room for sideheads on this dialog box.
UD	DEFAULT PARAGRAPH FONT	Format > Character > Default Paragraph Font (ESC, o, c, p)	Changes the text that has been selected back to the default paragraph font.
UD	DISCONNECT BOTH	Format > Customize Layout > Disconnect Both (ESC, Shift+c, Shift+b)	Disconnects two selected text frames.
UD	DISCONNECT NEXT	Format > Customize Layout > Disconnect Next (ESC, Shift+c, Shift+n)	Disconnects the selected text frame from the next text frame.
UD	DISCONNECT PREVIOUS	Format > Customize Layout > Disconnect Previous (ESC, Shift+c, Shift+p)	Use this to disconnect two text frames that you've just connected. *See Connect Text Frames.*
UD UB	DOCUMENT	Format > Document	Opens a submenu with the following options: • Numbering opens the Numbering Properties dialog box. • Change Bars opens the Change Bars Properties dialog box. • Footnote Properties opens the Footnote Properties dialog box. • Text Options opens the Text Options dialog box. • PDF Setup opens the PDF Setup dialog box. • Optimize PDF Size opens a submenu with the following two options: Options opens the Optimization Options dialog box and Optimize File opens a dialog box where you select the file you want to optimize. • Rubi Properties opens the Rubi Properties dialog box.
UD	EDIT COMBINED FONTS	Format > Document > Combined Fonts	Opens the Edit Combined Fonts dialog box where you can combine Asian and Western font families under a name of your choosing.

CODE	Name	Navigation	Description
UD	FONT	Format > Font	Opens FrameMaker's Font library.
UD UB	FOOTNOTE PROPERTIES	Format > Document > Footnote Properties (ESC, o, f)	This opens the Footnote Properties dialog box where you can set the properties for footnotes and table footnotes.
UD	INSERT CURRENT DATE	Format > Headers & Footers > Insert Current Date (ESC, o, h, d)	You must be on a Master Page to use this command. It inserts a current-date variable in the header or footer where your cursor is located.
UD	INSERT OTHER	Format > Headers & Footers > Insert Other (ESC, o, h, o)	You must be on a Master Page to use this command. It opens the Variables pod where you can select a variable to insert in the header or footer where your cursor is located.
UD	INSERT PAGE #	Format > Headers & Footers > Insert Page # (ESC, o, h, p)	You must be on a Master Page to use this command. It inserts a page-number variable in the header or footer where your cursor is located.
UD	INSERT PAGE COUNT	Format > Headers & Footers > Insert Page Count (ESC, o, h, c)	You must be on a Master Page to use this command. It inserts a page-count variable in the header or footer where your cursor is located.
UD UB	LINE LAYOUT	Format > Page Layout > Line Layout (ESC, o, l, l)	Opens the Line Layout dialog box where you can fine-tune the balance of text in different columns or text frames. If you place a checkmark in front of "Feather," FrameMaker will add space between lines and paragraphs up to the maximum you've indicated in the two fields beneath this.
UD	MASTER PAGE USAGE	Format > Page Layout > Master Page Usage (ESC, o, m, u)	Opens the Master Page Usage dialog box where you can designate what Master Page to apply to the Body Page your cursor is on or other options.
UD	NEW MASTER PAGE	Format > Page Layout > New Master Page (ESC, o, m, p)	If you're in the Body Pages view, the New Master Page dialog box opens to allow you to type a name for a new Master Page that will be created using the layout of the Body Page your cursor is currently on. If you're in the Master Pages view, the Add Master Page dialog box opens where you type the name of the new Master Page you want to create.

CODE	Name	Navigation	Description
UD UB	NUMBERING	Format > Document > Numbering (ESC, o, d, n) (ESC, e, n)	Opens the Numbering Properties dialog box. This is where you set the properties for volume numbers, chapter numbers, section numbers, sub-section numbers, page numbers, paragraph numbers, footnote numbers, and table footnote numbers.
UD UB	OPTIMIZATION OPTIONS	Format > Document > Optimize PDF Size > Options	Opens the Optimization Options dialog box where you can select settings that will optimize the size of your PDF files.
UD UB	PAGE SIZE	Format > Page Layout > Page Size (ESC, o, p, s)	Opens the Page Size dialog box where you can choose from common page sizes or create a custom page size.
UB	PAGE LAYOUT	Format > Page Layout	Opens a submenu with different options as follows: • Column Layout opens the Column Layout dialog box. • Line Layout opens the Line Layout dialog box where you can control the space between lines in your text. • Page Size opens the Page Size dialog box where you can change the size of your pages. • Pagination opens the Pagination dialog box where you select whether your pages will be single or double-sided. • Apply Master Page opens the Apply Master Page dialog box.
UD UB	PAGINATION	Format > Page Layout > Pagination (ESC, o, p, i)	Opens the Pagination dialog box where you can select if the document will be single-sided or double-sided, what page side the first page will be, and whether to delete empty pages, make page count even or odd, or leave them as is before saving and printing.
UD	PARAGRAPH CATALOG	Format > Paragraphs > Catalog (ESC, o, p, c)	Opens the Paragraph Catalog that lists all of the paragraph tags. Note that beneath the menu option for this, a list of paragraph tags being used in this document is displayed.
UD	PARAGRAPH DESIGNER	Format > Paragraphs > Designer (CTRL + m) (ESC, o, p, d)	Opens the Paragraph Designer panel.

CODE	Name	Navigation	Description
UD UB	PDF SETUP	Format > Document > PDF Setup (ESC, o, d, a)	Opens the PDF Setup dialog box where you can select various options for printing your document as a PDF.
UD	REORDER CUSTOM MASTER PAGES	Format > Page Layout > Reorder Custom Master Pages	Can only be accessed while you're in the Master Pages view. This opens the Reorder Custom Master Pages dialog box where you can move your custom Master Pages up or down in the Master Pages view.
UD	ROTATE PAGE CLOCKWISE	Format > Customize Layout > Rotate Page Clockwise (ESC, p, Shift+o)	Rotates the page clockwise where the cursor is located.
UD	ROTATE PAGE COUNTERCLOCKWISE	Format > Customize Layout > Rotate Page Counterclockwise (ESC, p, o)	Rotates the page counterclockwise where the cursor is located.
UD UB	RUBI PROPERTIES	Format > Document > Rubi Properties (ESC, o, r)	Opens the Rubi Properties dialog box where you can set the properties for any rubi text in your document.
UD	SIZE	Format > Size	Opens a list of different sizes of type that you can choose. Note that a checkmark is placed in front of the size of the type your cursor is placed on.
UD	SPLIT TEXT FRAME	Format > Customize Layout > Split Text Frame (ESC, Shift+c, Shift+s)	Splits the text frame at the point where the cursor is located.
UD	STYLE	Format > Style Plain Style (ESC, c, p, F2) Bold Style (CTRL + b) (F4) (ESC, c, b) Italic Style (CTRL + i) (F5) (ESC, c, i) Underline Style (CTRL+ u)	This enables you to apply a variety of styles to the selected text in your document.

CODE	Name	Navigation	Description
		(ESC, c, u) <u>Double Underline Style</u> (ESC, c, d) <u>Overline Style</u> (ESC, c, o) <u>Strikethrough Style</u> (Control+/) (ESC, c, s) <u>Change Bar Style</u> (Control+ Shift+h) (ESC, c, h) <u>Superscript Style</u> (ESC, c, Shift + +) (Plus + key) <u>Subscript Style</u> (ESC, c, -) <u>Small Caps Style</u> (CTRL + e) (ESC, c, m)	
UD	TABLE FOOTNOTE PROPERTIES	Format > Document > Footnote Properties (ESC, o, f)	Opens the Footnote Properties dialog box where you can set the properties for footnotes and table footnotes.
UD UB	TEXT OPTIONS	Format > Document > Text Options (ESC, o, t, o)	Opens the Text Options dialog box where you can set options such as smart quotes and smart spaces, line breaks with certain characters, and the properties of superscript, subscript, and small cap text.
UD	UNROTATE PAGE	Format > Customize Layout > Unrotate Page (ESC, p, Shift + u)	Reverses the rotation applied to the page where the cursor is located.
UD	UPDATE COLUMN LAYOUT	Format > Page Layout > Update Column Layout (ESC, o, u, p)	This is only available when you're in the Body Pages view. If the columns are aligned with the Master Pages, you'll receive only a message telling you that's the case.

Appendix I: Graphics Menu Options

This appendix lists the menu options for the Graphics menu of unstructured FrameMaker's document view. The Graphics menu is not displayed when you're in the book view. The options are listed in alphabetical order with shortcut keys (if applicable) and descriptions. Codes are as follows:

UD = Unstructured, Document view

Shortcut keys:

- Keys that are pressed one at a time are separated with commas.
- Keys that are pressed together are connected with a plus (+) sign.

Table 17: Graphics Menu Options and Shortcut Keys

CODE	Name	Navigation	Description
UD	3D Menu	Graphics > 3D Menu	When you select this menu option, a second menu opens that allows you to change various settings of a 3D object you've imported into your document.
UD	ALIGN	Graphics > Align (ESC, g, a)	Opens the Align panel. You can align the top, bottom, left, and right sides of two or more graphics by using this dialog box. Select the object that you want other selected objects to align with last.
UD	BRING TO FRONT	Graphics > Bring to Front (ESC, g, f)	Select the object that you want to be in front of other objects or text and select this option to bring it to front.
UD	DISTRIBUTE	Graphics > Distribute (ESC, g, d)	When you select this option, the Distribute panel becomes active. You can set the horizontal and vertical spacing between selected objects by using this dialog box.
UD	EDIT WITH ILLUSTRATOR	Graphics > Edit with Illustrator	When you select an object, and then select this option, you can edit the object using Adobe Illustrator if it's loaded on your computer.
UD	EDIT WITH PHOTOSHOP	Graphics > Edit with Photoshop	When you select an object, and then select this option, you can edit the object using Adobe Photoshop if it's loaded on your computer.
UD	EDIT WITH ROBOSCREENCAPTURE	Graphics > Edit with RoboScreenCapture	When you select an object, and then select this option, you can edit the object using Adobe RoboScreenCapture.

CODE	Name	Navigation	Description
UD	FLIP LEFT/RIGHT	Graphics > Flip Left/Right (ESC, g, h)	When you select an object (such as a line with an arrow at one end that is oriented horizontally on your page), and then select this option, the object is flipped horizontally 180 degrees.
UD	FLIP UP/DOWN	Graphics > Flip Up/Down (ESC, g, v)	If you select an object (such as a line with an arrow at one end that is oriented vertically on your page), and then select this option, the object is flipped 180 degrees.
UD	GRAVITY	Graphics > Gravity (ESC, g, y)	Gravity is a way to make objects be attracted to each other. If you select this option, and then draw or move an object close to another object that already exists, the object you're moving will be attracted to the other object and one of its handles (the closest) will "jump" to touch the other object. NOTE: When you select this option, a checkmark Is placed in front of the word "Gravity" on the Graphics menu to indicate that gravity is turned on. To turn it off, select it a second time. Also note that if both gravity and snap-to-grid are turned on, gravity will take precedence.
UD	GROUP	Graphics > Group (ESC, g, g)	After you've selected two or more objects, you can group them so they act like one object by using this option.
UD	JOIN	Graphics > Join (ESC, g, j)	If you select two objects that are joined at their ends (such as lines), and then select this option, the two objects will be joined.
UD	OBJECT PROPERTIES	Graphics > Object Properties (ESC, g, o)	Opens the Object Properties dialog box.
UD	RESHAPE	Graphics > Reshape (ESC, g, r)	When you select an object, and then select this option, you can change the shape of the object.
UD	ROTATE	Graphics > Rotate (ESC, g, t)	Opens the Rotate Selected Object dialog box. On this dialog box, you can select to rotate the object by a specific amount, clockwise or counterclockwise.
UD	RUNAROUND PROPERTIES	Graphics > Runaround Properties (ESC, g, Shift + r)	Opens the Runaround Properties panel. On this panel, you select how you want text to run around the selected object.

CODE	Name	Navigation	Description
UD	SCALE	Graphics > Scale (ESC, g, z)	Opens the Scale dialog box. On this dialog box, you can resize the selected object by percentages or change the size of the original object.
UD	SEND TO BACK	Graphics > Send to Back (ESC, g, b)	Select the object that you want to be in back of other objects or text and select this option to send it to the back.
UD	SET # OF SIDES	Graphics > Set # of Sides (ESC, g, n)	Opens the Set Number of Sides dialog box. On this dialog box, you specify how many sides you want an object to have and what the angle of the first side should be.
UD	SET POSTER	Graphics > Set Poster	A "poster" is the image that is displayed in your document to indicate a SWF media file. The poster is the first frame of the SWF media file. To activate the poster, right-click on the imported SWF file, and then click Graphics > Set Poster. If FrameMaker can't locate the frame to use, it inserts another image.
UD	SMOOTH	Graphics > Smooth (ESC, g, s)	Smooths the corners of a selected object (for example, the square corners of a rectangle).
UD	SNAP TO GRID	Graphics > Snap (ESC, g, p)	Activates an invisible grid that attracts objects to be aligned according to the grid. Objects will "snap" into place along the grid automatically if this option is selected. You set your grid settings on the View Options dialog box (View > Options on the menu bar).
UD	TOOLS	Graphics > Tools (ESC, g, Shift + t)	Opens the Tools palette.
UD	UNGROUP	Graphics > Ungroup (ESC, g, u)	Select the object that was created when you grouped two or more objects, and then select this option to ungroup those objects.
UD	UNSMOOTH	Graphics > Unsmooth (ESC, g, m)	When you select an object that you've previously "smoothed" the corners of, and then select this option, the corners return to the original shape.

This page is intentionally left blank.

Appendix J: Special Menu Options

This appendix lists the menu options for the Special menu of unstructured FrameMaker's document views. The Special menu is not displayed when you're in the book view. The options are listed in alphabetical order with shortcut keys (if applicable) and descriptions. Codes are as follows:

UD = Unstructured, Document view

Shortcut keys:

- Keys that are pressed one at a time are separated with commas.
- Keys that are pressed together are connected with a plus (+) sign.

Table 18: Special Menu Options and Shortcut Keys

CODE	Name	Navigation	Description
UD	ADD DISCONNECTED PAGES	Special > Add Disconnected Pages (ESC, s, p, a)	Most of the time, your document's Body Pages will be connected. When one page becomes full of text, the text automatically flows to the next page. There may be times, however, that you don't want this to happen. For example, if you're writing a document that has several text flows, you may want to insert some pages that aren't connected to the one previous to them. If you need to do this, Click Special > Add Disconnected Pages on the menu bar or press the keyboard shortcuts. The Add Disconnected Pages dialog box opens where you specify whether the disconnected pages come before or after the page where your cursor is currently located, how many disconnected pages to add, and what Master Page to apply to them.
UD	ANCHORED FRAME	Special > Anchored Frame (ESC, s, a)	Opens the Anchored Frame panel, which enables you to insert an anchored frame in several different locations.
UD	CONDITIONAL TEXT	Special > Conditional Text (ESC, s, SHIFT + c)	Opens a submenu where you can open the Conditional Text pod, show or hide conditional text, or show or hide conditional text indicators.
UD	CROSS-REFERENCE	Special > Cross-Reference (ESC, s, c)	Opens the Cross-Reference panel.

CODE	Name	Navigation	Description
UD	DELETE PAGES	Special > Delete Pages (ESC, s, p, d)	Opens the Delete Pages dialog box. If you only want to delete one page, type the same page number in both boxes. **NOTE**: All of the content on the deleted pages is deleted.
UD	EQUATIONS	Special > Equations (ESC, s, e)	Opens the Equations dialog box.
UD	FOOTNOTE	Special > Footnote (ESC, s, f)	Moves your cursor to the footnote section of your Body Page and inserts a footnote number.
UD	HYPERTEXT	Special > Hypertext (ESC, s, h)	Opens the Hypertext panel.
UD	INDEX OF	Special > Index of Authors (ESC, i, o, a) Subjects (ESC, i, o, s) Markers (ESC, i, o, m) References (ESC, i, o, r)	Selecting this option opens a second menu that lists the different kinds of indices you can create. When you select an option or press its keyboard shortcut, a message is displayed asking if you want this to be a standalone index or if you want to place the document and the index you're creating in a new book. If you select "yes" to the question asking if you want to create a standalone index, the Set Up XXXX Index dialog box opens. If you select "no" to the same question, a new book window opens with the document you're working on and a table of contents file added to it already and the Set Up XXXX Index dialog box opens as well.
UD	LIST OF	Special > List of Figures (ESC, l, o, f) Tables (ESC, l, o, t) Paragraphs (ESC, l, o, p) Paragraphs (Alphabetical) (ESC, l, o, Shift + p)	Selecting this option opens a second menu that lists the different kinds of lists you can create. When you select an option or press its keyboard shortcut, a message is displayed asking if you want this to be a standalone list or if you want to place the document and the list you're creating in a new book. If you select "yes" to the question asking if you want to create a standalone list, the Set Up XXXX dialog box opens. If you select "no" to the same question, a new book window opens with the document you're working on and a table of contents file added to it already and the Set Up XXXX dialog box opens as well.

CODE	Name	Navigation	Description
		Markers (ESC, l, o, m) Markers (Alphabetical) (ESC, l, o, Shift + m) References (ESC, l, o, r)	
UD	MARKER	Special > Marker (ESC, s, m)	Opens the Marker panel.
UD	PAGE BREAK	Special > Page Break (ESC, s, p, b)	Opens the Page Break panel, enabling you to choose whether you want to place the paragraph where your cursor is located wherever it fits or in another place as designated.
UD	RUBI	Special > Rubi (ESC, s, r)	Rubi text is small text that appears above the regular text. You also can use rubi text to add translations. Apply it by selecting the word or words that you want to place the smaller words or characters over, click Special > Rubi on the menu bar or press ESC, s, r, then type the text or characters that you want to appear above the other text. Set the properties for Rubi text by clicking Format > Document > Rubi Properties on the menu bar.
UD	STANDARD INDEX	Special > Standard Index (ESC, i, x)	Opens a message box that asks if you want to create a standalone index or place the document you're indexing and the index in a new book. If you select "yes" to the question asking if you want to create a standalone index, the Set Up Standard Index dialog box opens. If you select "no" to the same question, a new book window opens with the document you're indexing and an index file added to it already and the Set Up Standard Index dialog box opens as well.

CODE	Name	Navigation	Description
UD	TABLE OF CONTENTS	Special > Table of Contents (ESC, t, o, c)	Opens a message box that asks if you want to create a standalone table of contents for the document you're working on, or place the document you're creating a table of contents for and the table of contents in a new book. If you select "yes" to the question asking if you want to create a standalone table of contents, the Set Up Table of Contents dialog box opens. If you select "no" to the same question, a new book window opens with the document you're working on and a table of contents file added to it already and the Set Up Table of Contents dialog box opens as well.
UD	TRACK EDITS	Special > Track Text Edits Turn on or off (ESC, s, t, o) Preview Final (ESC, s, t, Shift + f) Preview Original (ESC, s, t, Shift + o) Preview Off (ESC, s, p, o) Accept Edit (ESC, s, t, a) Reject Edit (ESC, s, t, r) Accept All (ESC, s, t, Shift + a) Reject All (ESC, s, t, Shift + r)	Displays a second menu where you can choose various options for tracking changes made to the text in the selected document, book, DITA map, or documents.
UD	VARIABLES	Special > Variables (ESC, s, v)	Opens the Variables pod.

Appendix K: Table Menu Options

This appendix lists the menu options for the Table menu of unstructured FrameMaker's document view. This menu is not displayed when you're in the book view. The options are listed in alphabetical order with shortcut keys (if applicable) and descriptions. Codes are as follows:

UD = Unstructured, Document view

<u>Shortcut keys</u>:

- Keys that are pressed one at a time are separated with commas.
- Keys that are pressed together are connected with a plus (+) sign.

Table 19: Table Menu Options and Shortcut Keys

CODE	Name	Navigation	Description
UD	ADD ROWS OR COLUMNS	Table > Add Rows or Columns (ESC, t, a)	Opens the Add Rows or Columns dialog box.
UD	CONVERT TO PARAGRAPHS	Table > Convert to Paragraphs (ESC, t, v)	Opens the Convert to Paragraphs dialog box.
UD	FORMAT	Table > Format <u>Open Table Designer</u> (CTRL + t) <u>Row Format</u> (ESC, t, r) <u>Resize Columns</u> (ESC, t, z) <u>Custom Ruling and Shading</u> (ESC, t, x)	Opens a second menu that enables you to open the Table Designer and perform different actions to format your table. The second menu also shows you which table format is being used by the table where your cursor is located.
UD	INSERT TABLE	Table > Insert Table (ESC, t, i)	Opens the Insert Table dialog box.
UD	SORT	Table > Sort (ESC, t, s)	Opens the Sort Table dialog box.
UD	STRADDLE	Table > Straddle (ESC, t, l)	Merges two or more selected table cells. To reverse, select it and then press the same shortcut keys.

This page is intentionally left blank.

Appendix L: View Menu Options

This appendix lists the menu options for the View menu of unstructured FrameMaker's document and book views. The options are listed in alphabetical order with shortcut keys (if applicable) and descriptions. Codes are as follows:

UD = Unstructured, Document view

UB = Unstructured, Book view

<u>Shortcut keys</u>:

- Keys that are pressed one at a time are separated with commas.
- Keys that are pressed together are connected with a plus (+) sign.

Table 20: View Menu Options and Shortcut Keys

CODE	Name	Navigation	Description
UD	BODY PAGES	View > Body Pages (ESC, v, SHIFT + b)	Displays the Body Pages.
UD UB	BORDERS SHOW BORDERS	View > Borders View > Show Borders (ESC, v, b)	Shows or hides the borders on your document.
UD UB	COLOR DEFINITION	View > Color > Definitions (ESC, v, c, d)	Opens the Color Definitions dialog box.
UD UB	COLOR VIEWS	View > Color > Views (ESC, v, c, v)	Opens the Define Color Views dialog box.
UD UB	CONDITIONAL TEXT	View > Pods > Conditional Text	Opens the Conditional Text pod.
UD UB	CROSS-REFERENCES	View > Pods > Cross-References	Opens the Cross-References pod.
UD UB	FONTS	View > Pods > Fonts	Opens the Fonts pod.
UD	GO TO PAGE	View > Go to Page (CTRL + g) (ESC, v, p)	Opens the Go to Page dialog box where you first select whether you want to go to a Master Page or a Body Page. After you've made that selection, the Go to Page dialog box opens again with more specific settings.

CODE	Name	Navigation	Description
UD UB	GRAPHICS TOOLBAR	View > Toolbars > Graphics Toolbar	Displays the Graphics Toolbar.
UD UB	GRID LINES SHOW GRID LINES	View > Grid Lines View > Show Grid Lines (ESC, v, g)	Displays the grid lines on the document.
UD UB	HIDE ALL	View > Toolbars > Hide All	Hides all toolbars.
UB	HIDE CONDITIONAL TEXT INDICATORS	View > Hide Conditional Text Indicators	Hides conditional text indicators.
UB	HIDE GRAPHICS	View > Hide Graphics (ESC, SHIFT + v, v, h)	Hides the graphics in your document.
UD UB	MARKERS	View > Pods > Markers	Opens the Markers pod.
UD	MASTER PAGES	View > Master Pages (ESC, v, SHIFT + m)	Displays the Master Pages.
UD UB	MENUS – COMPLETE	View > Menus > Complete	When you select this, your menu bar changes to display all options.
UD UB	MENUS – MODIFY	View > Menus > Modify	Opens the Menu Customization File dialog box.
UD UB	MENUS – QUICK	View > Menus > Quick	Displays fewer menu options.
UD UB	OBJECT ALIGNMENT	View > Toolbars > Object Alignment (ESC, SHIFT + v, o, a)	Displays the Object Alignment toolbar.
UD UB	OBJECT PROPERTIES	View > Toolbars > Object Properties (ESC, SHIFT + v, o, p)	Displays the Object Properties toolbar.
UD UB	OPTIONS	View > Options	Opens the View Options dialog box.
UD UB	PARAGRAPH FORMATTING	View > Toolbars > Paragraph Formatting (ESC, SHIFT + v, p, a)	Displays the Paragraph Formatting toolbar.

CODE	Name	Navigation	Description
UD UB	QUICK ACCESS BAR	View > Toolbars > Quick Access Bar (ESC, v, q)	Displays the Quick Access Bar.
UD	REFERENCE PAGES	View > Reference Pages (ESC, v, SHIFT + r)	Displays the reference pages.
UD UB	REFERENCES	View > Pods > References	Opens the References pod.
UD UB	RULERS SHOW RULERS	View > Rulers View > Show Rulers (ESC, v, r)	Shows or hides rulers.
UD UB	SHOW ALL	View > Toolbars > Show All	If you select this, all toolbars are displayed.
UB	SHOW GRAPHICS	View > Show Graphics (ESC, SHIFT + v, v, s)	If you select this, the graphics will be shown.
UD UB	SHOW INSETS	View > Pods > Show Insets	Opens the Show Insets pod.
UB	SHOW/HIDE CONDITIONAL TEXT	View > Show/Hide Conditional Text	Shows or hides conditional text.
UD UB	TABLE FORMATTING	View > Toolbars > Table Formatting (ESC, SHIFT + v, t, a)	Displays the Table Formatting toolbar.
UD UB	TEXT FORMATTING	View > Toolbars > Text Formatting (ESC, SHIFT + v, t, e)	Displays the Text Formatting toolbar.
UD UB	TEXT SYMBOLS SHOW TEXT SYMBOLS	View > Text Symbols View > Show Text Symbols (ESC, v, t)	Shows or hides text symbols.
UD UB	TRACK TEXT EDITS	View > Toolbars > Track Text Edits (ESC, SHIFT + v, e)	Displays the Track Text Edits toolbar.
UB	TRACK TEXT EDITS	View > Track Text Edits	Opens a menu opens with options you can choose for tracking edits in your documents.
UD UB	VARIABLES	View > Pods > Variables	Opens the Variables pod.

CODE	Name	Navigation	Description
UB	ZOOM	View > Zoom	Opens a menu of zoom options.
		Zoom In (ESC, z, i)	
		Zoom Out (ESC, z, o)	
		100 percent (ESC, z, z)	
		Fit Page in Window (ESC, z, p)	
		Fit Window to Page (ESC, z, w)	
		Fit Window to Text Frame (ESC, z, f)	

Index

C

D

E

N

O

P

Q

R

S

T

U

V

W

Z

This page is intentionally left blank.

This page is intentionally left blank.

About the Author

Janet Underwood has more than twenty years of experience as a senior technical writer and trainer. She has developed technical documentation and training courses for major corporations in the computer, information technology, telecommunications, financial, and medical industries, as well as for government agencies such as NASA, the U.S. Army and the U.S. Navy. She began her career as an English teacher, and then worked as an editor and writer for several internationally known trade publications. She has won numerous awards for writing and documentation design and currently owns a technical writing and services business. She has taught technical writing skills to thousands of students around the world in her online classes. Her hobbies include playing the piano, reading science fiction, cooking unusual dishes, and tending to the never-ending needs of her Shih Tzu dogs.